Out of the mouths of children . . .

When a child speaks of a past life memory, the effects ripple far. At the center is the child, who is directly healed and changed. The parents standing close by are rocked by the truth of the experience—a truth powerful enough to dislodge deeply entrenched beliefs. For observers removed from the actual event—even those just reading about it—reports of a child's past life memory can jostle the soul toward new understanding. Children's past life memories have the power to change lives.

When a child speaks so innocently and knowingly about living before, and so calmly describes what happens after death and on the journey to rebirth, it is firsthand testimony to the truth that our souls never die. These memories present perhaps the best-documented evidence yet for reincarnation.

—CAROL BOWMAN

D1011758

Children's Past Lives

How Past Life Memories Affect Your Child

Carol Bowman

BANTAM BOOKS
New York Toronto London Sydney Auckland

This edition contains the complete text
of the original hardcover edition.
NOT ONE WORD HAS BEEN OMITTED.

Children's Past Lives

A Bantam Book

PUBLISHING HISTORY
Bantam hardcover edition / April 1997
Bantam paperback edition / January 1998

ISBN: 0-553-57485-X

Published simultaneously in the United States and Canada

Bantam Books are published by Bantam Books, a division of Random House, Inc. Its trade-
mark, consisting of the words "Bantam Books" and the portrayal of a rooster, is Registered in
U.S. Patent and Trademark Office and in other countries. Marca Registrada. Random House,
Inc., New York, New York.

PRINTED IN THE UNITED STATES OF AMERICA

OPM   10 9

*This book is dedicated
to the memory of Ian Ballantine,
whose vision and spirit continue
to change the world.*

Contents

Acknowledgments

My heartfelt thanks to all of the following for their help:

To my editor, Betty Ballantine, for her wisdom and patience, and for her many hours of work.

To Norman Inge for setting things in motion.

Applause for Elisa Petrini at Bantam for putting all of the pieces together.

Thanks to Kyle King for her magic; to Joseph Stern for a phone call; to Judith Wheelock for her efforts and insights; to Ellen Nalle Hass, Dr. Emma Mellon, Susan Garrett, Rosemarie Pasdar, Amy McLaughlin, and Michaela Majoun for taking time to read my rough drafts, and for making suggestions.

I am grateful to all of the parents who were willing to share their stories.

Thanks to Drs. Hazel Denning, William Emerson, David Chamberlain, Winafred Blake Lucas, and Colletta Long for sharing their cases and their good counsel. And to Henry Bolduc for his unflagging enthusiasm from the beginning; and Tineke Noordegraaf and Roger Woolger for their superb teaching.

My greatest appreciation and love to Sarah and Chase for letting me tell their stories.

My eternal gratitude to Steve, my co-author in life.

PART ONE

Past Life Stories

CHAPTER 1
Chase and Sarah

"Sit on your mom's lap, close your eyes, and tell me what you see when you hear the loud noises that scare you," instructed hypnotherapist Norman Inge.

My heart pounded with excitement. Maybe now we would solve the mystery of my five-year-old son's hysterical fear of loud noises. My mind raced back to an incident months earlier—to the Fourth of July, when Chase's unusual behavior began.

July 4, 1988

Every year my husband Steve and I hosted a big Fourth of July party at our house, which was a short walk to the best spot in all of Asheville for watching the city's fireworks. Our friends and their young children looked forward to joining us in our back yard for an afternoon of picnicking and celebration. The party always culminated with a walk down the hill to the municipal golf course to watch the grand fireworks display.

For weeks Chase had been talking excitedly about the fun he had had in previous years at our parties, and especially about the fireworks. His eyes got bigger as he remembered the bright colors in the sky. This year he was hoping for a long and spectacular show.

On the afternoon of the Fourth, our friends arrived with pot luck, Frisbees, and sparklers. The yard filled up fast, and kids were everywhere—hanging from the swing set, crowded in the sandbox, hiding under the back porch. Our quiet neighborhood was charged with the sounds of squealing, laughing children. Adults tried to relax on the porch while the children ran circles through the house and around the yard, usually with red-headed Chase in the lead.

Indeed, Chase lived up to his name. Always in motion, full of energy and curiosity, often unstoppable, it seemed we were always two steps behind him, trying to catch him before he knocked something over. Friends teased us about choosing the name *Chase,* saying we got what we asked for.

Our nine-year-old daughter, Sarah, and her friends retreated to a spot on the side of the house under the hemlocks and set up their own small table and chairs, just outside the range of watchful parents. For hours they entertained themselves, decorating their table with flowers and toy china, creating their own holiday party apart from the "wild" little kids. The only time we saw the girls was when they bustled back and forth from Sarah's room, modeling different dress-up clothes, jewelry, and hats on each trip.

When the sun sank low in the trees, throwing orange light into the back yard, we knew it was time to corral the kids and prepare for the march down the hill. I grabbed Chase as he ran by, washed the cake and ice cream off his face, and forced a clean shirt onto his squirming little body. Armed with blankets and flashlights, we joined the parade of people headed down our street toward the golf course.

Unexplained Fear

Chase, holding my hand tight, bobbed my arm up and down as he skipped along with the crowd. The older girls, Sarah's gang, formed their own giggling procession. They clutched the sparklers that we promised they could light once we got to the golf course. We reached our favorite spot just as the sun set behind the Blue Ridge Mountains in the distance, then spread our blankets on a strategic slope.

From the slope we watched the plain below—the lower nine fairways—fill with people. Soon blankets and lawn chairs were strewn everywhere. As the sky grew darker, boys and men set off firecrackers and Roman candles, filling the valley with flashes, bangs, and smoke. Nearby our children waved sparklers in the air, drawing bright circles and zigzag trails in the dusk; fireflies danced and blinked in approval.

Chase, pumped with excitement and sugar, ran up and down the hill with his friends until he finally ran out of steam and collapsed on my lap. We watched the noisy party below while we waited for the big show to begin.

Suddenly the cannonlike booms announcing the start of the fireworks reverberated off the hills, echoing all around us. The sky lit up and crackled with giant starbursts. The crowd around us oohed and aahed at the extravaganza of light and color against the black sky. Hearing the shots and booms at such close range added an exciting intensity to the show.

But Chase, instead of being delighted, began to cry. "What's wrong?" I asked him. He could not answer; he only wailed harder and louder. I held him close, thinking he was exhausted beyond his breaking point and that the loud noises had startled him. But his crying got deeper and more desperate. After a few more minutes, I could see that Chase was not calming down—his hysteria got worse. I knew I had to take him home, away from the noise and confusion. I told Steve that I was leaving with Chase and asked him to stay with Sarah until the fireworks were over.

The short walk home seemed long. Chase was sobbing so

deeply, he couldn't walk, and I had to carry him all the way up the hill. But even when we got home, he was still crying. I held him on my lap in a rocking chair on the back porch, amid the debris of the party, hoping he would calm down. When his deep crying softened enough for me to ask him if he was sick or hurt, he could only whimper and shake his head no. When I asked him if the loud noises scared him, he cried harder. There was nothing I could do but hold and rock him, while I watched the fireflies' silent show in our back yard. Chase gradually settled down and nuzzled into my chest. Finally, just when my arms were too stiff to hold him any longer, he fell asleep and I put him to bed.

Chase's unusual behavior puzzled me. He had never cried so long or so deeply in his short life. And he had never been afraid of fireworks before. This incident seemed out of character for Chase, who was not easily frightened by anything. I put it out of my mind by reasoning that he was frazzled from the long day, and maybe he had eaten too many treats, or something had just set him off—after all, things like this happen with children.

But a month later it happened again. On a hot August day, a friend invited us to cool off at their town's indoor swimming pool. Chase loves the water and was eager to jump in the pool. As soon as he entered the pool area, where the sound of the diving board and splashing and yelling echoed in the big hall, he began to cry hysterically. Howling and screaming, he grabbed my arm with both hands and dragged me toward the door. Reasoning with him was futile; he just pulled me harder. I gave up and took him outside.

We found a chair in the shade. I held Chase and asked him what was bothering him. He couldn't tell me, but he was obviously deeply disturbed, terrified of something. He finally calmed down, but even after he stopped crying, I couldn't persuade him to go back into the pool building.

As we sat outside, I thought back to the other time he had acted this way—on the Fourth of July. I recalled the sound of the fireworks reverberating in the hills, which had triggered his first attack of hysteria. Then I realized that the sound of the diving board reverberating off the bare walls of the pool building sounded the same. I asked Chase if he was frightened by the sounds. He sheepishly nodded yes, but still would not go any-where near the pool.

So that was it—the booming sounds! But *why* did Chase sud-denly have such a fear of loud noises? My mind tried to put all the pieces together. I couldn't remember anything that had hap-pened to him in the past that would cause such a severe reaction to booming sounds. And this was the second time it had hap-pened in a month. The fear seemed to come out of nowhere. Would it happen more often now, every time Chase heard a loud noise? I was worried! This could develop into a real problem, especially if I wasn't there the next time he became hysterical. I didn't know what to do, except wait and hope that he would outgrow this mysterious fear.

A few weeks later, we were fortunate to have a wonderful man and skilled hypnotherapist, Norman Inge, as our house guest. He was staying with us while he conducted workshops in Asheville on past life regression and did private sessions with some of my friends. With Norman as our teacher, we were all just beginning to explore the realms of past life regression.

One afternoon during his stay, Norman, Chase, Sarah, and I were sitting around the kitchen table having tea and cookies, laughing at Norman's stories. Something reminded me of Chase's irrational fear of loud noises, and I asked Norman about it. He listened to my story and then asked if Chase and I would like to try an experiment. Though I didn't know exactly what Norman had in mind, I trusted him and knew that he would be sensitive to my young son's limits. And since Chase was as eager as I was to solve this problem, we both agreed to try.

Still sitting around the kitchen table, Norman began. That moment, I realized later, was a turning point in my life. Up to that time I had never thought that children could remember their past lives.

Chase Sees War

"Sit on your mom's lap, close your eyes, and tell me what you see when you hear the loud noises that scare you," Norman gently instructed Chase.

I looked down at Chase's freckled face. *Nothing* could have prepared me for what I was about to hear.

Young Chase immediately began describing himself as a soldier—an adult soldier—carrying a gun. "I'm standing behind a rock. I'm carrying a long gun with a kind of sword at the end." My heart was pounding in my ears, and the hair on my arms stood up as I listened. Sarah and I glanced at each other in wide-eyed amazement.

"What are you wearing?" Norman questioned.

"I have dirty, ripped clothes, brown boots, a belt. I'm hiding behind a rock, crouching on my knees and shooting at the enemy. I'm at the edge of a valley. The battle is going on all around me."

I listened to Chase, surprised to hear him talk about war. He had never been interested in war toys and had never even owned a toy gun. He always preferred games and construction toys; he would spend hours at a time happily building with blocks, Legos, and his wooden trains. His television watching was strictly limited to *Sesame Street* and *Mister Rogers,* and none of the Disney movies he had seen depicted war.

"I'm behind a rock," he said again. "I don't want to look, but I have to when I shoot. Smoke and flashes everywhere. And loud noises: yelling, screaming, loud booms. I'm not sure who I'm shooting at—there's so much smoke, so much going on. I'm scared. I shoot at anything that moves. I really don't want to be here and shoot other people."

Although this was Chase's little-boy voice, his tone was serious and mature—uncharacteristic of my happy five-year-old. He actually seemed to be feeling this soldier's feelings and thinking his thoughts. He really didn't want to be there shooting at other men. This was not a glorified picture of war or soldiering; Chase was describing the sentiments of a man in the heat of battle who had serious doubts about the value of his actions and was terrified, thinking only of staying alive. These feelings and images were coming from someplace deep within him. Chase was not making this up.

Chase's body, too, revealed how deeply he was experiencing this life. As he described himself shooting from behind the rock, I could feel his body tense on my lap. When he admitted he didn't want to be there and shoot at other people, his breathing quickened and he curled up into a ball, as if he were trying to hide and avoid what he saw. Holding him, I could feel his fear.

Norman sensed Chase's distress with his role as a soldier who, in order to survive, had to kill other men. He explained to Chase, talking slowly, "We live many different lives on Earth. We take turns playing different parts, like actors in a play. We learn what it means to be human by playing these different parts. Sometimes we are soldiers and kill others in a battle, and sometimes we are killed. We are simply playing our parts to learn." Using simple language, Norman emphasized that there was no blame in being a soldier. He assured Chase that he was just doing his job, even if he had to kill other soldiers in battle.

As my son listened to Norman's assurances, I could feel his body relax and his breathing become more regular. The anguished look on his face melted away. Norman's words were helping. Young Chase was actually understanding and responding to these universal concepts.

When Norman saw that Chase had calmed down, he asked him to continue telling us what he saw.

"I'm crouching on my knees behind the rock. I'm hit in the right wrist by a bullet someone shot from above the valley. I slide down behind the rock, holding my wrist where I was shot. It's bleeding—I feel dizzy.

"Someone I know drags me out of the battle and takes me to a place where they took soldiers that are hurt—not like a regular hospital, just big poles, like an open tent, covered with material. There are beds there, but they're like wooden benches. They're very hard and uncomfortable."

Chase said that he felt dizzy and could hear the sounds of

gunfire around him as his wrist was being bandaged. He said he was relieved to be out of the fighting. But it wasn't long before he was ordered back into battle, and he reluctantly returned to the shooting.

"I'm walking back to battle. There are chickens on the road. I see a wagon pulling a cannon on it. The cannon is tied onto the wagon with ropes. The wagon has big wheels."

Chase said that he had been ordered to man a cannon on a hill overlooking the main battlefield. He was visibly upset by this order and repeated that he didn't want to be there. He said he missed his family. At the mention of his family, Norman and I looked at each other with raised eyebrows. But before we could learn more, Chase started to fidget and told us the images were fading. He opened his eyes, looked around the kitchen, looked at us, and smiled. The little-boy glow in his face had returned. Norman asked him how he felt. Chase chirped, "Fine." Then he hopped off my lap, grabbed another cookie, and ran into the other room to play.

As Chase pattered out of the kitchen, Norman, Sarah, and I looked at each other with our mouths open. I glanced at the clock on the stove: only twenty minutes had passed since Norman had told Chase to close his eyes. It felt like hours.

Norman broke our stunned silence to ask for another cup of tea.

We talked about the small miracle we had just witnessed. Norman was sure that Chase had remembered a past life. He explained that a traumatic experience in a past life such as being in war—and especially a traumatic death—can cause a phobia in the present life. Could this past life war experience be the cause of Chase's extreme fear of loud noises? Possibly. Norman said we'd have to wait and see if the fear went away.

Norman admitted that he had never worked with a child so young and that he was surprised at how easily Chase had retrieved his past life memory—no hypnotic induction had been needed, as with his older clients. Apparently, Chase's memories were close to the surface and needed only gentle encouragement to come out.

Sarah, who had been quietly absorbing everything that happened, suddenly bounced up and down in her chair, waving her arms, and piped in, "That spot on Chase's wrist, where he was shot—that's where his eczema is!"

She was right. The location of the wound Chase described was exactly the same location as that of a persistent rash he had suffered since he was a baby. He had always had severe eczema on his right wrist. Whenever he became upset or tired, he scratched that wrist until it bled. Sarah said that it sounded like Chase was "ripping his flesh" as he relentlessly scratched that one spot. I often bandaged his wrist to prevent his scratching and bleeding. Without a bandage, Chase would wake up with blood streaked on his sheets. I had taken him to several doctors because of the severity of his rash, but allergy testing, a food elimination diet, salves, and ointments failed to clear it up.

To our astonishment and relief, within a few days of his regression to the lifetime as a soldier, the eczema on Chase's right wrist vanished completely, and it has never returned.

Chase's fear of loud noises also totally disappeared. Fireworks, explosions, and booming sounds never scared him again. In fact, soon after the regression Chase began showing an intense interest in playing the drums. For his sixth birthday he got his first drum set. Now he's a serious drummer, filling the house with loud booming sounds every day.

Dolls Under the Bed

Nine-year-old Sarah had taken in everything Norman said, and during Chase's story she seemed to be in a trance herself, hanging on to every word. When we were finished processing Chase's experience, she asked Norman if he could try an experiment with her too. She confided to him that she had been struggling with her own terrible fear of house fires.

Like Chase's fear of loud noises, Sarah's extreme fear of fire was inexplicable. Though she admitted now that fire had terrified her as long as she could remember, Steve and I had become aware of it only a year earlier when, one evening, Sarah spent the night down the street at the home of her good friend Amy. The girls stayed up late and watched a movie on television that featured scenes of burning houses and buildings. Sarah was so distraught from seeing these images that Amy's mother had to bring her home in the middle of the night, waking us out of bed. Nothing like this had ever happened before; she had spent the night at Amy's many times.

When Sarah got home, her eyes were red from crying. She wept as she told us that she had cried uncontrollably when someone in the movie was killed in a fire. We were surprised by Sarah's reaction and asked her if this had happened before. She confessed through her tears that she was so terrified of fires—especially house fires—that she kept a bag packed under her bed with her favorite Barbie dolls and some clothes, ready for a quick escape. The revelation surprised us even more because this kind of precaution was totally out of character for our self-assured and independent Sarah. Where had the fear come from? I hugged her until she calmed down. Exhausted from her emotional experience, Sarah finally fell asleep. But she remained upset for days. Despite repeated assurances that she was safe, and even after reviewing escape routes from every room of our house, her fears became more pronounced. Sarah would become agitated even if we lit candles on the dining room table, and she insisted that we blow them out. She would not believe us when we promised that we would protect her if our house ever caught on fire.

As I had done with Chase's fear of loud noises, I reasoned at the time that Sarah would outgrow this fear. After all, many young children have irrational fears that dissipate naturally as they grow older. Besides, I didn't know what else to do. But now, seeing how Norman had worked with Chase, Sarah sensed an opportunity to get help with her fear of house fires. Norman agreed to try. Still sitting at the kitchen table, Norman instructed Sarah, "Close your eyes, feel the fear of fire. Now tell me what you see."

With her arms resting on the table, Sarah closed her eyes and squinted in deep concentration as she began describing what she saw. I, still trying to recover from the surprise of hearing my young son speak like an adult and describe war, didn't know what to expect from his older sister. All I could do was listen and watch.

Sarah described a simple two-story wooden house, shaped "like a barn" and surrounded by woods and farmland. A wagon road, overgrown with grass, passed in front of the house. She saw herself as a girl, about eleven or twelve years old (older than she was at the time). She said she spent most of her time working around the house helping her mother and sometimes helping her father with the animals. She didn't go to school because "they don't believe girls need education." She saw a younger brother who couldn't help with the work. Squeezing her closed eyes to see more details, she added that her brother may have been handicapped in some way.

Up to this point, Sarah told her story as an observer, objectively reporting what she saw, without any involvement or emotion. Then Norman suggested she "move ahead to the time when your fear of fire started." Sarah's perspective shifted. Now she spoke as the young girl, in the present tense, totally absorbed in the terror of her predicament.

"I wake up suddenly and smell smoke—I know the house is on fire. I'm scared. Panicked. Can't think. I jump out of bed. Flames and smoke everywhere. I run across the hall looking for my parents. Big flames cover the stairs and banister. Small flames shoot up through cracks in the floor. The bottom of my nightgown is on fire! I'm running into my parents' room. They're not there! Their beds are made. Where are they? I keep running until I'm trapped in the far corner of the room. I'm shaking as I stand in the corner. Why don't they save me? Why don't they get me out?"

Sarah paused for a moment to catch her breath. She was still leaning with her arms on the table, her eyes closed, her face contorted and pale. She was reliving this painful memory with all of her being, panicked like a trapped little animal, pressed into the corner of the room by flames and heat.

The terror in her voice drew me into her story. I felt the adrenaline pumping in my body, accelerating my heart and sending jitters through my veins. The air in the kitchen was taut with danger. Driven by motherly instinct, I shifted to reach out and comfort Sarah. But another instinct told me not to interrupt the flow and drama of her experience. I glanced at Norman for a sign. He sensed my question, nodded to assure me that Sarah was all right, and gestured for me to remain where I was. Sarah continued, crying with panic.

"A beam covered with big flames falls down right in front of me and breaks a hole in the floor. Fire is everywhere. There's no way out. Oh, it really hurts to breathe. I know I'm going to die!"

Sarah sat silently for a while at the kitchen table with her head in her hands. Her breathing slowed, her face relaxed. I discovered I had been holding my breath and let it out with a rush. A calm settled on the room. All was quiet, except for the purr of the refrigerator.

Norman waited, then softly asked Sarah, "What are you experiencing now?"

"I feel myself floating high above the treetops. I feel light, like air. I guess I'm dead. I don't feel any pain. I'm relieved that it's over. That was awful."

Norman asked Sarah if she could see her family below.

"There's my house—it's totally covered with flames. The roof is gone. I can see my family in the yard. My brother is sitting on the ground, and my father is holding on to my mother, who's crying and waving her arms at the house."

Sarah began to cry deeply as she described her family. She said she knew that they had tried to save her but were driven back by the heat and flames. They were devastated that they could not save their daughter. Clearly Sarah was deeply moved by the grief of her family. Through her sobs, with her eyes still closed, she said she realized that her family had really loved her after all. She now understood that there was nothing they could have done to save her life, and she was greatly relieved to know the truth. She admitted that she had carried into her present life the false belief that her parents hadn't tried to save her from dying in the burning house.

Sarah's sobbing gradually stopped. Norman and I sat silently and waited as she rubbed her eyes, then opened them and looked at us. She sniffled a few times and gave us a big smile. The panic and terror were gone. She looked peaceful.

She saw the worry on my face and assured me that she was all right. Then she recounted the last moments before her death. She said that it all happened so quickly—in just a few seconds—from the time she woke up to her last memory of the fiery beam falling in front of her and fire exploding all around. She explained that she had run into the corner of her parents' room out of pure panic, with no time to think of a way out of the house. Her only thought had been to find her parents. She admitted that her last moments had been filled with anger for her parents, believing they did not love her because they hadn't gotten her out of the burning house. She said again that she had carried that anger—her last dying thoughts—with her into her present life, misunderstanding what had really happened and confused by the sudden terror of her death. Then she explained that her current fear of fire was a reminder that she still had something unfinished from that lifetime to work out.

Norman and I were both amazed that we didn't have to interpret anything for Sarah. She understood intuitively, without prompting or explanation, the connection between her fear and anger at the time of her traumatic death and her present fear of fire. Many adults who remember past lives, Norman explained, are not as quick to process these connections between past and present. Sarah did it immediately on her own.

A few days later, Sarah unpacked the bag she had kept under her bed with her dolls and clothes. Her "irrational" fear of fire disappeared after that day, though she is still very careful when she lights a match.

Interlude

A few days after Chase and Sarah remembered their past lives, Chase entered kindergarten and Sarah began fourth grade. Chase looked forward to school every morning. He went to a small alternative school, Rainbow Mountain, that emphasized story-telling, music, and creativity. He loved dictating stories to the teacher and was especially proud of his saga of his two mischievous hamsters, Romeo and Juliet, which was displayed in the classroom for all to see. Each afternoon he came home and excitedly reported the progress the class was making on the life-size dinosaur habitat they were building with papier-mâché. Chase was thriving and growing.

Sarah began fourth grade in a new, experimental public school. She was placed in the accelerated program and spent some of her time in class doing independent projects, which made her feel grown up and responsible. Of course, as she started noticing the boys, she wished she could grow up faster. She spent more and more time on the phone with her friends gossiping about the constantly shifting alliances and affections among her classmates.

These new adventures in school upstaged the intensity of my children's extraordinary experiences with Norman just a few weeks before. The regressions, in their minds, quickly faded to the status of "something that happened."

On a few occasions Sarah, Chase, Steve, and I talked about their memories among ourselves and with a few close friends. But for the most part we kept it within the family. I was careful to protect my children from anyone who might laugh at them or accuse them of making up stories. I was afraid that mockery might shut Sarah and Chase down completely and that the door to their past lives, which had so miraculously opened, might close. I instructed them not to talk about their past life experiences with anyone unless they consulted me first. I assured them that what they saw was real, but I explained that most people would not understand and some people might even make fun of them. They readily understood and accepted this advice.

I thought often about their amazing past life memories, and had many questions. Do other children remember their past lives too? And if they do, are the memories as close to the surface and as easy to access as they had been with Chase and Sarah? How many other childhood fears and physical problems have past life origins? The questions kept coming. I wanted to find answers. But a few weeks later, Steve accepted a new job in Pennsylvania, and three months after that, in December, we sold our house and moved. Because of this upheaval in our lives, I didn't have the time or energy to pursue the answers to my questions—just yet.

Leaving Asheville was a loss for all of us, but it was especially hard on our children, who had been born there. We postponed the closing on our house until after Sarah's Christmas choral concert, where she sang a solo in *Dear Mr. Santa*. At the end of the concert, the children in Sarah's grade presented her with a bouquet of roses, and many of the little girls on stage broke into tears. We were heartbroken to leave so many close friends and such a comfortable community. Asheville had been good to us.

In suburban Philadelphia we moved into a centuries-old stone farmhouse surrounded by beautiful old trees and in a neighborhood with cul-de-sacs and streets that were safe for bikes and skateboards. Chase and Sarah entered public school, which was a new experience for both of them. Sarah was disappointed to find that students' desks were arranged in rows and that the children were forbidden to talk to each other during class, though she quickly adapted to public school mode and made the most of it. Chase rode the transition to the new kindergarten easily. Within a few weeks they were both making new friends.

After we were settled into our new house, Chase didn't mention his regression once. I thought he had forgotten about it. But one morning a few months later, while six-year-old Chase and I were enjoying breakfast together, he startled me with more information from his soldier's life. The conversation went like this:

"Mom, remember when I saw that I was a soldier with Norman?"

"Yes," I answered, surprised that he was bringing this up after so long. I could feel the goose bumps rippling all over my skin. I took a deep breath to calm myself as I looked Chase straight in the eye.

"Well, we talked funny," Chase said, looking right through me.

"What do you mean—did you speak English, the language that we speak?"

"Yes," he responded, squirming, looking a bit puzzled, "but we talked funny. We sounded different." He hesitated, groping for words to explain what he meant, and then said, "You know how black people talk?" I nodded. "Well, I was black."

After recovering from my shock, I managed to ask, in a more or less conversational tone, "Were you with other black soldiers?"

"Yes. There were black soldiers and white soldiers fighting together," Chase replied. I watched Chase's face. His eyes looked to the side. He seemed to be viewing images in his mind and reporting to me what he saw.

Remembering Norman's questions, I asked, "What else do you see?"

"That's it."

And that was that. Chase lost the image and went back to spooning his cereal.

I was caught off guard by Chase's sudden announcement and wished later that I had kept my wits about me and asked better questions, or had figured out a way to keep him talking. Was there more to be revealed about his experience as a soldier? Was his past life memory still affecting him in ways I didn't understand? Perhaps there were more issues and emotions from that lifetime that needed to surface. And why had this shard of memory surfaced spontaneously during breakfast? Chase's observations weren't prompted by anything we were saying or doing at the time, as far as I could tell. Had he been thinking about this? Had some incident in school triggered more memories? I didn't know. It was a mystery. I wanted to know the answers but realized that I needed to wait for another opportunity to ask Chase more questions.

I pieced together this new bit of information about being a black man with what Chase had described during his regression with Norman the year before: the battlefield, the description of the field hospital, the horses pulling cannons, and the gun with the sword at the end. And, I reasoned, since he spoke English and was black, the soldier Chase remembered was probably an American. This detail added a new twist to the story. Could he have been a black soldier in the Civil War? The Spanish-American War? World War I? Did they still use horse-drawn cannons in World War I? My limited knowledge of history failed me at that moment.

Coincidentally, the next day, *The Philadelphia Inquirer* featured an article, illustrated with photographs, about a local exhibit of memorabilia of black Civil War soldiers. I learned from the article that regiments of black soldiers had fought in the Civil War alongside white soldiers, just as Chase had said. I looked closely at the photograph of the black soldiers and then glanced at red-haired, freckle-faced Chase. I laughed, thinking God has a weird sense of humor.

This article gave me an opportunity to ask Chase more. Since he couldn't read at the time, I simply showed him, without comment, the pictures in the paper to see if they would prompt him to say anything. I watched his face closely as he looked at the photographs of the black Civil War soldiers posing in uniform. "Does this look familiar?" I ventured.

"Yeah," he responded matter-of-factly. He was not offering any more information, so I tried coaxing him by telling him how the article described black soldiers fighting in the Civil War alongside white soldiers, just as he had told me the day before.

"Do you remember anything else?" I asked him.

"No, not really." he said. This wasn't working. There had been a look on his face the day before—an energized, glowing look as he spoke of his memory. It wasn't there now. So I put the newspaper away and changed the subject. I didn't want to push him or betray how eager I was to know more. I wanted him to feel comfortable talking about his memories again, if they should resurface.

"Chickens Walk Free"

February 1991 was a frightening time for many of us. The conflict in Iraq brought the reality of war into our homes and, for the first time, into my children's lives. Although we didn't watch television, we anxiously listened to the radio and looked at newspapers as the fighting escalated. Everyone was feeling the tension.

One night, as we listened to the radio announce the first Scud missile attack on Israel, thunder crashed, lightning flashed outside our window and the power went off. We were all shaken, and Chase began to cry. Steve and I did our best to calm our children's fear that the war would spread to Philadelphia.

The day after the ground war began, I picked up Chase at school. He got into the car and announced, "They'll never make me fight again!" I wasn't sure if I had heard him correctly and asked him to repeat what he had said. Again Chase said, "They'll never make me fight again."

"What do you mean?" I asked, trying to figure out the context for his remark.

"I want to do another regression like I did with Norman that time when I was a soldier. There's more coming up. The kids in school keep talking about the war on TV, and I keep thinking about what I saw with Norman." Evidently the war news had triggered Chase's memory. This was the opportunity I had been waiting for.

During the ride home Chase explained to me that the school was decorated with yellow ribbons, showing unquestioned support for the American troops who were fighting. He described how the kids and teachers were uneasy about the war, but at the same time everyone was proud that America was leading the attack on Iraq. This glorification of the war, he explained, brought up uncomfortable feelings for him. He told me he knew these feelings had to do with the lifetime he had seen as a soldier. Chase's mature observation rang true. I agreed to regress him.

It had been two years since Chase last mentioned his past life as a soldier. During that time I had trained in hypnotherapy and studied past life regression techniques with Norman Inge and Dr. Roger Woolger. I apprenticed in guiding adults through their past life experiences and learned about the range of issues and trauma that can emerge during regressions. I also knew, from being regressed myself, that past life regression is a safe process. The unconscious mind, where past life memories reside, is selective in what it releases to the conscious mind: it will allow the person to go as deeply and as far as they need to go, and no further. I felt confident guiding Chase through a past life regression. I knew I could handle anything that came up.

I waited until we had a quiet stretch of time during the afternoon, then turned off the phone and made Chase comfortable on his bed. Remembering how easily Chase and Sarah had accessed their memories with Norman, I decided to follow his example and not use a formal induction technique. I simply told Chase to close his eyes, take some deep breaths, and "go back to the scene you saw with Norman when you were a soldier." This time, I took detailed notes as eight-year-old Chase told his story.

"Can't hear sounds, but can see it. I see horses coming in the valley. Men with guns with spears on the ends. I see myself crouching behind a rock, looking up at them. I'm feeling sad, scared, proud. There are soldiers on horses on my side. I'm now kneeling behind a rock. Waiting.

"There's a battle going on. Smoke everywhere. I'm not shooting, I'm waiting. I start to shoot at the enemy—I don't have any choice, I want to protect myself. The people on the horses are white, I'm black. White soldiers are on my side. There's too much going on. Confusion everywhere. I'm scared half to death. Oh—he gets my wrist with a shot. It hardly hurts. Everything goes black."

Chase was talking quietly in halting phrases and sentences, as thoughts and images poured forth in a stream of consciousness, not always in sequence. He appeared to be watching a continuous story in his mind, reporting only snapshots of the action. He was seeing and feeling much more than he could describe. At times he stopped talking, leaving gaps in his narrative. I encouraged him to continue with questions: "What are you experiencing?" "What happens next?" Without this gentle prodding he might have gotten bogged down in one spot.

As before, he was talking in his little-boy voice but with the seriousness and phrasing of an adult. Some of the words he used surprised me, because they were a stretch from his usual vocabulary, or words I had never heard him use before.

As he lay on the bed, Chase's body mirrored the changing scenes and emotions he was remembering. He was stiff as he described himself scared and waiting behind the rock in the battle. When he was hit in the wrist, he tensed up and stopped talking. His body relaxed when he reported that he "blacked out." This subtle body language added an extra dimension to an already fascinating account.

I encouraged him to continue: "What are you experiencing now?"

"Now I'm going back to fight with a bandage on my wrist. I see horses pulling a cannon, making a lot of dust. The cannon is on a wagon with big wheels—it's tied down with heavy ropes. There's chickens walking along the road. It's a time between fighting. I'm thinking how unhappy I am about going to war. I didn't know what I was getting into."

After a long pause I asked, "What happens next?"

"I'm back in battle. I'm shooting a cannon from the top of the valley. I pull a string, the cannon fires. I'm not loading it, though. I can't shoot a gun because of my arm. I'm scared shooting the cannon. Now I know how the others feel to be shot at. They're scared too."

Again Chase paused. I asked, "Do you know why you're fighting?"

"I don't know," Chase murmured.

On a hunch, based on his earlier comment "I didn't know what I was getting into," I asked Chase to go back to an earlier time before the battle. I wanted to find out about his life before the war, to understand why he kept saying that he didn't want to be there and shoot people.

"I'm at a house. It's mine. Sort of a cabin made of rough wood. The house has a front porch with a railing—a place to hitch horses. There's a rocking chair on the porch, and a door in the middle. I have two kids. I think I have a wife—I do. I'm happy. It's before the war. I was where the blacks are free. I see my wife—I see her from behind. She's in the house. She's wearing a blue dress with a white apron. She wears a dress with petticoats and black boots. She has straight hair she wears pulled back in a rag.

"I see a black man on the porch smoking a pipe—it's me. I'm not young—about thirty or something. I'm very happy in the town. I wasn't born there, but I was brought there as a baby in a covered wagon. I'm a painter and a carpenter, and I make pots and sell them and make models out of wood for a hobby. There's a green area behind my house with bushes around. That's my favorite place—that's where I make my pots.

"There's a dirt road in front of my house that goes to town. My town is a friendly town with wagons and farms. Chickens walk free. There are other black people who get along pretty well. The name of our town is something like Collosso." Chase strains as he tries to remember the name. "It's eighteen-sixty-something, at the beginning of the war.

"People are standing around a post where the roads meet—it's the center of town. There's a lot of excitement; they're talking about the war. I'm reading a notice attached to the post. The notice says 'WAR' and has little print. I'm not sure that I can read, but I know the notice is asking for volunteers. I get excited too, and I volunteer. I sign a paper. I don't know what the paper says. I can't read.

"I'm leaving my family. This is a sad time for me and my family, especially my kids. They're crying. I'm very sad. This is the saddest time of my life."

Again Chase stopped talking, as he felt the sadness. After a long pause, I asked, "And then what happens?"

"We're meeting with someone important, a general or something, after I join. He's talking about strategy. It's for my own good to listen. But I'm not paying attention—I'm thinking about my family. I feel totally pushed around, and I don't like it. People around me are more sad than scared."

Chase paused, then jumped back to the scene in the field hospital. "I'm hurt in the wrist. I'm under a big cloth held up by poles—it looks like a tepee or a covered wagon—wide open on the sides. It's very crowded. A lot of noise—war in the background, gunshots. Someone is putting bandages around my wrist. Others are screaming because they're in so much pain. I'm thankful I don't have as much pain as the others. I guess my wrist isn't that bad. I'm sad to go back to battle. I miss my family. I'm behind the cannon. I'm hit!"

Chase stopped speaking. I felt the energy shift—it felt lighter, like a breeze flowing through the room.

After a pause, Chase continued on his own. "I'm floating above the battlefield. I feel good that I'm done. I see the battle and smoke below. As I look down on the battlefield, everything is still and smoky—nothing is moving down there. I feel happy that I'm done. I get to go to a happier life. I float over my house. I see my wife and kids. I say good-bye to my family. They don't see me because I'm in spirit, but they know that I'm dead."

Chase looked peaceful. I let him enjoy the peace for a minute. Then I asked him what he had learned from his lifetime as a soldier. His reply amazed me:

"Everyone has to be in a war. It balances everything out. Not necessarily die in a war, but experience it. It teaches you about feelings. It gives you a sense of how other people feel. It's a bad place. I skipped World War II. I was up. I was waiting for my turn to go back to a more peaceful time. I had a short life in between."

I listened in wonder as my young son talked about universal balance and compassion. He spoke with a wisdom far beyond his eight years. His words and his tone of voice sounded as though they were coming from an old soul. I didn't know what to say. Where was "up"? Where was he waiting for his turn to come back? I wanted to hear more, but he was finished. The window to this mystery closed suddenly, and I knew I couldn't open it again.

Chase opened his eyes and lay quietly on the bed for a few minutes. He looked distant, but calm. I asked him how he felt. He said that he felt better now that he had remembered more. I gave him a hug and assured him that he was now safe, that he didn't have to fight again, and that we were all safe and together as a family. Chase liked that and hugged me back. He bounced off the bed and out of the room. Within a few minutes he was happily back at play in his own room with his newest Lego kit.

Layers of the Onion

Something extraordinary had happened that afternoon. I thought back to Chase's earlier protest: "They'll never make me fight again!" Now I understood what he meant. The memories of his lifetime as a soldier were all too real for him. The fear, sadness, and confusion of that peaceful man who became a soldier swelled close to the surface of Chase's memory, informing his present personality and his view of the world.

Chase's two regressions to that lifetime uncovered successive layers of emotions, thoughts, and images. Like the layers of an onion, once the first skin had been peeled away, the next was revealed. Norman had helped Chase bring the first layer of emotion to a conscious level: the layer of fear that was triggered by the loud booms, reminding him of battle. Once Chase reconciled his feelings about being a soldier and killing others in battle, the fear and the eczema—the stigma of his wound—disappeared.

The war in the Middle East triggered another layer of memory: the longing for his family. Chase's sadness changed to relief as he progressed further in the story to his death and had the opportunity to say good-bye to his family. He finally had closure on his life as a soldier. This enabled him to move beyond his personal tragedy to a universal understanding of the significance of war in a soul's development. His personal suffering transformed to spiritual awareness.

The consistency between this most recent version of the story and his first regression was remarkable. Although these two accounts were three years apart, Chase reported the same images and feelings almost word for word. His vocabulary had increased since he was five, adding a richer texture to the story but not changing it. The memory remained intact. He was seeing these images clearly in his mind, reporting what he saw.

Chase gave what sounded to me like an accurate portrayal of a Civil War soldier's life. His account of what it felt like to be in the middle of a confusing battle and to be "pushed around" was more realistic than the glorified version of war that is commonly depicted in movies and on television. The mundane details added color and realism to the story: chickens running free, his wife's black boots and multiple petticoats, the recruitment poster on a pole that was the center of town, enlistment papers he couldn't read, the field hospital made of poles and canvas, pulling a string to fire the cannon (which, I verified later, was how these cannons were actually fired). The cumulative effect of the details, the flow and cogency of his story, and the credible predicament of the protagonist would do credit to any novelist. Yet this was coming from an eight-year-old boy with virtually no exposure to the realities of war.

Most importantly, the benefits of these regressions were tangible. After this last regression Chase was immediately more confident and relaxed. He was no longer troubled by the war with Iraq, although we were all relieved when it was over a few days later.

CHAPTER 2
Prelude

A year before Norman Inge guided Chase and Sarah through their past lives, he regressed me through two of my own past lives. The regression healed a chronic illness and explained visions, obsessions, and dreams that had puzzled me since childhood.

If I hadn't experienced my own past lives, what happened with my children that day in my kitchen might not have been so meaningful. But because I had been through it myself I was able to quickly recognize my children's experiences as genuine. I was able to move beyond the simple fact that they were remembering their past lives, and pay attention to the subtleties of the process, such as how easily the memories surfaced and how naturally the children absorbed life lessons from the past. And I was primed to recognize the potential in this process for *all* children: I saw my children's regressions not just as an isolated event, but as an example of how other children might be helped.

Describing my regression shows what past life memories in

general look like, feel like, and how they sometimes ripple just below the surface of consciousness to influence a person's present life. Children's past life memories work in much the same way.

My Funeral

During the winter of 1986, when I was thirty-six, I was so seriously ill, I didn't know if I would survive. This was the third consecutive winter that I had battled pleurisy, asthma, pneumonia, and bronchial infections. I had so much difficulty breathing, Steve had to carry me up the stairs to our bedroom—the climb was too much for me. My wrenching, hacking cough echoed throughout the house, day and night.

Nothing stopped my cough, not even narcotic cough syrups and the formidable clutter of prescription drugs on my night table. I had so many different drugs to take at different intervals, I couldn't keep track of them. Steve tried to help by drawing a chart showing which pills to take at each hour of the day and night and posting it next to my bed. But it didn't work: I was so sick, I couldn't even follow the chart. Steve had to administer my pills to me.

My only relief came during short, fitful periods of sleep, and even those were interrupted by coughing spells. Continuously exhausted and heavily medicated, I was unable to care for six-year-old Sarah and three-year-old Chase. Steve divided his time between working, ministering to me in bed, and taking care of the children. As much as he tried, the laundry piled up, the litter of toys and Fisher-Price plastic people got worse, and Sarah and Chase weren't getting enough attention. My sense of order was destroyed, and I felt helpless to do even the simplest tasks.

I needed strict bed rest, either in the hospital or at home. I didn't want to go to the hospital, but I knew that I couldn't care for Chase and Sarah. So we called our parents and arranged for them to take our children until I got well. On a cold and icy January day, Steve drove down the mountain and put Sarah and Chase on the next plane to upstate New York. I was too sick even to worry about my family driving on the treacherous roads, and I was grateful to be alone without having to care for anyone but myself.

Our house had never been so quiet as it was during those days when the kids were away. As I lay in bed, my lungs strained with each breath, creaking like rusty hinges. My buzzing, medicated brain amplified all the sounds around me—the hissing of the radiator, cars approaching and passing on the street, the barking of our neighbor's terrier. When the wind blew hard, our old house creaked and moaned, and the tops of the hemlocks outside my windows bent in spasms. I was thankful, at least, to be out of the cold and in my warm bed. In the moments when I wasn't coughing, I stared at the frost patterns on the windows and watched them melt as the sun came around. Hours and minutes had no meaning; I marked time by the phases of dawn, daylight, dusk, and dark.

Late one afternoon, as the light in the room started to fade away and the shadows in the furniture grew deeper, I lay totally exhausted, aching for sleep. My coughing and fatigue had been battling it out all day, and my mind had been balancing for hours in the twilight zone between waking and sleeping.

Just as my body finally surrendered to fatigue and I began dozing off, I saw a vision of a frail middle-aged man. At first I saw only his face, the vision holding steady in front of my closed eyes, his deep brown eyes penetrating mine. I strained to hold on to this vision to see what it was, because it was so clear and real. As I focused on his face, the image grew. In the next moment I could see a complete picture of the man and the room he was in. He was lying in bed, dressed in a white gown, bolstered by many pillows. I could see and hear him coughing, gasping for breath, and spitting up blood into a handkerchief. A middle-aged woman in a long, full dress sat beside his bed with a deeply worried look on her face. As I too lay in bed struggling to breathe, his condition was eerily familiar.

The power of these images drew me in; they had a luminescence and vitality unlike daydreams. And I knew I wasn't sleeping, because I was aware of the barking of the dog next door. I forgot about my pain and coughing. My struggled breathing relaxed and slowed. I remained still, with my eyes closed, concentrating on the images, giving them all of my attention.

There was something haunting and familiar about the scene—the carved wooden bed, the white linens, the woman at his bedside, and the countenance of this dying man—especially his soulful eyes. As I allowed myself to sink deeper into the vision, it not only looked familiar, it began to *feel* familiar.

Then a bolt of recognition surged through my entire body, as if I had touched a live wire. I knew in that instant that I had been this man—that I had existed in another time and place. My body recognized the truth first, before my mind could register the fact. It was a staggered recognition, like running into a friend I hadn't seen in years, feeling the familiarity but not recalling the time or place where we had known each other until a few seconds later.

This sudden familiarity jolted me from head to toe. And when my mind finally acknowledged that I was watching myself in a past life, another realization hit me to complete the story: this man (or should I say *I*?) died of consumption in his midthirties—the same age that I was now in my present life.

I took a minute to absorb this new realization. When I did, the images of the movie in my mind segued to the next scene: his funeral—a procession of carriages and horses, and men and women in ornate nineteenth-century dress. From an aerial view above the treetops, I saw the procession move through the elaborate stone and iron gates of a cemetery. The cemetery looked like a park, green with beautiful arching shade trees and crowded with mausoleums. Again my perspective shifted. At close range I saw the woman in the long dress, who had lovingly nursed this man at his deathbed, holding a handkerchief to her veiled face. The sight of this grieving woman let loose in me ripples of unspeakable sorrow and fear. I struggled to quell these unwelcome feelings, which broke my concentration. Just as quickly as the images had formed, they faded.

I opened my eyes and looked around my bedroom, anchoring myself back in the present. Some light still came in through the curtains. The neighbor's terrier was still barking.

Then another wave of realization hit me: if I had indeed been this man who died at the same age as I was now, and with a similar affliction of the lungs, was I destined to repeat the same pattern? Would I soon die? Was this a vision of my own imminent death? I was terrified. I couldn't bear the thought of dying and leaving my two young children and my husband alone.

My mind raced on. Was I simply hallucinating from medication and fatigue? I preferred to think that I was just imagining all of this—that it would all go away. But the intense feelings these images evoked were too compelling to dismiss. The emotion was too familiar, like something I had once known but forgotten. And the image had the clarity and body of a waking vision, not the shifting disorder of a dream or hallucination.

But what was I to do with this information? If I was repeating a pattern from a past life, was there any way I could change the pattern and break my cycle of illness?

As soon as Steve got home that evening, I told him all about my vision. He didn't know what to think. But if my revelation about a past life might cure me, he was happy to give me the benefit of the doubt. The next day I sent him to the local library to find books on reincarnation that might shed light on this mystery. He found books on religion and theological discourses on reincarnation but nothing that told what it meant to actually remember a past life. He returned to the house empty-handed and disappointed. I would have to find the answers on my own, somehow.

"At the Still Point of the Turning World . . ."

In the days that followed, I lay in bed unable to do anything. I was too sick to read, and to my great disappointment, talking on the phone for more than a couple of minutes triggered painful coughing spells. All I could do was watch the hemlocks bend outside my window, follow the patterns of sunlight as they crawled across the walls—and think.

Questions about reincarnation and death swirled in my restless mind. The vision of my death and funeral in that past life was alive in my memory, and I shuddered every time a cold premonition of imminent death passed through my body. Now, because I was so sick, understanding the implications of reincarnation was suddenly and immediately relevant to survival in my present life.

I thought back to my Jewish religious training as a child, to see if I had forgotten anything that might help me now. I could never fathom an existence that simply ended at death. I had always thought that it didn't make sense that each person was born once into inequitable circumstances, lived, died, and that was the end of it. But Judaism never adequately answered questions about death and afterlife for me, and never mentioned reincarnation. Nor did the Christianity of my neighbors, as far as I could tell.

When I was a little girl, our rabbi once said something in a sermon that I never forgot: "With a twist of God's wrist, you could have been born in India, dying of starvation." I questioned: Why? How does God decide who gets a good life and who gets a hard life? I was lucky, I thought, but why weren't the others? I felt uneasy thinking that our fates were merely God's whim. It just didn't make sense to me as a child.

To add to my confusion, my Catholic playmates scared me with their visions of heaven, hell, and purgatory. Death, as they described it, was terrifying because your soul might end up in the wrong place forever. And according to them, the road to heaven was not an easy one. Only a few perfect people made it. What if I did something bad—would that condemn me for eternity?

One rainy day when I was about seven, some neighborhood children and I were playing house in my garage. The little girl who lived next door informed me, "You will certainly go to hell because Jews do not accept Jesus Christ as their Savior." Well, that made me furious. That wasn't fair at all! At that moment I decided that their version of the afterlife was all wrong. Since they didn't even give me a chance because I was Jewish, I wasn't going to believe what they said about what happens after we die. That settled that!

My thoughts drifted to another time—to a literature course at Simmons College, in the late 1960s, when I was first introduced to T. S. Eliot's poetry, and especially his masterpiece, *Four Quartets*. My professor, Conrad Snowden, a tall, stately black man of imposing intelligence, held the *Four Quartets* before us like Moses with the Ten Commandments; we trembled in our seats at the sight. He mesmerized us with a magical and passionate reading of the entire work. The cryptic words of the *Quartets* sang in my ears: "In my end is my beginning . . . to be conscious is not to be in time."[1]

Those two phrases in particular I couldn't get out of my head, like a popular tune that wouldn't go away. The truth in the lines tugged at my mind and nagged me to understand them. "In my end is my beginning . . . to be conscious is not to be in time." For months I carried the *Four Quartets* in my knapsack everywhere I went, hoping to penetrate the mystery of those lines.

That summer some friends and I took a trip to Plum Island, a wildlife refuge of pristine dunes, beaches, and marshlands on the coast north of Boston. We stayed up all night laughing, telling stories, eating Chinese food, and playing games in the darkened dunes. The night sky was perfectly clear; the stars sparkled more brightly than they ever did in the hazy sky above Boston. As the first light colored the sky over the ocean, I decided I had had enough talking. I left the circle of my friends and drifted to a dune where I could sit quietly by myself to listen to the surf and watch the sun rise.

As I watched the first splinter of orange sun peek over the horizon, I noticed a strange buzzing sound in my ears, and everything I looked at started to sparkle and wink. The horizon began to shimmer. Then suddenly everything changed in a way I had never experienced before. My exhaustion, the hypnotic sound of the surf, the sparkle of the new sun on the water, and other forces unknown conspired in the moment to transport me to a different state of consciousness.

I wasn't just seeing with my eyes—I was perceiving everything around me. I was seeing, sensing, becoming, being the sand, the waves, the endless orange and pink sky. My body was still sitting on the dune, but I can't say "I" was sitting on the dune because suddenly I was all energy, and everything around me was all the same energy, flowing within me and without me. What I normally thought of as solid matter was now a seamless reflection of all this golden energy. My body seemed to melt away totally. I became one with the sand and the surf—and then, for a moment, with all of creation. I felt tremendously expanded and alive. I was worlds more than the "me" in my body, more than the "Carol" personality that I had always thought was my limit. Joy and relief filled my mind as I understood—really understood—that I was a part of something greater than the finite me.

In a flash I realized that this energy I felt within myself could never be destroyed—it would always exist. Only the body dies, while this essence that was everywhere but somehow still centered in my body continues forever. "At the still point of the turning world. Neither flesh nor fleshless; Neither from nor towards; at the still point, there the dance is . . ."[2] T. S. Eliot was finally making sense!

My moment of revelation, this blissful epiphany, was sharply interrupted when a bolt of lightning streaked across the sky. My friends came over to where I was sitting and said that we had to leave, a storm was approaching the island. (The storm never came.)

On the way back to Boston, I tried to describe my "eternal moment" to my friends. They couldn't tell if I was joking or serious. Try as I would, I couldn't describe it; it sounded too fantastic, even to me. But it wasn't fantasy, it wasn't a joke, and it wasn't an illusion. It was real—so real, I was stirred for days by the experience and I never forgot it. To this day I can still put myself back on that beach and see and feel the indescribable joy of that blessed moment.

The next day I walked around Harvard Square, still in a daze from my extraordinary experience, frustrated that I couldn't put it into words. I wandered into one of my favorite haunts, the Sphinx Book Store and, without thinking, walked over to a shelf and randomly pulled down a book. I opened it in the middle and began reading. The words on the page electrified me. They perfectly described my indescribable experience on the beach. "Thine own consciousness, shining, void, and inseparable from the Great Body of Radiance, hath no birth, nor death, and is the Immutable Light."[3] The book was *The Tibetan Book of the Dead.*

In the next weeks I put aside the *Four Quartets* and dove into *The Tibetan Book of the Dead.* I discovered that it isn't about death so much as it is about the part of us that never dies—our consciousness.

To the Buddhists, consciousness is an uninterrupted continuum that always exists, even after we die. And rebirth is a fact of life. The *Book of the Dead* describes the stages of consciousness experienced immediately before and after the moment of death, after the soul leaves the body, and as the soul travels the path back to the womb door to be reborn. This ancient text, written by Buddhist sages, is a guidebook intended to be read to a person who is near death and to the departed soul after it leaves the body. It gives detailed instructions for the soul's journey through these stages of consciousness after death and before rebirth, called the bardo states.

The most significant phase of the soul's passage, according to the *Book of the Dead,* is the time surrounding death. At the moment immediately following death, the soul is most aware of the full scope of its divine and timeless nature, being one with the Great Body of Radiance. The language that resonated with me so completely when I first picked the book off the shelf was describing this grandest moment of illumination. It spoke to me because, for an instant on the beach, I had peeked into this bardo and understood the timelessness of existence.

Reading *The Tibetan Book of the Dead* led me, in turn, to study other Eastern texts like *The Upanishads* and *The Bhagavad-Gita.* I was seeking to understand, from any source I could find, more about the continuum of consciousness and the workings of reincarnation. *The Upanishads* speak about rebirth using poetic images: "Like corn, a man ripens and falls to the ground; like corn, he springs up again in his season."[4]

But these Buddhist and Hindu texts, though amazingly wise, the culmination of centuries of spiritual wisdom, were somehow unsatisfying. The insight I sought from them was buried in complicated religious doctrine I couldn't relate to. The Eastern texts stress a disciplined life of right action as the only path to enlightenment and freedom from rebirth. But this disciplined life was defined in terms totally foreign to my culture and lifestyle as a college student in Boston in the heady days of 1970. I could never imagine myself living the disciplined life of a monk.

Then one morning back at college, in a daze, I stumbled into the right class and discovered the nineteenth-century English Romantic poets Wordsworth, Coleridge, and Blake. These poets shared visions akin to the Buddhist and Hindu sages. I was relieved to find Eastern mysticism in Western literature, originating from people whose culture and language were similar to mine. These poets wrote of the immortality of the soul—the essence within all of us that is timeless, eternal, and divine: "I saw no God, nor heard any, in a finite organical perception; but my senses discover'd the infinite in everything," wrote William Blake.[5]

After reading those words, I spent the next three months writing a paper comparing William Blake's poetry to the teachings of *The Tibetan Book of the Dead.* Writing this paper became a holy quest to clarify and explain the wisp of enlightenment I had experienced on the beach.

All this study and exploration into the meaning of death and reincarnation answered some of my questions and gave me a new framework for my beliefs. But I was frustrated: I couldn't see how to use it to guide my life. If a part of me had always existed in other lifetimes with other experiences, how did it affect me now, in a practical day-to-day sense? And if patterns of thought and experience persist from lifetime to lifetime, how do we change these patterns? These were important answers that I didn't have. For as I lay sick in bed, with images of a dying man in my mind, reincarnation was becoming a personal reality. I needed to know more—my life depended on it.

The Screen of His Impressive Talent

I didn't die that winter. From the time I had the vision, my health began to improve. Of course, it could have been the medication and the bed rest that reversed my illness. I didn't know. As the coughing subsided, I was able to sleep for longer periods of time—blessed, uninterrupted sleep. I regained my energy day by day. About this time Sarah sent us a letter from upstate New York to tell us that her grandparents were taking good care of her, but she wrote: "when Grandma and Grandpa tuck me in at nite I don't feel right. I can't wate intile I come off the plain and see you."

I knew I was getting better when my thoughts began to shift to more mundane matters, such as getting the house cleaned, catching up on the laundry, and getting in shape to keep up with Chase. A few weeks later when Steve returned from the airport with Chase and Sarah, I hugged them tight and long, thinking back to the dark days when I thought I might never see them again. I was so happy and so thankful.

By the time the daffodils appeared in our yard, I had returned to full health. I couldn't remember a more joyous or beautiful spring. Asheville was gloriously vibrant with the pink, purple, and red azaleas, and white dogwood blossoms floated like constellations of stars in the woods. I appreciated the sunny warmth more deeply than I ever had before, and I thanked God with every painless breath I took. As the spring and my good health blossomed, my fear of illness and death faded like a bad dream. But when fall came, and the nights turned colder and the flowers began to go to seed in my garden, I again worried about my health, not knowing if I could survive another winter like the last one. I thought back to my vision and hoped that the morbid scenes and the premonition of death had dissolved forever—though deep down I knew they hadn't. I sensed that something still had to be resolved, but I didn't know what or how. I prayed for understanding, and for health.

In October our close friend Rosario, to whom I had confided my sickbed vision, called me with exciting news. He had just met a hypnotherapist from Florida, who was staying in Asheville doing past life regressions. Perhaps this man could help me understand my vision and break my cycle of illness. Without hesitating, and not really knowing what past life regression was, I called the hypnotherapist, Norman Inge.

On the appointed morning—a crackling clear fall day with the sweetgums and maples in full color—Norman Inge appeared at my front door. I was immediately fascinated by his impish smile, sparkling eyes, and tinseled silvery hair. We chatted, and Norman explained his unusual background. He told me that he was a native Hawaiian and descended from a long line of kahuna—spiritual healers of the Hawaiian islands. In the tradition of the kahuna, Norman had learned the native wisdom of his people from his father and grandfather. He combined this traditional wisdom with training in hypnotherapy and neurolinguistic programming, expanding his virtuosity for healing. I was so intrigued by what Norman was telling me that I forgot about the butterflies in my stomach.

Norman began my session with a simple relaxation exercise. While I reclined on my couch with eyes closed and listened to a tape of soothing music, he instructed me to focus on my breathing and consciously relax each part of my body. Soon I was totally relaxed. Then Norman led me on a brief visionary journey through a peaceful landscape, followed by a descent down an imaginary stairway. He suggested that when I reached the bottom of the stairs, I would find myself in another lifetime.

Faint images immediately came into my mind—images of the same frail man I had seen months earlier when I was sick in bed. Norman coached, "Describe what you see—bring the images into sharper focus." As I followed Norman's suggestion, the pictures changed from fuzzy impressions to clear and colorful, full-bodied images. Sometimes the scenes moved along in succession, like a movie. Other times the frame froze as I directed my attention to my feelings in that scene.

As Norman guided me along, the images changed from the dying man to a scene from his early childhood. "I see myself as a baby. I'm wearing a gown and sitting in a high chair. My mother is feeding me porridge. I see my family eating around the table, my father and my sisters." I described to Norman how it felt to be a baby bathed in love, content and nurtured.

The skeptical voice in my mind interrupted, chiding, "You're just making this up." But the compelling energy of the images and emotions was stronger than my doubting mind. This skeptical voice soon quieted and disappeared as I was pulled deeper into the experience with Norman's words: "What are you experiencing? What are you feeling?"

After a few minutes of this focusing, I wasn't just watching a movie in my head; I was the main character in the story, engaged in a full sensory experience. I could "see" through this man's eyes, I could "hear" through his ears, I could feel love swelling in his heart, and I knew what he was thinking. Even more amazing, I could easily shift my perspective from that of an observer, to being in the body of the character I saw—or be in both places at once. I could jump out of my body and observe myself from any angle of the room. In this altered state I possessed a surreal omniscience. I had access to everything this man knew, understood, and remembered, plus I enjoyed a broader overview, an understanding of the patterns in his life beyond what even he knew.

At the same time that I was engrossed in the visions, I was still aware that I was in the room with Norman, lying on my couch. I could hear my telephone ringing in the background, but the ringing sounded far away and had no significance. It was as if I were fully awake while dreaming, consciously directing my attention to the dream. I was in a sensory paradox, straddling two realities.

The scene in my mind progressed, and I saw myself as a boy of ten. I was in a room with an arched ceiling and tall windows. A glissando of sunlight fell from the window onto the grand piano in the center of the room. Next to me stood an older gentleman who laid his hand on my shoulder. I knew that this kindly man was my beloved piano teacher. Warmth filled my body as I looked at him and as I thought about my family and my music. My life was a fusion of love and music. I was happy.

"Then what happens?" asked Norman, breaking the enchantment of my reverie.

"A decision has been made that I should go away to a city some distance from my home to study music. I am honored to go." I felt a tightening in my chest and tears coming to my eyes as I saw myself saying good-bye to my family and my piano teacher.

"Move ahead to a later time," encouraged Norman.

I saw myself, in my late twenties or early thirties, standing next to a piano in a large, square room with heavily draped French doors and crowded with well-dressed people. The room felt hot and stuffy and smelled (all of a sudden I could smell) musty. I stood next to the piano chatting with a circle of admiring women. As the women pressed close, I could smell traces of their perfume, and I was aware of the scent of my own talcum powder.

I smiled as I saw another scene in which I was walking down a broad carpeted staircase with an elegantly dressed woman on each arm. I saw rich colors in the long, full dresses on the women and in the sparkling crystals of a chandelier hanging over the curving staircase. The scene had a velvety texture of elegance and civility. I held my shoulders back with the pride of an admired performer as I glided gracefully through the chattering crowd.

But this pride was undermined by sadness and an unbearable longing. "I feel torn. I enjoy their admiration, but they never see who I really am. They can't see beyond my talent. They can't see me." I could feel the emptiness in my stomach as I longed for the nurturing and love I had left behind with my family. "I have many friends," I continued. "They love the music I play. But I have no one who really loves me deeply." I felt myself getting weak, and I curled into a fetal position on the couch.

Then I was back to the scene of this man on his deathbed, coughing, barely able to breathe, exhausted—the same scene I had seen months before, when I myself lay sick. A woman, who I sensed was my sister, sat next to my bed, lovingly attending to my needs. I could feel in my own body his exhaustion and the pain in his lungs, as I recalled my own illness of the previous winter. At this point Norman sensed the opportunity and asked, "What are the emotional reasons for your illness? What is it that you need?" Without thinking, I replied, "This is the only way I can get the attention and nurturing that I need. My life is out of balance." Although I was answering from the point of view of this man, I sensed that what I was saying was significant to my present life as well. But I wasn't sure how.

Norman saw it, though. While I was still in a trance, he

helped me understand that my present life was almost the inverse of my past life as this man. As a musician, he could express his creativity fully through his music, but he lacked the loving relationships he needed to be a complete and balanced person. The screen of his impressive talent made it almost impossible for people to see the real person, or get close to him. His illness was an extreme expression of his need for love and nurturing.

My life, on the other hand, was rich with a loving, lively family and good friends. However, as the mother of two small children, all of my time and energy were spent taking care of the kids and the house. I felt suffocated. I had no medium for expressing my creativity, no higher purpose beyond loving my family. I had no time to feed the explorer, the artist, and the teacher in me that I had totally neglected since getting married and having children. In that moment, with the paradox of my past spread before me, I understood that I needed to bring creativity and purpose into my life in order to be balanced and complete—and healthy.

Norman then guided me through this man's death. I could see the sister sitting at his bedside when he finally died. I watched the scene as an observer in the room. I saw a look of relief come over his gaunt face as he died and left his sick, drained body behind. At the same moment I felt a tingling lightness in my own body.

Then my perspective shifted from being at the deathbed scene to a vantage point above the funeral procession—the same view I had seen months before when I was sick. I felt myself as the disembodied spirit of that man floating above the crowd, watching the mourners below, witnessing my own funeral. I was deeply moved by the assembly of friends who honored me at my death. Suddenly my vision zoomed in on my sister standing among the mourners, holding a handkerchief to her face, crying. I felt sad for her; I wanted her to know that I no longer suffered and that I was grateful for her loving care. At Norman's suggestion I said good-bye to her and thanked her for her love.

Broken Dreams and Vanished Years

The images of that man's life faded. Without pausing, Norman suggested that I go to another lifetime. I immediately saw the image of a young girl, about eleven or twelve, playing a grand piano before a small audience. She wore a blue-gray dress, white stockings, and a floppy white bow in her shoulder-length hair. She was playing in a recital. I knew that her performance pleased her parents and other stiffly dressed adults in the room. Norman's voice flowed into my awareness: "What are you experiencing?"

"I am playing for these people so they can determine whether I should go on to the Conservatory. I know I play well. It's easy for me. It is decided that I should go on with my studies. It's a great honor to go to the Conservatory. I'm sad about leaving my family—I'll be far away and I'll miss them. But I do look forward to my studies, my music.

"I see my father, mother, and younger brother at a train station. Everything is dark brown or sooty gray. My father leans over and kisses me, my mother cries, my little brother looks lost. I have one brown square suitcase that I take with me."

"Where are you, and where are you going?"

"I'm leaving Poland to study in Vienna." This information leaped into my mind, startling me.

I next saw myself in my late teens walking down a corridor in a building. The ceilings were very high with hanging lights and glass windows above the doors. "This is where I study music. I have many friends here, and I'm happy. This is now my home."

The images progressed to the next scene, and at the same time my mood changed—my happiness melted into fear. "I see myself in a narrow apartment—I am in my mid- to late twenties, with two small children. A grand piano fills one corner of the room. The door opens, and a young man wearing a beret walks in. I know he is my husband. He looks worried. The words 'It's too late' come to mind. I know that whatever he tells me has something to do with our being Jewish. My husband, who is a teacher at the university, speaks out against German policies. From the fear in his eyes, I know we're in trouble. I don't want to see what happens next."

Norman said, "Go on."

I curled up on the couch and held my knees; my stomach felt queasy, and I had to push out every word to describe what I saw next. "I see my two children, a little girl of about two and a boy about six. I'm holding their hands as we stand on a cobblestone street with many other people. I am wearing a maroon coat. There is a high stone wall behind us. My husband is gone—I don't know where he is. They've taken him somewhere. The Germans are rounding us up. I'm scared for me and for my children."

I began to cry as I told Norman what I was seeing. Waves of sorrow swept through me. I shivered from cold as my plight got worse.

"We're beside a train. Soldiers and dogs—German shepherds. I'm holding my little one on my hip and my son is gripping tight my free hand. Shouts and confusion, lines of people. No one really knows what's going on."

I sensed that something terrible was happening beyond anything the images showed. I began to moan and cry, but Norman gently urged me again, "Go on." I cried more deeply as I lay there on my couch, unable to speak. I had enough presence of mind, though, to ask Norman for Kleenex to blow my nose and dry my eyes.

My body was seized with dread and I resisted looking at the next scene. After waiting a long time for me to cry it out, Norman again pressed me to continue.

"I'm in a camp. Everything is gray. I walk around numb. I don't know what's going on anymore. I don't know what happened to my children or my husband. My family is gone, my music is gone. My spirit feels dead. I don't want to live anymore. Then I'm floating. I look down on an icy room with concrete walls. I see myself lying in a pile of twisted bodies. I've been gassed."

As I describe these last cold images, my voice is flat and emotionless. Then the images fade. "What a waste" is all I can add. "What a waste."

Norman saw that I had had enough and ended the session with the suggestion that I come back to the present time, remembering everything I had experienced. After he was satisfied that I was fully back in my body and had calmed down, we talked briefly. Then he left.

I lay on the couch for a few minutes, barely able to think, totally drained from all the emotion and crying. I was moved in indescribable ways by these memories, especially by the woman who died with her family in the Holocaust. I now realized that I had been carrying the shadow of this woman's grief with me my whole life. What a relief to finally let it go! I felt lighter and clearer.

I walked outside and sat on the front stoop. About three hours had passed since Norman arrived, and the day was peaking in full glory, the sun high in the sky and warm, the October air refreshing and cool. I thought about my regression and the lives stretching behind me and the lives yet to come. I realized how glad I was to be in this life, in this body, in this moment on Earth.

In the days that followed, as I absorbed the lessons of the regression, I could feel how the past life memories added a new dimension to my life. The vapors of past images that had trailed me all my life had now congealed into solid conscious memories. My notion that there was more to me than just my experience in this life was confirmed. I was certain now that a part of me had survived death and would again. My beliefs about reincarnation and the continuity of the soul, those high-minded ideas from my college days, were becoming a part of my walking-around reality. This confirmation made me feel saner and happier.

Two weeks after my regression with Norman, my father died unexpectedly after routine surgery, putting my new understanding of life and death to the test. His sudden death shocked and saddened all of us. I flew to New York immediately, and Steve and the kids followed, driving up the next day. They described to me later how they sang "Going Down the Road Feeling Bad" and thought about Grandpa all the way up Interstate 81.

At the gravesite I stood and listened to the rabbi reading from Ecclesiastes, taking comfort in the poetry and wisdom of the words: "To everything there is a season, and a time to every purpose under heaven." I thought about my own funeral and the deaths that I had seen in the regression, and about how I had floated out of my body. I wondered, "Can my father see us now? Where is he? What is he feeling?" Suddenly the hairs on my arms stood on end; my whole body was energized. I sensed that he was there with us in the cemetery. I remembered the words from *The Tibetan Book of the Dead,* intended to be read to a person immediately after their death: "O nobly-born . . . now thou art experiencing the Radiance of the Clear Light of Pure Reality. Recognize it." I imagined my father hearing these words and understanding what they meant.

Just then something strange happened. As my father's coffin was being lowered into the ground, my brother's yarmulke flew off his head and fell into the crack between the coffin and the earth wall of the grave. But no wind had blown to knock it off his head. We all looked at each other and wondered the same thing, "What was *that?*" Steve and I looked at each other in wide-eyed silence. Could it be a sign from my father? Some of us believe it was.

"I Am More Than My Body"

In the following weeks and months, as I washed dishes, folded laundry, and drove the kids around town, past life images drifted through my mind. New insights came to me in flashes and reinforced my understanding of how the lifetimes I had seen related to my present life.

In the light of my new understanding, scenes and feelings from early childhood began to make more sense: my love of music and the piano, my horrified fascination with the Holocaust, the pattern of illness in my lungs. A childhood game took on new significance: my friend and I used to cower under my basement stairs pretending we were hiding from the Nazis, taking cans of food with us so that we wouldn't starve—surely an odd game for young children to play. Thinking back on it now, the connection was obvious.

I finally understood another mystery from childhood. Ever since I was very young, I had a recurring dream of a woman with medium-length brown hair wearing a maroon coat, a black hat, and carrying a shoulder bag, walking down a boulevard with a stone wall in the background. The image was bright and clear, so vivid that I never could forget it. I remember thinking as a young girl that I was going to be that lady when I grew up.

This dream recurred frequently over the years and was always the same. But the last time I had it, just weeks before the regression with Norman, it progressed and changed. That time I knew that I *was* this woman. Again I was walking down the boulevard dressed in exactly the same way, but then I continued and approached a palatial building with a square central courtyard—the vision was so graphic and complete, I could draw a diagram of the building the next day. I entered a dark room in the right wing of the building. The room had a high ceiling, massive antique furnishings, and heavily draped windows blocking out the sunlight; I clearly remember the rich patina of the old wood wainscoting.

I approached three men in uniform behind a desk—one man was seated, while the others stood to either side. I addressed the seated man behind the desk, politely asking for the whereabouts of my husband. My inquiry was met with silence. They acted as if I wasn't really there. In frustration I banged my fist on the desk, demanding attention, and furiously yelled at them in German—a language I do not speak. They laughed at me with contempt and physically forced me out of the room. I left the building, humiliated and scared. I was thinking, "How will I care for my children alone?" I saw myself slowly walking away from the building, with my shoulders slumped and my head down.

With the German words floating in my mind, I bolted up in bed. I shook Steve awake and told him about the dream, rushing to repeat those phrases in German still clear and distinct in my ears. Within seconds, though, the words slipped away. But the feeling of foreboding stayed with me for hours.

The woman I saw in my recurring dream was the same woman I had seen in my regression to the Holocaust life. Apparently, beginning when I was a very young child, these fragments of memory had seeped from my unconscious into my dreams. Before I had the regression, I had no idea what the images in the dream meant; after the regression, I never had the dream again.

Another incident from my childhood now became clear. When I was three or four years old, I was sitting in our living room playing on the floor. To this day I can still feel the warmth of the morning sun pouring through the window and the scratchy wool carpet under my legs. My mother came into the room and put a classical piano record on the record player. Suddenly I forgot about my toys; I was swept up in the music. I knew the music! I could hum along, anticipating the notes, the melodies, the shifting harmonies. I sat and listened, so overwhelmed with joy that I began to cry. I felt myself and the whole room getting larger; I felt expanded, merging with everything around me. I knew in that instant that I was *more* than my body. Though this euphoria lasted only a couple of minutes, the timelessness and magic of that moment has always stayed with me.

I am more than my body. Looking back years later, and with the benefit of new insight from my regression, I now understood what had happened that day. The piano music my mother put on the phonograph must have been a composition I had performed hundreds of times in either of my past lives. The familiar sounds triggered my soul's memory of that life and propelled me, for that moment, into a consciousness that was much older than the four-year-old girl playing on the carpet. "To be conscious is not to be in time." I had that experience as a small child. I knew it again—the same experience, only grander—as I sat on a beach near Boston many years later.

"Only Through Time Is Time Conquered"[6]

The winter came and went, and to my profound delight I remained healthy all through the coldest months for the first time in years. In March we had a freak snowstorm, the biggest snow-fall of the winter. A foot of powdery snow turned the mountains into a sparkling wonderland and the golf course near our house into the steepest, fastest sledding hill in the city. We bundled up the kids, and they spent the day speeding down the fairways on truck inner tubes.

That night Steve and I waited until Chase and Sarah were asleep, then crept off to have our own party in the snow. It was a beautiful, starry winter night. Teenagers had built a huge bonfire in a sand trap at the top of the biggest hill, and the light from the fire reflected off the white snow, illuminating the slope for night sledding. Steve and I piled on the inner tube together and headed down the icy hill. We flew down the hill, spinning around and careening backward over bumps, laughing and screaming all the way. Eager for the next ride, I ran back up the hill, breathing the cold air deep into my lungs. Suddenly I flashed back to the winter before, when I was so sick I could hardly breathe at all. In this moment I knew I was really healed. I said a prayer of gratitude to the winking stars overhead—and hopped on the inner tube for another ride.

Why was I healed? It had something to do with recognizing patterns from the past and understanding how they carried over from life to life. One pattern was clear. In each life I had died with trauma to the lungs: as the man, I died of consumption; as the woman, I died with gas in my lungs. Somehow the traumas of those two deaths were still lodged in my lungs, and as long as they remained unconscious, they continued to affect me. But by reliving these deaths through the regression, bringing them to conscious awareness, and crying out the pain, the trauma was released. I could breathe again.

Yet there was more to it than that. The physical traumas also pointed to unfinished business, to deeper lessons I had to learn. The regression to the life of the admired pianist brought to con-sciousness an issue of choice—of balancing creative fulfillment with the need for love and intimacy. Seeing this helped me set a new course for my life.

The Holocaust life showed a different kind of unfinished busi-ness. At the time of my death in the gas chamber, I was less than human, my soul was numb. The tears of grief for my family and my wasted life had frozen in my body. A lifetime later, the immense pressure of that grief welled below the surface of my awareness, even pushing into my childhood dreams. Now, bringing the truth to consciousness, I could finally cry and grieve for the lives lost long ago, setting that part of my soul to rest. What a blessed relief.

I also knew that my sickbed supplication, my life-and-death question, "What does reincarnation mean for my life?" was finally answered. The answer was direct and practical: reexperiencing my past lives released the grip of the past and gave me a fresh start in the present.

I was lit! That one regression had given me health *and* new purpose. It was a discovery I had to share. I talked about my regression and past lives with friends, strangers, relatives—anyone who would listen. A dozen of my friends, sparked by my excitement and my example, wanted to try past life regression with Norman Inge.

That is how Norman came to be sitting in my kitchen having tea with Chase and Sarah and me that August afternoon. Looking back, years later, I can see that a special blend of ingredients—Norman's masterful skill with past life regression, my own profound healing from remembering past lives the year before, and my children's isolated, unexplained fears—converged in my kitchen to create the right conditions for a small miracle.

My eyes were opened, my life changed direction, and my future was set the moment Norman gently instructed Chase to "sit on your mom's lap, close your eyes, and tell me what you see when you hear the loud noises that scare you."

CHAPTER 3

Musings on the Playground

A few weeks after Sarah and Chase's regressions, it was my turn to volunteer at Chase's preschool. I stood on the playground amidst swirls of squealing, laughing children. I watched Chase's young classmates—mostly four- and five-year-olds—in every corner of the playground, playing tag in the brilliant fall sunshine, feeding and stroking the rabbit in its hutch, climbing on bars and elevated platforms, and swinging as high as they dared on the swing set. A small group of kids gathered in an old motorboat that had found its permanent home on the playground, yelling commands and waving their arms to others who were trying to board the vessel. Two girls in colorful, flowing capes danced across the yard, singing and moving to their own graceful rhythm.

I glanced around looking for Chase—his flaming red hair made him easy to spot in any crowd. He was climbing on the monkey bars with some other children, pulling a reluctant little boy up with him onto the platform. My mind began to play too:

if Chase had been a black soldier wounded in battle, who had these other children been before? Would *they* remember? If I asked them who they had been, would they tell me stories about their lives as an Eskimo villager, a peasant farmer in Russia, or a herdsman in Africa?

My gaze wandered around the playground, resting on one little girl who was kneeling in front of the rabbit hutch, talking earnestly to the rabbit. Close by, the two dancing girls leaped from behind a tree, giggling. I momentarily drifted back to my own childhood, recalling the many conversations I had had with my imaginary friend, a human-sized rabbit named Betty. I knew even then that Betty was make-believe, but I enjoyed our relationship as much as if she had been a real friend. We spent many pleasant days together riding around the neighborhood on my tricycle. (Betty rode on the back.) And I recalled other childhood fantasy adventures. My friends and I spent many hours making forts on the banks of the Hudson River, bravely defending ourselves from warrior tribes. I felt the magic of these childhood fantasies ripple through me again as I watched the children totally absorbed in their play.

Chase caught my attention as he zoomed by on his way to the schoolhouse, yelling out to me that it was story time.

As I walked back to the classroom, I marveled at how rich the fantasy lives of these children are. I thought how past life memories seem, on the surface, to resemble fantasy: in both, the child can experience being a different person in a different time, seeing things that nobody else can see, talking to people that don't exist. The more I thought about it, though, the more I saw that it is easy to distinguish between the two. A child engaged in fantasy play constructs a temporary reality that shifts and changes at will. He can easily switch personae and settings, playing the role of a dashing soldier heroically defending a fort in one moment, and a merry baker making pies for the King and Queen of the World in the next. In these fantasies glaring inconsistencies are thrown into the mix too—a combination of what a child believes to be true of the role he is playing, peppered with unbounded imagination and impossible magic. The result is a jumble of fact and fiction.

When Sarah and Chase remembered their past lives, however, they saw another type of reality—an intact and *consistent* inner reality with only plausible details. And these memories had the ring of truth. Nobody in them had any magical powers to save the day. On the contrary, the events they described were tragic beyond anything they had experienced or seen in this life. They were not playing; they were not having fun in made-up adventures they could direct and control.

I sat on the floor of Chase's class on a carpet square and listened while his teacher read the story of a mouse and his motorcycle. I studied the children sitting next to me. Some listened, rapt and enchanted; others lay quietly on their carpet squares with their eyes closed. One little boy fidgeted on the floor, pulling at the frayed ends of his carpet square as he spun around in place. I marveled at the diversity of personalities in this one small class, and I could not stop wondering who these children had been before and what their souls had experienced. How much of this diversity was a consequence of past lives? I scanned the young faces in the room. In light of these reflections, their childish features took on a deeper interest.

I looked over at Chase sitting between his best friends, Henson and Mari. His eyes were big but tired. I ached for the hardships he had endured as a soldier, wounded on a battlefield far from home and family. I felt warm love swell inside me for my son as I thought how far his soul had come from the cold horror of that long-ago battle to this cozy classroom, safe among gentle friends. I smiled to myself, then pushed these intriguing thoughts aside, for it was time to put our carpet squares away and go home.

Buzzing with Ideas

A few days later my friend Cathy Sky and I did lunch. Cathy was a preschool teacher and the mother of three children; she was also a musician and a writer with a quick mind. During the days of my illness, she visited with hot soup and helped care for the kids. She knew about my regression with Norman and had watched my remarkable recovery. This lunch was my first chance to fill her in on what had happened with Norman and my kids, and to air the musings that were dancing in my brain.

A half hour later, when I finally stopped talking, I noticed that Cathy had finished her lunch and I had barely taken a bite of mine. She hadn't said a word the whole time. She startled me by asking, "Well . . . is it safe?"

Safe? That question had never crossed my mind. My kids' regressions had been so gentle, so natural, I couldn't imagine how it could be dangerous. Both Sarah and Chase had moved in and out of their memories easily. Both had been playing happily only minutes after their regressions, and they never confused their past life experiences with their present reality. Sarah, in particular, was lucid about the significance of what had happened. With a flourish of my fork, I concluded, "The fact is, their lives are much better for it. Their fears have gone away and Chase's eczema was healed." Cathy saw my point.

Over dessert Cathy and I recalled several children we knew who had phobias. We thought of one small child who was terrified of water, whose mother could not coax him into a swimming pool. Could he have drowned in another lifetime? Would his fear go away if he simply remembered his past life?

Excitement rose in me as we followed this line of thinking. Not just fears, but any traits could be the result of past lives. We talked of children we knew who had unusual talents, odd interests, or quirky behavior that puzzled their parents. She told me the story of a three-year-old girl in her class who sat on the playground crying in front of a small hole she had dug and covered with leaves. When Cathy asked her what was wrong, she said, "I'm crying for my children who died in the flood." Cathy questioned the girl's parents about this remark, but they couldn't explain it either.

Running with the possibilities, Cathy and I jumped to another idea. How often do we find children in families who seem to be totally different from each other and from their parents? We had both felt the uniqueness of our own babies when we held them for the first time; the seeds of personality were already there at birth. We could *feel* it. Maybe this uniqueness is not solely the result of random combinations of the parents' genes. Maybe it's also due to traces of past life personality and experience that children bring with them to this life. And maybe our children are much more than blank slates to be written upon by experience, as science has led us to believe for so long.

In the middle of one of these grand speculations, Cathy suddenly realized that she was late and dashed off. She left me alone at the table, sipping my coffee, buzzing with ideas.

"Dangerous Territory"

Not everyone was as excited as Cathy was about these ideas. Other friends I told about my adventures with past life regression were less receptive. Some entertained the idea that reincarnation was possible, and that karma offered the best explanation for the inequities of life. But when faced with my personal account of how recalling past lives heals, and especially when they heard that my kids were involved, they were skeptical. They coolly implied that I was somehow mistaken and suggested that there must be some other explanation for what had happened.

Others were embarrassed for me, fearing that I was stepping off the edge of reason. For them, reincarnation is on the fringes of the supernatural, as suspect as any of the headlines on the supermarket tabloids. And to subject my children to it! One friend in particular warned me, "You're moving into dangerous territory. You may not be able to get back." I tried to argue that it made sense to me and confirmed truths I had suspected all my life. "What's more," I pointed out, "I'm better, and Sarah and Chase are better." I could see I had no chance of convincing her, so I let it drop.

This resistance and criticism made me realize that I needed validation from other sources—solid, credible documentation of past life memories—to offer to skeptics. I felt they would be more able to accept what I was so excited about if I could cite research to back up my own experience. If only I had a whole book of cases and explanations to hand to my incredulous friends.

The more I thought about it, I wanted a book that would give *me* a reality check too—that would confirm what had happened to me and my children, and help me understand how it all worked. Surely, I thought, there must be books available about past life regression with children. Others—professionals with university degrees and study grants—must have researched and documented what I was discovering quite by accident and on my own. But who and where were these others? How could I find them?

CHAPTER 4

The Moment
of Death

Unfinished Business Propels the Memories

I began my search by returning to the religion and philosophy
shelves in the local library that Steve had searched a year earlier,
just in case he had missed something. But poking through these
old editions was frustrating and fruitless and left me sneezing
from the years of accumulated dust. Nothing in these academic
artifacts had anything to say about how remembering a past life
can heal.

Maybe a newer book would be more relevant. With Chase in
tow, I headed for my favorite eclectic bookstore and café in
downtown Asheville. After some coaxing, Chase agreed to sit
in the children's section while I rushed to search through the
store's selections on reincarnation and mysticism, wedged somewhere between astrology and Buddhism. A few titles looked in-

teresting: I found books by Fiore, Sutphen, Wambach, and Moody, and quickly flipped through each of them. Meanwhile, Chase had already lost his patience for sitting still and had begun to play hide and seek with a little girl among the tall stacks of books. I could hear their squeals of excitement moving around the store, and I knew it was only a matter of minutes before something came crashing down. So I grabbed Fiore, Wambach, and Moody, completed my purchase, and made a fast getaway with Chase.

Dr. Wambach and the History of the Four-Pronged Fork

Dr. Helen Wambach's *Reliving Past Lives* was just the objective proof I was looking for to offer to my critics. She devised an ingenious experiment to prove that past life memories are real.

But Dr. Wambach hadn't set out to be a past life researcher—she'd begun as a conventional psychologist and scientist. Her interest in this unusual field began as a quest to explain an unsettling personal experience—an intense déjà vu—that she had one day while visiting an historic Quaker museum in New Jersey. As she climbed the stairs of this old building, she was overcome by a distinct feeling of being in another time and place. "I entered the small library room and went automatically to the shelf of books, reached for a particular book, and took it down. I seemed to 'know' that this had been my book, and as I looked at the pages, a scene came before my inner eye. I was riding on a mule across a stubbled field with this book propped up on the saddle in front of me. The sun was hot on my back, and my clothes were scratchy. I could feel the mule moving under me while I sat in the saddle, deeply absorbed in reading the book propped before me. I seemed to know the book's contents before I turned the pages."[1]

Dr. Wambach was profoundly shaken by the unmistakable feeling that she had been in another body in another lifetime.

This feeling was new and foreign to her. At that time she considered herself to be a respectable psychologist and college instructor, and she had always believed that psychic phenomena could be explained away as meaningless fantasies and delusions. But the vividness of her déjà vu was too real to dismiss. She had to find out more about it. She suspected that it might have been a glimpse of a hidden reality, a peek at a dimension of the mind never admitted to in psychology books. And she had a hunch that understanding this new dimension might be immensely valuable in her therapy practice.

This personal experience changed Dr. Wambach's ideas about the potential of the mind, but it didn't diminish her faith in scientific method. Her training required that she study the phenomenon objectively and rationally.

She started by reading everything she could find on psychic phenomena and past life recall. Then she began to use hypnosis to regress student volunteers to past lives. With each regression she became more intrigued. Her subjects went through deeply emotional experiences that convinced them—and her—of the reality of their past life memories. They described anonymous lives from all parts of the world and all periods of human history matter-of-factly, and in rich detail. Most of the historical facts from the regressions that she was able to research—details of clothing, food, climate, and architecture, for example—agreed with what historians knew of life through the centuries. She was amazed at how accurate the memories were. Her subjects made no errors even on obscure details that took her hours in the library to research and verify.

But proving the reality of past lives was elusive. She could not accumulate enough names, dates, or hard facts in the individual cases to build a solid proof that her skeptical scientific colleagues would accept. She couldn't see how to prove conclusively that her subjects hadn't somehow concocted their stories from prior knowledge.

Then she looked at the patterns in the data. One pattern in particular struck Dr. Wambach as significant and gave her the confidence to plow ahead. Half of her subjects, she noticed, reported at least one life in which they had died as very young children. This mirrored the historical fact that in primitive societies nearly 50 percent of children died before reaching the age of five, and it confirmed to Dr. Wambach that these stories were not self-serving fantasy or images gleaned from books or movies. What would be the advantage to the ego to fantasize a life cut pitifully short by famine or disease?

Taking a clue from this observation, Dr. Wambach changed her method. From her scientific training she knew that the broad behavior of groups quantified in statistics was much more reliable and convincing than isolated cases, no matter how impressive those individual cases were.[2] So instead of working to document a few lifetimes as conclusively as possible, she decided to gather data from a large population of subjects to see if the patterns that emerged would reproduce broad patterns of historical fact.

Dr. Wambach had discovered before that she could regress a group of a dozen or more people as easily as she could regress one person. She also had discovered that her subjects could remember everything they had experienced during the regression, even if they did not talk while in trance. Building on these discoveries, she began to regress groups of volunteers. She hypnotized each group in exactly the same way and gave them the choice of eleven specific periods in history to visit, ranging from 2000 B.C. to 1945. She did this three times with each group. While the subjects were in trance, she directed them to observe their surroundings and took them through a typical day in that lifetime; then she guided them through their deaths and the after-death state. No subjects talked during the regressions or before they had answered a standard list of written questions.

The questions asked the subjects to record what they had seen and experienced during their regressions: what they wore on their bodies and feet, the color of their skin and type of hair, the climate and landscape, the dwellings and structures they saw, the food they ate, and the utensils, tools, and money they used. Other questions gathered data on their deaths: where they died, how old they had been, the cause of death, and what happened *after* they died.

Following prudent scientific methodology, Dr. Wambach took pains to prevent errors and distortions. The volunteers were strangers to each other before the experiment, and they weren't allowed to talk until after the questionnaires had been completed. She designed the questions to expose subjects who were fantasizing or improvising answers, and she screened the replies on each questionnaire for internal discrepancies and historical anachronisms. When she was finished, she had 1,088 completed questionnaires. She had expected that 10 to 20 percent of these would be tossed out for inaccuracies or discrepancies, but to her surprise only eleven had to be discarded—less than 1 percent!

Of all of her subjects, 70 percent remembered a past life. She compiled and analyzed their responses, reconstructing the geographic location, culture, climate, race, and social status of the lives her subjects remembered. She drew charts and graphs, and wrote summaries of her findings. The final result is an amazing correlation, point by point, between the composite of the subjects' past life recalls and historical fact:

Male and female: The subjects reported an almost even split between the two sexes, with 50.3 percent male and 49.7 percent female across all the time periods. This result came despite the fact that 78 percent of her subjects were women, and that most subjects switched gender seemingly at random from lifetime to lifetime.

Rich and poor: Not one of her subjects remembered being a known historical personality or anyone worthy of even a good fantasy. There were no Cleopatras, Napoleons, Galileos, or Marie Antoinettes. Most lives were dreary, ordinary, and hard. The primary occupation, in almost every time period, was farming and gathering food. The great majority went through their lives wearing homespun garments, living in crude huts, and eating bland cereal with their fingers from wooden bowls.

She found a consistent ratio of rich to poor lives: for all time periods, the upper classes were never more than 10 percent of her sample; middle classes (the craftsmen and merchants) fluctuated between 20 and 34 percent; the lower classes (peasants, primitives, soldiers, and slaves) were never less than 60 percent. During the bleak periods of history, when civilization was at an ebb, the proportion of desperately poor rose to as high as 80 percent.

Race and geography: Even though almost all of Wambach's regression subjects were middle-class Caucasians, most of them remembered at least one life as a member of another race—African, Asian, or Indian. And the fluctuations in the numbers and locations of the different races accurately reflected the shifting densities of population through history and across the globe.

Many of the white subjects who remembered previous lives in the twentieth century reported that they were black or Asian in their most immediate past life. This rules out genetic memory as an explanation for the phenomenon.

Food: The majority of subjects reported eating bland foods, like gruel made from cereal grains, roots and berries gathered by the primitives, and an occasional tree fruit or vegetable. Meat was rare—beef wasn't mentioned at all until 1500—and many of the subjects reported tasting spoiled food. Most of the wild game they sampled was small animals that tasted greasy.

As an example of the high degree of detail, Dr. Wambach's results trace the evolution of eating utensils from crude spoons and scoopers to the three-pronged fork, which first appeared in her surveys in 1500, and then to the modern four-pronged fork, which first appeared around 1800. The majority of her subjects, however, reported eating with their fingers.

On the basis of the body of data gathered from more than a thousand regressions, Dr. Wambach was satisfied that she had proven statistically that past life recall under hypnosis accurately reflects the past. She was convinced that these results were not the products of the subjects' wishful fantasies, but were memories of real past lives.

Death Throughout History

You can imagine how I welcomed this information. It was just the kind of objective data I was looking for to help me sway my more rational friends about the reality of past lives. In *Reliving Past Lives* I had evidence to challenge the common notion that past lives are merely superstitions, fantasies, or something to joke about at parties.

But the part of Dr. Wambach's research that intrigued me the most was what had happened to her subjects when they died. That was new information—a statistical analysis of the death experience throughout history.

As with the other data, Dr. Wambach divided the causes of death into categories and graphed them over the centuries. Of the total deaths reported, 62 percent were from natural causes such as old age and disease; 18 percent were violent deaths by murder, suicide, or attacks by animals; and deaths from unknown causes made up the remaining 20 percent. Many of the subjects were under thirty years of age when they died, which matches what we know of the average life span through history.

Even more interesting was the statistical breakdown of what the subjects experienced when they died:

• For 90 percent of her subjects, death was the best part of the regression. Again and again they reported how pleasant it was to die.

• Seventy-nine percent experienced a deep calm and peace after death, and many felt a joy in being released from the body—so much joy that they wept during the regression.

• About 20 percent described floating above their bodies

after death and watching the commotion around the body they had left behind.

• Two-thirds soared up toward a bright light after leaving their bodies; 25 percent said that they found themselves in darkness first, then went into the light.

• A majority reported that they had lost their fear of death in their current life.[3]

Not everyone accepted death so peacefully, though. The remaining 10 percent of the subjects reported highly charged negative emotions surrounding the death. Each of these subjects had died violently or suddenly, in an accident or a war, or in great fear. An example shows how a very sudden death can result in confusion and disorientation: "I was hit by a car while I was running across the street. I seemed to continue running across the street, and wasn't really aware that I was dead. Then I felt very frustrated and lost, because I didn't understand what was happening to me."[4]

If the dying soul felt any grief, it was not for the self but for the people left behind. The saddest deaths of all were those of parents who left behind young children that needed to be cared for, or mothers who died during childbirth, which happened often throughout history.

Hints of Healing

In passing, Dr. Wambach observed a fascinating by-product of the experiment. In the weeks after the group regression, some of the subjects reported to her that their lifelong phobias had disappeared. These phobias were *always related to the mode of death* they had experienced in their past lives: a fear of water disappeared when the subject remembered drowning; another subject lost his fear of horses when remembering a death caused by a horse; and a woman with recurring dizzy spells and an irrational urge to run found these were eradicated after she remembered being pursued by angry townspeople and chased over a cliff to her death. Wambach concluded that traumatic deaths fraught with negative emotions *probably* cause phobias in the present life. But that was as far as she went with it.

Perhaps even more significantly, many of Dr. Wambach's subjects were freed of their phobias without any guidance or intervention from a therapist and without any preconception that these memories could heal. Neither Dr. Wambach nor her subjects had anticipated that they could rid themselves of phobias by remembering their past lives. It just happened. And Dr. Wambach was as surprised as her subjects were.

This tidbit struck me as the most important news in the whole book. If the healing happened without the intention or expectation of the subjects or therapist, then this hinted that the healing effect of recalling past lives is both powerful and universal. *Just by remembering past lives, people could heal themselves of phobias.* They didn't even have to know that it was possible.

But Dr. Wambach didn't give this insight more than a passing comment in her book. In her effort to find empirical evidence of past life memories, she left unanswered many questions that I had found particularly intriguing. For example she made no attempt to explain *how* or *why* past life memories connect to our present lives. In her pursuit to find patterns in the statistics she had amassed, she passed over the intense emotions that, to me, seemed to be at the heart of the phenomenon. And she said nothing about children.

Dr. Fiore and a Backward Discovery

You Have Been Here Before, by Dr. Edith Fiore, was a welcome find indeed. It was the first book I had found that focused on the *healing* benefits of past life regression.

Like Dr. Wambach, Dr. Fiore had never believed in past lives—had never even thought about the subject—until she discovered it quite by accident and on her own. She trained as a clinical psychologist at Mount Holyoke College, the University of Maryland, and the University of Miami. Her nine years of studying psychology stressed the superiority of scientific method and objectivity. She was taught to "deal only in observables." Despite this training, she became convinced from the writings of Freud that the way to really help people was by bringing to light their hidden motivations—things that were *not* readily observable. So when she opened her psychotherapy practice in California, she began using hypnosis, which she found to be a shortcut to motivations buried in the subconscious mind.

Dr. Fiore followed Freud's method of age regression. While her patients were in a hypnotic trance, she would suggest that they scan back through the years to the source of their current problem, usually an emotional trauma of some kind. Once the forgotten trauma was brought to consciousness and worked through, the symptoms that had brought the patient into therapy would clear up. Using this technique, she found that complex problems that had formerly taken years to resolve without hypnosis now could be cleared up in a matter of months.[5]

Surprisingly, she found that some lifelong problems could be traced back even *further*—to events in the first few months of life, during the birth experience, or in the womb. At the time this was a truly radical concept, ridiculed by conventional psychologists who held the then-current view that infants' brains were not developed enough to carry memory. Yet when Dr. Fiore's patients recalled these very early experiences, their chronic emotional problems, such as guilt, or their physical symptoms, such as headaches or asthma, disappeared.

One day Dr. Fiore stumbled upon something even more extraordinary. While using hypnotic age regression to discover the source of a patient's crippling sexual inhibitions, she gave the suggestion that he go back to the source of his problem. She was totally unprepared for his reply.

He said, "Two or three lifetimes ago, I was a Catholic priest." Then he gave a vivid and emotional description of his life and sexual attitudes as a seventeenth-century Italian priest. Because Dr. Fiore knew that this patient believed in reincarnation, she reasoned that this "lifetime" was nothing more than a colorful fantasy. But the next time she saw him he reported, much to her surprise, that he was not only healed of his sexual problems but felt much better about himself in general.

Soon after this session the same thing happened again. Another client she was regressing with hypnosis unexpectedly jumped back to a past life and described a death that perfectly explained the problem that had brought her into therapy. Again Dr. Fiore was not convinced that her patient's past life memory was real, or that her patient was not merely fantasizing a past life cause of her problem. But six weeks later the patient returned to report that her problem had completely disappeared.

Nothing in Dr. Fiore's Protestant upbringing had prepared her for this. She was taught that we live only one life on Earth. And her scientific training taught her to be skeptical of anything that couldn't be proven. But she was a healer, deeply committed to helping her patients, and she couldn't ignore the fact that they were getting better by remembering these apparent past lives. Despite her beliefs or the beliefs of her patients, past life stories healed. From that point on she routinely used past life regression with her patients.

People came to Dr. Fiore for help with all sorts of problems. She always probed first for a cause in the patient's present life. When she couldn't find one, she searched their past lives. Often at the root of these problems was a past life story, particularly a death. The death experience, she found, was the event *most* responsible for the person's symptoms and problems. When patients got dramatic relief from their symptoms, often it was as a direct result of reexperiencing the death while under hypnosis.[6]

One of Dr. Fiore's cases shows how this works. A successful businessman and lawyer was so terrified of heights that he completely avoided air travel and would not even drive over mountains. This fear, by putting limits on his travel, was hurting his career. After trying traditional therapies without success, he sought Dr. Fiore's help as a desperate measure to conquer his fear. In a dramatic, highly emotional regression, this man remembered being a workman fixing a tile roof on a European church. He slipped on a tile and slid down the roof, clinging on to a gutter to break his fall. He relived each terror-filled second as he slowly lost his grip on the gutter and fell to his death, becoming impaled on the wooden scaffolding below. After he fully reexperienced and processed this gruesome death in several regression sessions, he was free of his crippling fear of heights.[7]

Dr. Fiore found that not just phobias but physical symptoms too could be traced to horrible past life deaths. For example, migraine headaches, chronic back and neck problems, and stomach disorders could be traced to deaths in which the patient was clubbed in the head, guillotined, hanged, or shot or speared in the same place on the body. Physical ailments could also be the consequence of dying while in the grip of strong emotions—anger, guilt, sadness, or fear. These unresolved feelings kept the memory alive and showed up as physical symptoms in a later life. Once the trauma was reexperienced under hypnosis, though, and the emotions processed with Dr. Fiore's guidance, the physical reminder of the past life experience cleared up and the symptoms disappeared.

I turned these revelations over in my mind and compared them with what had happened with Chase. His feeling of guilt that had originated *in another lifetime* had continued to afflict him, not as guilt in this life but as a physical symptom—the eczema— on the same spot where the bullet had pierced his wrist in the past life. And once he had a chance to revisit the past life and process the emotions, the eczema had disappeared. This seemed incredible to me at first, but here it was validated as a recurring phenomenon in Dr. Fiore's book.

Her cases validated my own past life memories as well. I could imagine my own story in *You Have Been Here Before*, shuffled among the others. Her cases had the same qualities and feel as my past life stories. They had the same unexpected turns of everyday life and the same mundane details that made them ring true. They were textured with deep emotions: sadness, joy, anger, love. Reading them, I felt I was eavesdropping, they were so personal. I remembered being moved in the same way as I listened to Sarah and Chase tell their stories that day in my kitchen. These were stories of real people groping through real lives and struggling to come to grips with real deaths.

Remembered Death Experiences

"I have helped more than a thousand people die. All in my office." Dr. Fiore's claim at first seems glib. But it's true. Almost every patient who remembered a past life also remembered the death experience that had ended that life. The reports of remembered deaths were amazingly consistent with each other, with the reports of Dr. Wambach's regression subjects, and with the reports of near death experiences in Dr. Raymond Moody's *Life After Life.* Everyone who remembered dying described a continuation of consciousness after death; their awareness didn't cease when their heart stopped beating. Their perceptions remained viable. They could still see, hear, sense what was happening to them and around them. Any physical or emotional pain they had been feeling at death was gone, hunger was satisfied, thirst was quenched. They felt whole again.

At the moment of death, they felt themselves leaving their bodies, suddenly feeling lighter, floating like a feather, rising up into the air, looking down at the scenes they had left below. Patients reported watching their own funerals from above the treetops, just as I had done in my nineteenth-century death. Many entered a celestial realm of bright light and bathed in its warm, loving presence. Angels and light beings appeared. Some heard sounds—buzzing, humming, even celestial music. Others were welcomed by deceased friends and relatives in spirit form. For many, this was true bliss. Invariably the transition was a peaceful one, filled with indescribable beauty and grace, prompting some to weep for joy while still in trance.

By remembering their deaths, many of Dr. Fiore's patients gained a new confidence in life. They weren't afraid of death anymore. They understood that death is not an end, it's another beginning. For all, the remembered death experience was a source of profound inspiration that changed how they lived their lives.

Dr. Wambach found that over 90 percent of her subjects had the same pleasant experiences, almost word for word. Is it possible to penetrate one of life's greatest mysteries through regression? I believe so. My remembered death experiences were almost identical to those described by Dr. Wambach's and Dr. Fiore's patients. Sarah's description of her after-death state was similar: "I feel myself floating high above the treetops. I feel light, like air. I guess I'm dead. I don't feel any pain. I'm relieved that it's over." Chase remembered floating above the battlefield, feeling good that his life was done, that he could now move on to a happier life.

When I finished reading Dr. Fiore's book, I realized that it was the reality check I had been looking for. Here was a clinical psychologist with years of training in the empirical sciences describing the same types of past life stories, the same death experiences, and most importantly, the same healing effects of past life memories that I had discovered in my family. It gave me the confidence to push on. The answers were coming; my search was bearing fruit.

But I still had many questions about *how* the healing worked. Little did I suspect that I would find more answers in my friend Cathy's kitchen.

Dr. Roger Woolger: Searching for Soul and Spirit

Cathy invited me to her house one morning for a cup of espresso and "girl talk." By the second cup we were flying. Our voices were getting louder by the minute, and her husband, Patrick, who was trying to concentrate in the next room, couldn't help overhearing our animated conversation about past lives. He poked his head around the door and said he had given up trying to work, could he join us?

"What a coincidence," he said in his mellifluous Georgian drawl. "My good friend Roger just published a book about past lives. Which reminds me of a story . . ."

Patrick, an entertainer who can't resist an opportunity to tell a story, launched into Rabelaisian tales of the "good old days in

Vermont" when he and Roger had hung out together. His yarn grew more and more outrageous and funny, until we pleaded with him to stop because we were so worn out from laughing. Then he strolled over to his bookshelf, handed me his friend's book, and with a cynical grin said, "*You* might like this. Personally I think this past life stuff is a bunch of crap. I can't believe that y'all believe this!" Cathy and I looked at each other—and burst out laughing again. What irony that Patrick, the teller of outrageous tales, should be surrounded by crazy people who actually believed this "crap."

That evening, after the kids were in bed, I opened the book, *Other Lives, Other Selves—A Jungian Therapist Discovers Past Lives*, by Roger Woolger, Ph.D. After hearing Patrick's tales about the author, I didn't know what to expect. But I was immediately swept up in the swift current of Dr. Woolger's writing. Here was a book that combined all the streams of ideas I had been swimming in for years—past lives, T. S. Eliot, hypnotic regression, William Blake, healing. Most gratifying of all, it featured my old companion, *The Tibetan Book of the Dead*. Dr. Woolger made sense out of all these ideas and added new depth to my understanding of past lives. When I finished it, I called Cathy in disbelief: "Patrick's *friend* wrote this? It's really brilliant, and so well-written!" I was impressed that Patrick had such an erudite friend. "Yes," Cathy admitted, "Patrick does have some remarkable friends."

Like Dr. Fiore, Dr. Woolger is a therapist, interested first in the healing power of past life memories. In addition, Dr. Woolger is a consummate scholar with a scope of vision much broader than psychology. His book goes beyond reporting past life therapy as a singular clinical technique. He elevates it into the context of the ageless study of the mind, and by showing how past life memories underlie every person's makeup, he challenges the most basic and sacred premises of modern psychology. Combining ideas from Western psychology, ancient Eastern mysticism, his own regression experiences, and his direct observation of thousands of regression patients, he builds a comprehensive model that explains *how* past life memories work.

I read the book a second time. Dr. Woolger made no mention

of children but, I reasoned, if I could understand well the dynamics of past life memories as they affect adults, then I could extrapolate them to children.

Dr. Woolger begins the book with his own story. He grew up in England, just miles from Stratford-on-Avon, surrounded by the spirit of Shakespeare. Drama cast its spell on young Roger, and he originally intended a career as an actor. Instead he found himself at Oxford University, in a world where experimentalism and sterile statistics reigned supreme. He graduated with a joint degree in behavioral psychology and analytic philosophy. But his studies left him disillusioned and questioning: "What have statistics to do with the heart and the soul, with the supreme spiritual achievements of mankind?" In an attempt to find answers outside the "materialistic straightjacket of Western thought," he immersed himself in Hinduism and Christian mysticism, and in the process earned a Ph.D. in comparative religion from London University. But studying religion yielded only dry, philosophical constructs—soul and spirit in name only—when what Dr. Woolger was looking for was practical applications of these ideas that he could use in his personal and professional life.

Dr. Woolger continued his search in Zurich, at the Jungian Institute. Carl Jung, known for expanding Freud's vision of the unconscious, created a theory of psychology that allowed for the mysteries of spirit and soul. In Jung, Woolger had finally found a philosophy that nourished both his intellectual and his spiritual sides.

After Zurich, he came to America to teach at the University of Vermont, and stayed to open a psychotherapy practice. One day a colleague asked if he would be willing to experiment with a technique for regression to past lives. Although skeptical, his advanced sense of adventure got the better of him, and he agreed to try.

To his great surprise, in this first regression Dr. Woolger vividly recalled a life in thirteenth-century France as a mercenary in the papal army. He found himself in the midst of unspeakable horror, as the inhabitants of entire French villages were massacred and burned in the name of the Church. Repulsed by the cruelty, the soldier had a change of heart and deserted the army, but was captured and burned at the stake as a heretic himself.

This regression opened Dr. Woolger's eyes and changed his life. It explained terrifying dreams he had had of torture and killing, which no amount of psychotherapy had been able to erase. And with this single stroke, another mystery was solved: he finally understood that a severe phobia of fire that had plagued him all his life was caused by being burned at the stake in this past life. This session was so powerful and had such immediate results that he and his colleagues began to experiment in earnest with past life regression techniques, swapping sessions with each other. They collected all the information they could find on hypnotic regression and past lives, pooled their insights, and refined their methods. When he had gained enough confidence in the technique, Dr. Woolger changed his practice to feature past life therapy.

Serious Healing

Dr. Woolger and Dr. Fiore, both trained in traditional psychotherapy but coming from different sides of the Atlantic, were finding the same thing: past life therapy works. Their patients were getting better.

As in Dr. Fiore's book, the stories that emerge in Dr. Woolger's therapy sessions have the ring of truth, with none of the disjointed characteristics of fantasy. Most of the past lives his patients report are of obscure persons—peasants, slaves, soldiers, craftsmen, traders, hunters, food gatherers. The accounts are always told from the puny perspective of the individual living in that time, never from the omniscient perspective of history. The threads of stories that run through these lives are plausible and continuous, as in a real life, no matter how bizarre the twists of fate. All of the stories are peppered with mundane details, which I was beginning to recognize as a hallmark of true past life memory.

But it is the *psychological* truth of the story that matters most to Dr. Woolger. He tells his patients that it doesn't matter if they believe in reincarnation for past life therapy to be effective. It works regardless of belief. Therefore he is not concerned with the historic proof of these lives. He seldom probes for specific names, dates, or historical details. He actually discourages his patients from thinking about proof at all, warning that it could be a distraction, draining vital energy from the healing power of the story. "A past life memory is not an end in itself," he stresses, "but a means to the emotional catharsis, self-understanding, and healing that are the true goals of psychotherapy."[8]

Like Dr. Fiore, Dr. Woolger helps his patients trace the source of their current problems to past life stories. But where most of Dr. Fiore's cases usually demonstrate a simple one-to-one, cause-and-effect relationship between past life and present life, Dr. Woolger shows how complex both the cause and effect can be. The source of a problem can echo back through multiple past lives, each life adding another layer of complexity to the problem. He shows how a series of past lives can create a tangled skein of emotional, physical, and mental problems in the present. For example, a phobia may be accompanied by a physical symptom; being hanged for speaking out against the authorities could result in a chronic neck pain *and* a fear of speaking in public. Chase's phobia of loud noises and his eczema both stemmed from being traumatized in battle. Dr. Woolger is a master at unraveling these knotty issues, and he explains how he does it in his book.

People come to therapy because they have specific problems for which they are seeking relief. Dr. Woolger shows that by uncovering a patient's past lives, a wide range and variety of these problems can be solved.

For example, Dr. Woolger has seen a long list of phobias—unexplained fears—cured by regressions to past lives. Underlying each phobia is usually a specific and corresponding past life trauma, most often a death. But he has also found that past life therapy cures a host of other fears—neurotic fears, such as eating disorders, acute insecurity, depression, poor self-image, and obsession with money.

Some physical complaints can be traced directly to a specific past life injury: hanging or strangling manifest as neck or shoulder aches, disembowelment can result in intestinal problems, dying of smoke or gas shows up as weak lungs or allergies. Physical symptoms can be caused not only through wounds to the flesh, but by penetrating blows to the psyche as well: headaches can come from intolerable mental choices, sinusitis from a failure to grieve, back troubles from carrying too much guilt.

Ideas and thoughts can transcend death. The last thought that occupies the mind at the very moment of death can imprint on the soul and dominate the person's thinking in the next life. Dr. Woolger calls this a life script (similar to what some psychologists call a dominant myth or personal theme). These life scripts can shape a person's disposition, expectations, and motivations, coloring all perceptions of how the world works and how people should act.

For example, the life script "It's not safe to go out in the world" could result from dying in a surprise attack. "I'm not good enough" could stem from any serious failure in a past life. "It's all my fault" could come from making any kind of immediately fatal error. Dying as a child in any accident where the parents were nearby could result in the life script "You didn't protect me."

It is not only death traumas that carry over to the present. The second most common category of trauma (after violent death) is separation and abandonment. This is a sad theme that runs through all of history: being separated as a child from parents during war; abandoned in the wilderness in time of famine; or separated from loved ones who are sold into slavery. Being permanently separated from parents or family can so violate a person's psyche that the loss dominates the mind through to death, even if the death is many years later. This trauma can manifest in later lives as insecurity, an inability to trust others, extreme possessiveness, or separation anxiety in a baby.[9]

Difficulties with personal relationships and family struggles can also be deeply rooted in past life scenarios. The same people weave in and out of our lifetimes, reappearing over and over again to finish business from the past. We come back to replay the same themes, switching roles and changing gender from life to life. The relationships range from loving to hateful, and everything in between. The issues can be among groups of two, three, or any number of people.

Positive relationships, I believe, are the most common. A former husband can now be a beloved daughter, or a former loyal friend can be your mother. Generally, if there was a positive relationship in the past, it continues to be good in the present. It's true that love survives, even though the roles may change. Falling in love with a soul mate is not just a romantic notion—it happens.

But Dr. Woolger's book is about serious healing, and his patients come to therapy burdened with serious relationship problems. When regressed, they often describe feuds and vindictive squabbles spanning many centuries and many lifetimes. Old scores between parent and child, master and slave, victim and victimizer, siblings, spouses, lovers—the list is endless—are re-energized and replayed in the present life. Dr. Woolger gives one case where a father and daughter flipflopped through *six* different lives, and another where bitter reprisals between a trio—mother, daughter, and granddaughter in this life—could be traced through *eight* past lives.[10]

Why All the Tragedy?

Something bothered me about the cases in Dr. Woolger's book. They seemed to be excessively bloody and violent. Boiling at the core of his patients' past life traumas is a seemingly endless variety of rape, murder, suicide, torture, accidental death, and disaster. Why all the tragedy? Maybe it is because such atrocities have been more common than we realize through the centuries, and past life regression is an uncensored window on these dark and anonymous corners of history. These past life stories are anything but sugarcoated versions of the past.

But I realized there is another reason why this gore is necessary. Dr. Woolger's patients came to him with serious problems that were crippling their lives—problems that, in most cases, had resisted conventional therapy. The past life source of such a severe problem had to be a violent death, or a trauma so heart-wrenching that it permanently scarred the psyche. The more horrible or sudden the death or the more profound the trauma, the more likely it would cling to the soul and scar a future life.

This insight helped me to understand that Dr. Woolger's cases, full of such tragedy and pain, are *not* a cross section of *typical* lives. Dr. Wambach's survey found that 62 percent of lives end in a peaceful death. Dr. Woolger's cases are the extreme ones from the other 38 percent.

As Dr. Wambach shows, fulfilled and happy lives do occur, and they leave their positive traces as talents, virtues, wisdom, loving relationships, and a propensity for more happy lives. Dr. Fiore found evidence of these too. But happy lives do not cause problems that bring people into therapy. "It would be as valuable to someone in distress to focus on happy past lives," Dr. Woolger says, "as it would be for a physician to treat a hurt leg by examining the healthy one."

I believe that this principle holds true for children's memories too. The majority of them are benign and do not cause problems in future lifetimes. But as Sarah and Chase taught me, children can carry the scars of past life trauma in the same ways that adults do. Their deaths were no less horrible and their last moments no less grisly than any of the adults regressed by Drs. Wambach, Fiore, or Woolger. After all, Chase died amidst the slaughter of a Civil War battlefield, and Sarah perished as flames seared her flesh. Memories of such tragedies are not reserved for adults only.

Widening the Frame of Psychology

Dr. Woolger does much more than show the range of problems that can be treated with past life therapy. His book is about how and why past life therapy works. He explains it, generally, by demonstrating that past life therapy is not an isolated technique, but rather an extension of conventional psychotherapy. He shows, point by point, how the dynamics and principles of Western psychology apply across many lifetimes.

For example, he is fond of a particular quote from Jung: "A complex arises where we have experienced a defeat in life," to which Dr. Woolger asks, "Which life?" He modernizes Jung's dictum to say, "A complex arises where we have experienced a defeat in *any life.*"[11]

Traditional Western psychology, beginning with Freud, believes that everything we experience in this life is recorded in the unconscious mind—a metaphor for all of the forces in our psyche outside our conscious awareness. These unconscious forces shape, direct, and color everything we think, feel, and do. Dr. Woolger is saying, simply, that experiences from past lives are also floating in the unconscious soup. Traumas, thoughts, and emotions from past lives are dumped into the soup along with material originating in this life. Once they are in the unconscious, *all* these memories follow the same laws and can affect us in the same ways. Any severe trauma—whether it is from two years or two lifetimes ago—if forgotten and repressed, can cause problems. This also means that forgotten and repressed traumas can be healed in the same way: by being made conscious. Therapy is the process of hunting for the original traumas and bringing them out in the open.

From Dr. Woolger's point of view, the domain where traditional psychologists search for the causes of problems is too narrow. Their search is limited within the frame of a single lifetime. They look back no further than birth.

Past life therapists have demonstrated that it pays to widen the frame of psychology far beyond a single lifetime, to include all of the patient's lifetimes. In this widened frame, birth is not an absolute beginning, the start of the time line. Instead it's a transition, a door through which an experienced soul enters carrying the baggage and lessons of past lifetimes. In this new paradigm the old idea of tabula rasa—the belief that our mind at birth is a clean slate to be written on by experience alone—is destroyed. Nor is death the end of the time line, the end of all consequences, like turning off a TV, case closed. Death too is a transition, a doorway the soul passes through on its journey to more lifetimes.

But death is more than a doorway. It is also a psychological event, a trauma with psychological consequences.

This is a new idea. Conventional therapists have no experience treating the psychological consequences of a person's own death. Past life therapists have gained some experience, but even they have much to learn because the idea is so new. This is why Dr. Woolger draws guidance from the great Eastern psychologists, the Buddhist and Hindu sages—and particularly from the authors of *The Tibetan Book of the Dead*—who have been studying and writing about the moment of death for centuries.

Buddhists write about mind, just as Western psychologists do. But they begin with the radically different premise that consciousness exists outside the physical body and continues after death. This idea of the continuation of consciousness is difficult for Westerners to comprehend because we have been taught that the mind ceases at death. But reports from those in the West who have had near death experiences, in addition to reports of remembered death experiences from past life regressions, support what Eastern mystics have been saying for thousands of years.

Buddhists observe and describe the stages of mind as it goes through the entire cycle from life to life, including the moment of death and the interval between lives. According to sacred Buddhist teachings, the moment of death is the peak psychological moment—the supreme bardo in the entire cycle of life, death, and rebirth.

The Moment of Death

At the moment of death we drop our physical bodies and all of our mental barriers. The illusions of the physical world dissolve, and we come face to face with what the Buddhists call the "Clear Light of Reality" and the "true nature of Mind"—the base essence of the universe and of our own inner nature both being the same. "To realize the nature of mind is to realize the nature of all things."[12] This is a timeless, ageless essence that is untouched even by death.

This heightened consciousness makes the moment of death a golden opportunity for the soul to progress in its spiritual journey. It is possible in this moment to open our hearts and embrace the truth of our divine nature, and to release any negativity or trauma from the life we are leaving—and from any other lifetime—and thus advance to a more favorable life.

It is a perilous moment too. Thoughts at the moment of death can be "magnified out of all proportion and flood our whole perception."[13] So if the mind is full of petty and negative thoughts, they will be amplified and will dominate our consciousness from that point forward, influencing the particulars of the next incarnation.

Dr. Woolger discovered this too from observing his therapy patients. In his search for the cause of present-life problems, he discovered that death is the psychological event that has the most bearing on a person's well-being in subsequent lives. Many problems in the lives of his patients could be traced directly to the imprints from unresolved thoughts and feelings, usually negative ones, surrounding the moment of death. These thoughts and feelings don't just die with the physical body. Instead, they coalesce to form a soul memory—a composite of images, thoughts, and feelings around the highly charged experience. As Dr. Woolger explains, "The heightened consciousness that occurs at death imprints with exaggerated intensity the dying thoughts, feelings, or sensation on whatever we call the vehicle that transfers our essence from one lifetime to another."[14]

In traumatic deaths especially—sudden or horrible deaths—we have no way to come to terms with our lives or our death; nor do we have time to make amends to people, say goodbye to loved ones, or finish up our business on Earth. We are not at peace. *We die incomplete.* If we are preoccupied at the moment of death by negative emotions—hate, fear, guilt, blame, resentment, anger—they somehow intensify all other sensations, including the body sensations of the death and the messages flashing through the mind. It is these *emotions* that glue all the other impressions to the soul and bind them to travel intact to the next life.

If we die incomplete, we leave that lifetime with what Dr.

Woolger calls "unfinished business of the soul." We pass through death's door carrying our unresolved issues with us and an urge to finish what we have left undone. These issues, begging to be resolved, are what manifest as problems in another lifetime. Unfinished business propels the memories.

Through regression therapy and the healing intelligence of the unconscious mind, we have the opportunity to go back to the moment of death and reverse its effects. Exactly how this works remains a mystery, but thousands of successful past life regressions offer evidence that it does.

The Moment of Death in Therapy

The crux of Dr. Woolger's therapy method is the reenactment of the moment of death. This is the point where the real healing happens.

He typically works with a client over several sessions to comprehend the full complexity of the problem, gradually peeling away the present life and past life layers surrounding the cause of the problem. The climax of these sessions comes when he guides a patient step by step through the death and the after-death state of omniscient illumination. He directs them to examine each supercharged thought, feeling, and body sensation throughout the process.

At the moment of death, Dr. Woolger asks questions to focus the patient's awareness on the details of the experience: "What is happening? What are you thinking? What are your *last* thoughts? What are you feeling?" He probes for connections and patterns: "How is this trauma held in your body? What is your body saying?" This can be a time of great catharsis for the patient, as strong emotions that were frozen in the past at the time of death well to the surface and are released—usually with lots of crying. Once they do, the energy that held the memory dissipates, and the negative thoughts, feelings, and sensations that were fixed to the memory become "unglued" from the soul.

This after-life state is an extremely lucid time for the patient, an opportunity to fully understand and resolve important issues from the past life. Dr. Woolger asks, "Is there anything unfinished in that lifetime? What do you need to do to let go of it?" Using techniques from psychodrama and gestalt therapy, he encourages his patients to dialogue with characters from other lifetimes. In this way apologies can be made, forgiveness extended, new understanding gained, guilt assuaged. He makes sure that the death process is finished, all issues are resolved, and all questions answered, before bringing the patient out of the trance. The patient must consciously know that these memories, and everything else that goes with them, are in the past, finished, and never have to be played out again. This closure is the goal of the regression.

Dr. Woolger wraps up the session by discussing with the patient what just happened. They review the past life story, drawing parallels with the present life. He shows the patient ways to integrate these new insights into day-to-day life, and how to use the knowledge to change old patterns. He may suggest the patient use daily affirmations such as "I am now safe," "I am worthy of love," or "I can trust other people" to reinforce the new understanding.

The dramatic case of Edith, a client of Dr. Woolger's, illustrates how going back to the moment of death can disengage a past life pattern that was causing a chronic disease.

Edith, a dancer in her late twenties, suffered from a degenerative disease called lupus erythematosus, causing painful stiffness in her joints. During a workshop with Dr. Woolger, she vividly recalled being a young Russian man, an anarchist, who was engaged in an uprising against palace guards who were suppressing food riots by the poor. This man's father had been slain a few days earlier in one of these riots. In a fit of vengeance, this man and his friends planned an attack on the palace barracks with a homemade bomb. One night, with a bomb hidden beneath his coat, he furtively approached the barracks. But before he had a chance to throw the bomb, it went off in his hands.

At this point in the regression, Edith fully identified with this young man and his feelings. When Dr. Woolger urged her to tell what she was experiencing, she burst into tears, almost screaming, telling him that she couldn't bear to look and see what had happened. Horrified, she said that she saw her body: the bomb had blown off her arms and legs. This man died slowly, knowing that his arms and legs would never work again. Dr. Woolger then suggested to Edith, "Be aware of your last words as you are dying, and go to the point where your heart finally stops beating." Edith replied, "My arms and legs will never work again. Oh, no!"

Edith suddenly made the connection between this painful past life death and her fear of progressive degeneration from the lupus.

Dr. Woolger skillfully guided Edith: "Were there any other thoughts you had been holding in your arms and legs before you left them?" Edith described her anger toward the men who killed the young man's father and how he had wanted them to suffer for what they did. Edith began to cry as she realized that her vengeance had turned on itself, and it was the young man who ended up suffering. With this realization she agreed to let go of her anger. She took a deep breath, and her body, which had been reexperiencing the pain, went limp. When she sat up and opened her eyes, the pain was gone from her joints.

When Dr. Woolger saw Edith six months later, her lupus was in remission, and she was able to dance again.[15]

Typical Kids, Typical Deaths

Dr. Woolger's book assured me that what Chase and Sarah had experienced was not unusual but typical. Although he didn't say anything specifically about children's memories, his model of healing, and especially the case of Edith, explained what had happened with my children. *Their past life deaths were incomplete.*

When Sarah relived her death in the house fire, she again felt the strong emotions of her last moments before she died. She hadn't had a chance to cry, say good-bye to her family, or finish her life. She died incomplete. She was confused and angry at her parents, believing that they had abandoned her, and she was terrified of the flames engulfing her. Once she finally allowed these painful emotions to come to the surface, cried, and expressed her anger toward her parents, the emotions dissipated. In a moment of clarity, she could see that her parents had tried to save her, and she understood that they were really not to blame. She let go of her anger.

I remember that moment as we sat with Sarah in the kitchen: we could almost feel the surge of energy leave; the anger and fear seemed to just blow out of her. And when the anger left, so did her phobia.

In Chase's case, a catharsis was not necessary for his fear of loud noises and his eczema to be cured. Awareness and understanding were all he needed the first time with Norman Inge. The process was gentle and not highly emotional. Apparently it wasn't time for Chase to see his death in that lifetime. He went just so far, and the memory faded.

But as it turned out, his story was still incomplete. The unsettled emotions of his war experience continued to reside in him, and three years later they were triggered by the immediate reality of the war in the Persian Gulf. His sadness about leaving his family surfaced along with the rest of his story, including his death on the battlefield. He finally had closure on that life when he experienced his death and moved into the after-death state. He gained the detachment he needed to resolve his feelings and leave that lifetime behind, where it belonged. His death was finally complete.

Dr. Woolger's healing model helped me understand what had happened with my children. But something still puzzled me. My children's memories had a quality different from the dark and complex cases of adults in *Other Lives, Other Selves*. Sarah's and Chase's past life deaths had been every bit as tragic and horrible as theirs, but my children's traumas seemed to be closer to the surface, requiring only a light and gentle touch to bring out and resolve. It was as if their memories were only surface cuts that just needed air to heal, whereas Dr. Woolger's patients suffered from deep wounds that needed major psychological surgery. What *was* this different quality? I turned this question over in my mind many times.

Perhaps I was missing the obvious: children's memories *are* closer to the surface. Children haven't lived through enough years and experiences to layer over and thoroughly embed these issues into their personalities. Very young children, especially, don't have the additional layers of belief and cultural conditioning glazing over their memories, obstructing their own awareness, and leading them to believe that remembering past lives is impossible. Since there aren't as many layers and barriers for their memories to pass through, it is much easier for children to access and resolve problems from the past. They can accomplish in a few minutes what it takes an adult many sessions and the guidance of a therapist to do.

CHAPTER 5

Trance Is Easy

Leaving the Outside World Behind

After we moved to Philadelphia, I talked to Norman Inge on the phone. I had stored up a host of questions, and now I bombarded him mercilessly with them. He saw that I was on a quest, and he wanted to help me, so he made me an offer: if I could visit him in Florida, he would begin to train me to do regressions. The only condition was that I continue my training in hypnotherapy when I returned home. I wanted to accept Norman's offer, but I wasn't sure how I could manage a trip to Florida. Steve was on the road with his new job—who would watch my kids?

As luck would have it, a few weeks later my mother called to say that she was going to stay with her good friend in Florida, and invited the kids and me down for a visit. Her friend, I found out, lived only a short drive from Norman's home. It took two seconds to figure out that I could go to Florida, take the kids to Disney World, and then train with Norman while my mother spent time with her grandchildren. Treats all around.

Finally, after weeks of Chase asking "Is it time to go to Disney World yet?" the big day arrived. Chase, Sarah, my mother, and I entered the Magic Kingdom, leaving the outside world behind at the gate. Disney World was all we expected it to be—dizzying and magical, a world unto itself. Indefatigable Chase ran from one adventure to the next, with Sarah trailing close behind. My mother and I rallied, following up the rear, fortifying ourselves with iced tea and coffee. The kids were on their best behavior, despite the long waits in line for the attractions. They were in a state of wide-eyed bliss as we rode trains, went underwater in a submarine, and sailed through the Caribbean in pursuit of pirates. When the haunted house ride got stuck in the middle of the graveyard for a scary ten minutes, Chase thought it was the best part of the trip.

I had my own taste of magic. I was climbing the walls of the pioneer fort in Frontierland trying to keep Chase in sight when I heard a distant voice shout, "Carol?" I turned around and saw a friend from Asheville who had been regressed by Norman, one of the only people in the world I knew personally who had been regressed to a past life. Strange, we both thought, that we should run into each other in Frontierland, miles from home. I told her that I was in Florida to train with Norman. She remarked, "That figures."

In two days we had covered about every inch of the Magic Kingdom. The kids reluctantly reentered the real world of Florida; my mother and I were more than ready.

The next day I left the kids with my mother and drove to Norman's. As I wound my way through the sandy lanes that led to his home; I spotted a large white bird flying ahead of my car. It seemed to be leading me. When I got out of the car, I noticed it had settled in a tree next to Norman's house. Norman opened the door to greet me and looked up at the bird.

"Did you see that?" I greeted him. "He led me to your house."

"Yes," he laughed with a gleam in his eye, "he visits here

occasionally." I could tell that my time with Norman was going to be very interesting.

We spent the next two days talking about healing, the subconscious mind, kahuna shamanism of Hawaii, and hypnotism. We kept coming back to the question of how to open the flow of memory. I flooded Norman with questions: How had Sarah and Chase accessed their memories so quickly without formal hypnosis? Is it possible to hypnotize children as you do adults? If we tried to regress Sarah and Chase again, would they go to the same lives or to different lives, and if different, would these be traumatic lives too?

Hypnosis, Norman explained, is nothing more than a state of focused concentration. We go in and out of hypnotic states all the time, shifting our focus from without to within. For example, when we are deeply engrossed in watching TV, a movie, or reading an exciting novel, we shut off our awareness of the sounds and activity around us. We go into a light trance. Sometimes, when driving a car on the interstate, our attention lapses, we plunge into our thoughts, then discover too late that we have driven past our exit. This is also a light trance. Certainly a part of us manages to drive the car and stay on the road, but our conscious awareness of what we are doing is temporarily suspended.

So it is with hypnotic trance states. Conscious awareness is suspended to some degree while the mind is occupied by inner thoughts, images, and feelings. The conscious mind doesn't turn off completely; it is always monitoring. That is why during a regression a person can ask for a Kleenex, or get up to go to the bathroom, and maintain the trance until they get back to the couch.

Norman stressed that trance is the same for children. If anything, *children go in and out of trance more easily and more often than adults.* If you watch children, especially very young children, you may notice that their eyes look bigger and their breathing changes as they stare vacantly for short periods of time. They seem to be off in their own world, not aware of what is happening around them. Actually, they are in a light trance state, their focus directed on an inner reality. What exactly are they experiencing in this state? We don't really know. But some psychologists believe that the brightest and most creative children are those who stare frequently, without interruption. So not only is this a safe and natural process for children, but it appears it may benefit them as well.

With adult clients, Norman explained, he uses a variety of techniques—relaxation, breathing, guided imagery—to assist them in shifting their focus from external to internal sensations. Closing the eyes and focusing on breathing start the process. The internal focus is then deepened by having the client imagine a beautiful scene, or other inviting image, that engages the mind. As the client loses touch with outer sensory distractions, a transition is made, and the client's inner reality begins to take on a life of its own. The conscious mind then "takes a break" while the subconscious mind becomes dominant.

Once the client is in a trance, Norman makes a suggestion such as "go back to a past life" or "go back to the time when your problem began." These suggestions act like keys to unlock experiences held in the subconscious, the storage vault of memories. If the key fits, the door to memory will open. Sometimes, though, the door will not open. Either the therapist hasn't found the right key, or the client for some reason isn't ready to delve into past life memories and the door is barred. Some people's conscious minds are simply too strong to relinquish control, and they fight the process. These are the minority who cannot be hypnotized. If nothing works after trying different techniques, it's best not to push. The client's resistance is there for a reason—protection—and it should be respected. This process can't be forced.

"I Hate Camp"

After hours of delicious talk about hypnosis and the amazing healing intelligence of the unconscious mind, Norman's afternoon appointment arrived. This client, Charles, had agreed to let me sit in on his session as Norman's apprentice. He had come to Norman because he was curious: he wanted to try a past life regression to learn more about himself; he didn't have any particular problem he was trying to solve.

Norman began by interviewing Charles about issues in his life. I was all ears and eyes; I didn't want to miss a thing. He asked Charles about the happiest, saddest, and most memorable events in his life. He took a physical history too, inquiring about injuries, surgeries, illnesses—anything Charles could think of.

Charles sat in the big reclining chair in Norman's darkened office. Although Norman hadn't yet done a hypnotic induction, Charles closed his eyes and went into a deep reverie, recalling scenes from earlier in his life. His most traumatic memory was from childhood, when his parents sent him away to overnight summer camp. How he hated it! Charles was so distressed that he ran away and took a train home by himself. When his father found out what Charles had done, he was furious and whipped him with a belt. That was the only time in his life that Charles remembered being physically punished by his father—and he never forgot it. In fact, Charles cringed as he told us this story so many years later.

Charles couldn't think of anything else in his life that was particularly significant or troubling. So Norman began a hypnotic induction with Charles to ease him into a past life. I listened carefully to Norman's words and focused intently on Charles's face, watching for changes as he slipped into trance.

Norman, softening and slowing his voice, told Charles to close his eyes and focus on his breathing. He asked him to imagine himself in a beautiful and peaceful outdoor setting. Moving smoothly from one image to another, he suggested that Charles find an opening in the ground with stairs descending into the earth. He suggested that he descend the stairs, one by one, until he found himself in a luminous chamber below the ground. One, two, three . . . nine, ten. In this chamber were many doors. Each door represents a lifetime he had lived. He could choose any lifetime to visit simply by walking up and opening one of the doors.

I sat perfectly still, watching and listening for something to happen. I could hear my heart pounding louder and faster inside my chest.

But nothing happened; Charles remained silent. Norman asked him, slowly and patiently, "Describe what you see around you." Nothing. "What are you feeling in your body?" Nothing. "Look down at your feet. What are you wearing on your feet?" Still nothing happened. Norman tried a different technique for focusing Charles on his inner vision. Nothing happened. He tried another, and another. Charles strained to cooperate. He did everything Norman suggested. But he continued to report that none of the images he saw were anything but ordinary thinking pictures.

But as I watched and listened to Norman talk to Charles, something odd happened to me. I began to feel a churning in my stomach—I couldn't tell if it was excitement or fear. A rush of energy like a chill moved up my spine. A great sadness swept over me and filled my body. I felt an irresistible urge to cry. I tried to hold back, for fear of interrupting Charles's session, but the tears started streaming down my cheeks. I wiped them away, took a deep breath, and tried to collect myself. What on earth was happening to me?

Norman, concentrating too closely on Charles to notice my state, was about to give up. He was reassuring Charles, telling him that clients don't always go back to a past life during the first session. Nothing to be ashamed of.

Suddenly, on an overwhelming hunch, unable to hold back any longer, I broke my silence. "Charles," I said, "it's strange that you had such a bad experience in camp as a child, because the same thing happened to me when I went to Girl Scout camp. I cried and cried the whole time. I was miserable. I hated camp. And I thought something was wrong with me because everyone else seemed to like it! Now, I know that it was because *summer camp* reminded me of my own death in a *concentration camp*."

No sooner were the words out of my mouth than Charles clutched his chest and began gasping for air. Norman, not missing a beat, recognizing immediately what had happened, fired at Charles, "What's happening?"

"I smell gas . . . can't breathe . . . being suffocated." Charles pushed out each word, barely able to speak.

"Where are you?" Norman asked. Charles began weeping uncontrollably. I could see the images of his life and death in my own mind, even before he said anything. Through his sobs he described in detail the terror he was feeling as a young man, crammed in a cold, dark room with others. He smelled gas filling the room and suddenly felt a stinging and tightness in his chest. Then he left his body.

Silence. (Except for my sniveling.) Norman handed each of us a Kleenex.

When Charles had calmed down enough to speak, Norman asked him to go back to an earlier time in that life. Charles recounted his life as a young man, a Polish Jew, who had been forced from his home with his parents and neighbors. He remembered an oppressive and terrifying journey by train from his home. Eventually he found himself in that room, gasping for air, as the gas filled his lungs.

Norman encouraged Charles to continue describing his life, again taking him through his death in the gas chamber until his chest pains went away and he could breathe freely. After going through the past life death again, he was at peace.

We had another surprise. Once Charles came out of his trance he exclaimed, "That's why I get anxiety attacks! For no apparent reason my heartbeat accelerates, I get pains in my chest, and I gasp for air. When I was a child, my parents took me to one specialist after another, but none of the doctors could find an organic problem. They even took me to a psychiatrist, but he couldn't help me either. Now it all makes sense—the anxiety, the chest pains, and my difficulty breathing. It's from my death in the concentration camp. That overnight camp reminded me of the concentration camp—I couldn't stand it! Now it all makes sense!"

After the session, Charles and I gave each other a big teary hug. We looked at each other in wordless comprehension, sharing our gratitude for such a profound experience—for such a deep connection.

Norman and I walked Charles out into the bright sunlight to say good-bye. After he drove away, we laughed to realize what a perfect learning session that had been for me, better than anything we could have planned. Since Charles hadn't responded immediately to suggestions to go back to a past life, I had had the opportunity to see Norman go through his entire repertoire, mustering techniques he didn't ordinarily use.

And more importantly, I had learned to trust my intuition. Apparently I too had gone into trance when Norman did the hypnotic induction. Since I had been concentrating on Charles, I somehow tuned in to his memory, first emotionally—the crying—then visually, when I saw him in the concentration camp. I trusted my intuition and offered this key to Charles's memory. It fitted perfectly, and Charles's memory came out. Norman explained that it is not uncommon for a past life therapist to do this with a client. Sometimes a therapist will "image along," seeing what the client is seeing and picking up on the emotions of the memory.

By now it was early evening, the sun splintered through the tall palms, and a breeze ruffled the landscaping around Norman's condo. I was emotionally spent from the experience, my mind thoroughly saturated with new ideas. And I was famished. Norman and I and his wife, Joyce, went for a wonderful dinner at a nearby Thai restaurant. I recall every dish tasting unusually delicious, I was so hungry. Then, after dinner, Norman took me to a bookstore where he occasionally taught classes in past life regression and healing. I was surprised and happy to see in one room so many people with an interest in past life regression. But Norman had another surprise for me that night: within minutes, he had us all singing an authentic Hawaiian song and dancing the hula!

Sarah Rules

The next morning, when Sarah and Chase heard about my adventures, they were disappointed that they had not had a chance to spend time with Norman. They were most upset that they didn't get to see him dance the hula. So I called Norman, and we hatched a plan. Early the next day, Norman picked us up, baggage and all, and took us to his house a few hours before we had to leave for the airport.

Chase and Sarah took a few minutes to thoroughly check out Norman's condo, looking for pets, toys, or a swimming pool. Finding nothing especially interesting, both children sat unusually still on the couch. Then, with a twinkle in her eye and an irresistible sweetness in her voice, Sarah asked Norman if he would do another regression with her. Norman and I smiled at each other. What a great idea!

We followed Sarah into Norman's office. I told Chase that he could watch, but he would have to sit quietly until Norman was finished. Chase promised that he'd be good—he was as curious about what was going to happen as I was.

Norman instructed nine-year-old Sarah to make herself comfortable in the reclining chair, as he closed the blinds to block out the intense morning sunshine. He asked Sarah if she was having any problems like she had last time, or if she had any questions about her life. I wondered what Sarah would say. No, there was nothing special she wanted to find out. She was just curious.

I was waiting to see what Norman would do, since Sarah had no specific issue to address. The last time he had done this, he had used her fear of fire as the key to the memory. But since there was nothing specific to go on this time, would he use the same hypnotic technique he employed with the adults?

Norman put on a tape of soothing music—synthesizer and flute. He told Sarah to close her eyes and picture a beautiful place outside—her favorite place in the world. Her closed eyelids began fluttering like butterflies. Her face lit up. Norman didn't need to go any further. "Where are you, Sarah? What are you experiencing?" he asked in a soothing voice.

Sarah described herself as an adult male in Egypt, a long time ago. She saw herself sitting on a stone seat in an open room with stone pillars, surrounded by people she said were her servants. As Sarah described this scene, she sat stiffly in the reclining chair, with her arms resting squarely on the arms of the chair. The softness had left her face; her expression was as stony as the scene she described. Her voice surprised me. It still sounded high like Sarah's little-girl voice, but the inflections and slow cadence were those of a person in the habit of being listened to and obeyed.

"How do you feel about having this power?" Norman said, probing to see if wielding power was the reason her unconscious had chosen to show this life.

"I like it. I use it well. My people like me," she responded proudly.

At this point Chase started to fidget. I put my finger to my lips, reminding him to be quiet. He made a face. I pointed toward the door. He got up quietly and closed the door gently behind him, his eye peeking through the crack as it closed.

Sarah described a lifetime as a powerful male potentate. She spoke of this man's feelings for his people. He was concerned about what his subjects felt toward him, and about using his power wisely. He relied upon the advice of others, weighing all sides of questions that came before him. He valued most the guidance of one adviser in particular, who was also his closest friend. Sarah began to cry a little as she described the death of this friend. She said that he had a stone erected in his friend's honor. When he needed advice on difficult matters, he would go to the stone, place his hands on it, feel his deceased friend's presence, and receive guidance from him.

Norman suggested, "Go to the stone now. Put your hands on it." I could see Sarah's face light up—she began to glow and perked up in the chair, her eyes still closed. "Yes," she said, "I feel his energy." I looked at Norman. He nodded at me and smiled. Yes, she was really experiencing this.

Sarah said that nothing of importance happened during the rest of this man's life, save the daily task of ruling his people. He had a wife and children whom he loved but who only figured in the background. Sarah did say that when this man died, his duty and power would be passed on to his eldest son. He was at peace with that thought.

"Do you have any regrets about this lifetime?" Norman asked.

Sarah's lower lip began to quiver. The tight expression on her face melted, and tears welled up in her closed eyes. She brushed them away, trying to maintain her composure.

"What is it?" Norman asked.

"It's my sister. I feel guilty about my sister."

"What happened to your sister?" Norman encouraged her.

"According to Egyptian law, I had every right to inherit everything after my father died. But my sister was jealous. She and her husband stole something valuable from me—a statue, I think. That wasn't right. She shouldn't have done it—it was against the law of the land. I was angry when I found out. She heard that I knew and fled with her husband during the night. She never came back. I never saw her again. I missed her the rest of my life."

Sarah began to cry. "I should have followed my heart and not the law of the land. But I had no choice. I had to be an example to my people. It was the law. I'm sorry to have lost my sister."

"Do you know your sister in this life? Is she someone you know now, in another form?"

"It's Chase," she said, without hesitating. "I chose to come back with him this time so we could learn to be fair with each other." Her mouth curled into a little smile. "That's funny," she said. "He had very straight red hair in that lifetime too. Almost everyone else had black hair."

Sarah opened her eyes and smiled broadly.

"Is that why you go out of your way to share with your brother," I asked, "even when he bothers you?"

Sarah gave her arms a big stretch and hopped out of the chair. "Yeah, I guess so," she answered with an impish grin, brushing off the comment as she would a fly from her shoulder.

Sarah had always gone out of her way to share with Chase. Steve and I were continually amazed and gratified at how tolerant and considerate Sarah was of her busy little brother. I chuckled to myself, thinking that we had attributed these virtuous qualities in Sarah to our good parenting. Now it seemed that there was a lot more to it than that.

We all walked out to the kitchen, had a drink of juice, stepped out onto the terrace, and squinted in the brash Florida sunshine. Chase had been waiting patiently for us. He was on his extra-good six-year-old vacation behavior, for he never knew what treat might be in store for him next. And he certainly didn't want to miss an opportunity for some fun.

Norman looked at his watch and said that we had time for one more regression. He asked Chase if he would like to have a turn;

he didn't want Chase to be left out. After all, Sarah was still beaming. Chase said, "Sure."

Dirty Toes

We all walked back into Norman's office. This time Chase sat in the reclining chair. A little boy in a big chair.

Norman began, "You just went to Disney World, didn't you? Tell me about your favorite ride there." Chase described how he liked the cars in the haunted house that went fast and suddenly jerked sideways.

"Okay," Norman continued. "Close your eyes, and imagine that you're on one of those cars, traveling very, very fast, spinning around and around and around." Chase gripped the sides of the big chair. His eyelids fluttered rapidly, his mouth was slightly open, his breathing quickened. "This car goes around and around and suddenly stops. And when it stops, you step off and find yourself in another lifetime—any lifetime that you want."

"I'm a man. I'm wearing brown pants"—Norman winked at me, while Sarah had her eyes closed and was listening carefully—"and a big white shirt—it's big, not like a regular shirt. I have sandals on. . . . I can see the leather straps. I can see my dirty toes. It's hot and dusty. It's dry. A woman . . . my wife . . . is standing next to me. She has a dress on with a big white hat that sticks out on the sides. I have a little boy. I make toys for him out of wood. I have a dog too. I'm very happy."

This was the second time I had heard my little boy mention having a wife and family. It still sent shivers up my arms and shoulders.

"What kind of work do you do?" Norman asked.

"I make things for people out of wood. I like my work. I'm very happy."

"Does anything happen to you in this lifetime?" asked Norman.

"It's a good life. I really like my family."

"Does anything happen in that lifetime that's important?"

"I work. I like my work. My son grows up and works with wood too. We carve things. It's a good life. I really like my family."

"Is there anyone in that lifetime who is with you now, as a different person?" Norman was probing, trying to figure out if there was anything that was unfinished from this lifetime, or that explained anything about Chase.

"Yes, my son. It's my friend, Henson."

I thought of Henson, who always followed Chase around at school, and smiled to myself, trying to imagine Henson as Chase's son. Henson's mom and I loved it when the boys got together to play after school because they were so kind to each other and never fought.

"Is there anything else about that lifetime?" It was getting late, but Norman wanted to make sure that he left nothing unfinished with Chase.

"Yes. My dog. I miss my dog from that lifetime. I was really mad when my parents gave away our dog before I was born. I wanted to have a dog again. I remember that I was sad when they gave the dog away."

"You knew what was happening *before* you were born?" Norman clarified.

"Oh, yeah. I knew they were giving away the dog, but I couldn't tell them that I wanted to keep him, because I wasn't born yet." This was an interesting twist. Yes, we had owned a dog, a big German shepherd that we had to give away because we moved from the country into town. Had Chase really been aware of this *before* he was born? Can children really know what is happening in the outside world while still in utero? I stored that question away for later.

It was time to go. Norman confirmed to Chase that it was good to remember such a happy lifetime, that those good feelings were his to keep all his life. Then he told him to open his eyes. Chase's eyes popped open exceptionally big. He rubbed them, scanned once around the room, then climbed over the arm of the big chair to the floor and scooted out the door. By the time we got into the other room, he was smiling brightly and asked if he could put his feet in the pool on Norman's patio.

When I told them we had to leave, both kids moaned. They were sorry to say good-bye to Norman: he was so much fun. I knew exactly how they felt.

On the plane ride home, I realized that Norman had done it again—and so had the kids. But this time was different from that day in my kitchen. The way Norman accessed the memories was different. The first time, Sarah and Chase had specific fears that Norman could use to bridge back to their past lives; this time, with no particular issues to work from, he employed the same generic induction he uses with adults—relaxation and guided imagery. With Chase he chose an image—the spinning car from Disney World—that Chase could relate to as a transition back to the past; and it worked. Without specific instructions where to go but through her own subconscious selection process, Sarah went back to a lifetime of unfinished business with her brother. And in her own words, she told us that she had *chosen* to be with Chase again to heal the rift between them. Would this insight affect their relationship in any way? That remained to be seen.

Chase's benign memory of his lifetime as a woodcarver was a study in the mundane. It explained his deep friendship and affection for Henson, but there wasn't anything noteworthy about it. Perhaps this benign memory was an act of gracious balance, a relief from the weight of his traumatic war memory.

I was relieved to learn that Sarah and Chase had some past life memories that were pleasant, not painfully tragic like the last time. Surely, fulfilled and blessed lifetimes live within us to temper the tragic ones. William Blake's words came to mind: "Joy & Woe are woven fine, A Clothing for the soul divine."

Past Life Heaven

I returned from Florida with a renewed dedication to my research (as I boldly began to call it). I also came back with a long reading list from Norman. I read and read: books about Dr. Milton Erickson, considered by many to be the grand master of hypnotists and healers, books about neurolinguistic programming, and of course, books about past lives and past life therapy. To fulfill my agreement with Norman, I found a hypnotherapist in Philadelphia who agreed to tutor me in the fundamentals of hypnosis.

I got Dr. Roger Woolger's address from Patrick and Cathy and wrote to tell him how much I valued his book and a little of what I was learning about children's past life memories. I added that I hoped we could meet someday. He responded by sending me a schedule of his training workshops. Listed on it was a weeklong training program he was giving that summer in beautiful upstate New York. No question about it: I was going!

In late June I dropped off Chase and Sarah at my mother's and continued up the Hudson Valley to the site of the training, in the hills close to the Vermont border. The workshop was held in a large rustic lodge by a lake, a peaceful site away from telephones and distractions where we could concentrate on nothing but past life regression. I joined a group of fifteen people comprising therapists, psychiatrists, a social worker, a lawyer, educators, a midwife, and a yoga teacher from Costa Rica. I was in past life heaven. All week I regressed others, was regressed, and talked about past lives.

We watched Roger demonstrate his techniques with members of the group, bringing the principles in his book to life. I saw participants of the workshop move through an incredible range of emotions and sensations as they experienced their past lives. They were crying, moaning, laughing, and rolling on the floor all week. I was amazed at how deeply people plunged into their past life stories, and how powerful and elegant Roger's techniques of induction were. He seldom uses formal hypnotic induction. Instead, he uses images, recurrent thoughts and phrases (life scripts), body symptoms, or feelings as a bridge to the past life story. Since these memories have several components—mental, emotional, and physical—by closing one's eyes and focusing on any one of them, a full past life story can emerge.

For example, if someone describes their problem as the recurring life script "I never feel safe," Roger will tell the person to repeat the phrase many times, while still focusing on the breath.

"I never feel safe. I never feel safe. I never feel safe." With this repetition, images and feelings begin to well up into the patient's awareness and take on a life of their own, coalescing into a vivid past life story. The same can be done with feelings: a patient is instructed to "give words to the feelings and repeat these words until an image that belongs to the story comes to mind."

Finally I fully understood the mechanics of how Norman had accessed my kids' memories that first time in my kitchen. He had used a bridging technique when he said, "Tell me what you see when you hear the loud noises that frighten you" and "Close your eyes and tell me what you see when you feel your fear of fire." He was using their fears, and the sensory cues that triggered them, as a bridge to their past life stories.

I soon had a chance to experience these techniques firsthand. Toward the end of the week, we paired off and worked with partners. My partner and I found a private corner of the lodge, and I lay down on my cushion on the floor. She asked me to choose a deep concern that I wanted to work on and describe it to her. I told her how uncomfortable I felt when Roger called on me to address the whole group. I've always been deathly afraid of any kind of public speaking. She told me to stay with that thought. I did. I confessed that, in fact, I had always felt that I didn't fit into any group of people—I always felt like an outsider, even as a child. "Fitting in" had *always* been a big issue with me and caused me uneasiness in many situations. Using this cue, she told me to close my eyes, take some deep breaths, and continue to repeat the phrase "I don't fit in."

"I don't fit in. I don't fit in. I don't fit in." Images began to form. "I don't fit in. I don't fit in." Very quickly I found myself in another body, in another place. I saw myself as a young boy—about twelve—sitting on a hard wooden bench in a square, primitive building. I was in school; other boys were on the bench too. My clothing was coarse and plain and scratchy. Immediately it came to mind that I was in Pennsylvania in the late 1700s in a religious community—possibly Amish. And I knew what the problem was. I was a clever and imaginative child, and I was totally out of place in this austere, God-fearing community. At the moment I entered this vision, I found myself daydreaming, barely aware of the schoolmaster's steady drone.

Suddenly I felt a stinging blow across my hands that brought me crashing back to the dreary reality around me. The dull schoolmaster had whipped my hands with a switch. I could feel the pain in my hands, but it didn't compare with the wound to my soul. What was I doing here? I didn't fit in at all. Why did I stay here? I hated this repressive life that bound my spirit and bridled my expression. Their strictures were killing me.

In the next scene I saw myself climbing an old cherry tree. I not only saw it, but I could feel the raised bark under my fingers. And I could feel the hemp rope I carried over my shoulder. My mind was made up. I couldn't back down now. I began to cry. I was racked with guilt thinking about my parents. I prayed for their forgiveness and for God's mercy. I felt the scratchy rope around my neck. I hesitated before jumping off the limb, distracted by a burning sensation across the back of my hands where I had been struck by the schoolmaster. The burning changed to an electric tingling. My hands felt alive. So much energy was surging through them that they began to hurt. I jumped, and my last breath was cut short by the rope cinching my neck. Everything went dark. My last thought was a plea to God that my spirit would be free to express itself. My last feelings were of the choking in my throat and the immense energy in my hands.

Out of the darkness a distant voice startled me. My workshop partner asked, "What is happening?" Then I saw a vision of myself in the nineteenth-century lifetime, the elegantly dressed man, playing the piano with unearthly grace. The full expression of my spirit flowed effortlessly through my hands. My hands were alive, but my lungs were weak from disease. I struggled for each breath I took—as if the tightness of that noose were still choking my neck. The connections between the two lives filled my awareness with an awesome speed and clarity.

By the end of the week, all of the people in the workshop were drained and weary from all the intense emotional experiences. We had had enough high drama for a while. Amazingly, though, most of us felt lighter and happier for it—even giddy. We celebrated the end of the workshop with a sumptuous dinner accompanied by wine from a local winery. To lighten things up, and to do what he loves best, Roger entertained us with his perfect renditions of Monty Python routines—complete with exaggerated and authentic British affectations. He had us all rolling on the floor. By that time, though, we were used to it.

Double Spontaneous Memories

While I was busy with my self-directed course of instruction, Sarah and Chase were preparing their own curriculum for me. My next lesson was strictly *not* by the book.

Sarah and Chase befriended a boy, John, who lived nearby and was the same age as ten-year-old Sarah. The three kids flew around the neighborhood on their bikes, shared Nintendo tips, and concocted adventures in the woods. Seven-year-old Chase adored John and followed him everywhere. I was glad that my kids had found a friend that they both liked.

This peace and harmony didn't last long, though. Sarah grew jealous of Chase and John's friendship, and she taunted Chase by telling him that John didn't really like him. She said that John only hung around with him because he was bored. Predictably, Chase's feelings were deeply hurt. Sarah, who should have had better things to do, would not abide by my admonishments to "leave them alone!"

One Saturday afternoon Chase and John collected big cardboard boxes and spent the day busily cutting and taping. Chase ran around the house plundering drawers and closets for building materials. I poked my head into the room to see what all the commotion was about. They were both hunched over a huge cardboard model of a castle, adorned with towers, windows, doors, and a working drawbridge. The model took up most of the floor in the room, and scraps were everywhere. I was so delighted they were making their own fun, rather than playing video games, that I curbed my natural cleaning instinct and left the room without even mentioning the mess.

Sarah occasionally popped her head into the room to see what they were doing, then sullenly retreated to her room.

Later, after John had left, Sarah again teased Chase about John. This time he exploded. He began crying hysterically, ran to his room, and threw himself on the bed; Sarah ran down the hall to her room and slammed the door. I heard the commotion and rushed upstairs to see what was going on. I went into Chase's room first to comfort him; I'd deal with Sarah later, I thought. Chase was facedown on the bed, sobbing. My attempts to console him didn't work. He continued to cry.

Then, through his sobs, he told me that images were coming to him of a lifetime during "castle times." I wasn't sure where he was going with this, but I encouraged him to let the images come and tell me what he saw. "I'm a young woman. I have a long dress on. I'm in a room in a kind of stone castle. I'm very, very sad. I'm dying of a broken heart."

By this time Chase had rolled over on the bed and was lying still, telling me his story. His sentences were halting, coming in fragments, and barely audible. I leaned close so I could hear what he was saying.

"You're dying of a broken heart?" I encouraged him to continue.

"Yeah. I'm betrothed"—his word—"to a young man, but I don't love him. I love someone else. My father wants me to marry him so he'll get more land. He isn't thinking about me at all; he's just thinking about the land he'll get. I don't want to marry the man he picked for me, so I tell him. My father gets really mad at me and locks me in my room so I can't leave. I don't eat. I don't want to live anymore. My heart is breaking. I die of a broken heart." After a few seconds of silence, Chase added: "Sarah was my father, and John was the man I wanted to marry."

The whole time, as Chase's story was unfolding, Sarah was jumping up and down on the minitramp in her room; I could hear the screeching of the minitramp springs. Suddenly she stormed into the room and blasted, "I had every right to do that as her father. It was the law of the land!" She pivoted around on her heels, raced out of the room, and pounded down the stairs.

It took me a few long seconds to figure out what had just

happened. This was extraordinary! Sarah had somehow tapped into Chase's memory, triggering her own recollection of that lifetime. At that moment I wished that I could be in two places at once.

Chase was calming down, so I told him that I would be right back. I ran downstairs and found Sarah sitting on the living room couch with her arms folded across her chest and her chin jutting out defiantly. She stared straight ahead, without looking at me, with tears streaming down her cheeks, and repeated, "I had every right to do that as her father. It was the law of the land."

"How do you feel about your actions now?" I asked, not sure how to keep this going. Sarah burst into sobs. "I should have followed my heart. Not the laws. I was wrong to try to force her marriage."

"Why don't you tell Chase how you feel about that now?" I offered. With tears still streaming down her face, Sarah ran back up to Chase's room and explained to him how she was sorry for what she had done so long ago. She now knew that it was wrong. Chase, whose face was red from crying, sniffled and listened to Sarah's explanation. He accepted her apology with a hug. Within minutes they were hugging each other and getting silly. The crying and conflict had passed.

I left the room and hurried to find Steve and tell him what had just happened. This was amazing: both Sarah and Chase had *spontaneously* and *simultaneously* remembered the same lifetime they had shared as father and daughter. Although the roles and setting were different this time, Sarah, Chase, and John were still acting out this old conflict. Prompted by Sarah's taunting, the old story had broken through to the surface, first for Chase, then for Sarah.

For an instant, the doubting voice in my mind wondered if this drama could simply have been a creative way of working out their conflicts, fabricated from bits of fairy tales and Disney stories. Perhaps. But Chase's story was too consistent and his reactions too realistic for a fantasy. How had Chase known the word *betrothed* and used it so accurately in his story?

I knew in every cell of my body that this was real. It was becoming familiar territory. What surprised me, though, was that these memories came up spontaneously. I hadn't said anything to prompt them. Adding to this mystery, how had Sarah known exactly what was happening with Chase at that moment? She could not possibly have heard his hushed voice from behind her closed door. She was actually remembering the same lifetime from her own perspective, reacting in character. Her story dovetailed perfectly with Chase's.

Sarah's role in this drama reiterated the theme of "following one's heart instead of the laws of the land," the same as in the Egyptian lifetime when Norman regressed her in Florida. The thematic consistency between these two stories was significant. In light of the Egyptian lifetime she remembered, when she and Chase had a falling out as brother and sister over inheritance, this memory made perfect sense. Apparently they have been playing out this familial pattern of rivalry over inheritance for lifetimes. Each time they are together, they switch roles, gender, and modify the script, but fail to come to a resolution. Sarah identified this pattern and her desire to resolve her issues with Chase in her regression with Norman: "I chose to come back with Chase this time so we could learn to be fair with each other." What an unusual and refreshing perspective on sibling rivalry! As in some of Dr. Woolger's cases of entangled relationships between family members, these themes can play out repeatedly over lifetimes until the issues are resolved and the cycle is broken. Hopefully, by understanding the pattern, Sarah and Chase will be able to move beyond it in this lifetime.

After that afternoon, Chase and John gradually became less involved with each other, which seemed more appropriate to the difference in their ages. Sarah left them in peace. Both of them soon forgot what all the fuss was about.

What remained for me were more lessons about how these memories work. Beyond the personal significance of this double memory, I was intrigued by the way Sarah had "tuned in" to what was happening with Chase, triggering her own memory of that lifetime. There was some sort of telepathy between them. I had experienced this telepathy myself when I was training with Norman and intuitively "saw" and "felt" Charles's concentration-camp memory. Here it was a second time.

Even more significant was that both children spontaneously remembered the same lifetime they had shared. The memories burst forth on their own, without any prompting from me or anyone else. I thought about what Norman had said: *"Children go in and out of trance all the time."*

Seeing what had just happened with my children, I wondered if other children have spontaneous past life memories as well.

CHAPTER 6

Dr. Ian Stevenson

Rumors of a Gold Mine

As I sought out and read every book I could find about past lives and reincarnation, I repeatedly came across references to Dr. Ian Stevenson. They would refer to this professor almost in an off-hand way, citing a statistic, or in a footnote. All that I could put together from these scant reports was that Stevenson was the head of the department of psychiatry at the University of Virginia School of Medicine, and that he had documented thousands of children who spontaneously remembered their past lives.

I had to know more. Surely a medical doctor with thousands of cases of children's past life memories would be able to answer my questions about the healing effects of these memories. But nowhere could I find a full discussion of his work. This was strange. Past life writers knew of Stevenson. Why, then, were they not exploring and promoting what sounded to me like a wealth of information on past life healing, and the closest thing to scientific proof of reincarnation? This indifference, to me, was like ignoring rumors of a gold mine.

Now that my own two kids had had spontaneous past life memories, I decided it was time to track down these rumors and discover for myself what Stevenson was all about.

I called my local bookstore to order two titles I had found listed in a bibliography, *Twenty Cases Suggestive of Reincarnation* and *Children Who Remember Previous Lives.* Sorry, they told me, but these were academic books that could only be ordered from the University of Virginia. When I finally reached a person at the University Press who could fill my order I must have sounded excited because she remarked, "I rarely talk to customers as enthusiastic as you are about our academic books." From that day on, the sound of the mail truck signaled the start of my daily jog down to the mailbox.

Finally, when the volumes arrived, I ripped open the package and leafed through them as I walked back up the hill to my house. Skimming the pages I saw chapter headings like "Types of Evidence for Reincarnation" and "Variations of Cases in Different Cultures" and "The Child's Behavior Related to the Previous Life." I let out a squeal that startled the robins into flight when I spotted the charts in *Twenty Cases:* extensive tabulations printed sideways (I had to turn the book around to read them), comparing dozens of facts that each child had remembered of a previous life to an actual person who had lived before.

I made a cup of tea, mentally trashed my to-do list for the day, and went to my favorite reading chair. I flipped through *Twenty Cases* and read at random. Everywhere I looked I found one fascinating case after another.

For example, I saw the case of Parmod, a two-and-a-half-year-old boy from India who remembered owning a large soda and biscuit shop in another town. When his family took him to the town, he led them directly to the biscuit shop and demonstrated how to fix a complicated soda machine that had been purposely disconnected to test his knowledge.[1]

Three-year-old Michael Wright of Texas amazed his mother

with specific details of a fatal automobile accident that he claimed had killed him. The life he remembered was of his mother's high school boyfriend, who no one in the family ever mentioned. The boyfriend had died in an automobile accident—precisely as little Michael had described.[2]

When Sukla of India was a year and a half, she would cradle a block of wood and call it Minu, her daughter. Over the next few years, Sukla remembered enough details of her past life for her family to be able to take her to her former village. Sukla led them to her former home and was reunited with Minu, a girl whose mother had died when she was a baby.[3]

The books were full of cases as fascinating as these. In each, a young child, usually two or three years old, without prompting from anyone, recalled enough specific details of a past life for his former identity to be established. Then Dr. Stevenson investigated the case and verified that the child had not learned about the remembered person by any normal means, leaving past life memory as the only explanation.

These books were revolutionary. Why wasn't Dr. Stevenson's work better known?

After an hour of reading, I was sure I had found the answer. His approach is severely academic. I had to struggle to follow his categorical reasoning, and to sift through the pedantic verbiage and long discourses on methodology. Even after two cups of Darjeeling tea, my eyes were threatening mutinous sleep. Yet occasionally I would see just enough glint of story or sparkle of insight to keep going. I began to suspect that buried under these layers of dry argument was a mother lode of evidence and observation I could use to underwrite my own quest to understand children's memories.

But as I read more, I became increasingly disappointed and upset to discover that Dr. Stevenson was not at all interested in the healing potential of these memories. I had assumed that since he is a psychiatrist, he would be interested in healing. But apparently he isn't. I snapped the book shut in frustration and took a nap.

Proof Is the Point

Over the next few days I tried hard to understand Dr. Stevenson's approach to these memories. Finally, it dawned on me what the problem was; when I stopped assuming and looked to discover what he was really doing, his work began to make sense. I saw that he is, first and foremost, an empiricist. His mission is to gather data and publish it unadorned for others to examine; he assiduously avoids drawing conclusions or making claims. He writes exclusively for his peers—other scientists, academics, and researchers—and the tortuous academic style of these books is simply Dr. Stevenson addressing his tribe in their native dialect.

Dr. Stevenson overlooks issues of healing in his drive to answer a much larger question that has puzzled man since the beginning of time: *What survives bodily death?* Thanks to his enormous life-long effort, for the first time in the history of science we have objective evidence for proof of reincarnation—evidence that suggests strongly that something of our personality *does* survive bodily death.

When I understood this, my frustration melted. My feelings turned to gratitude for what this man has done, for his years of painstaking effort in his quest for empirical evidence, and for the enormous legacy he is providing with his research. I felt respect, admiration—even awe—when I finally comprehended the full significance and implications of his work. With my new attitude, the story of how Dr. Stevenson began his quest, and how he went about building such a solid case for reincarnation, suddenly became utterly fascinating.

Dr. Stevenson is a medical doctor and a psychiatrist, but early in his career he became disenchanted with both Freudian psychoanalysis and behavioral psychology. An iconoclast, he dismissed both theories of the mind as misguided, limited, and unscientific, at a time when they were both the darlings of the intellectual community.[4] He began to explore other theories for how personality develops, and through this quest discovered parapsychology. Parapsychology is a branch of science that seeks objective proof for advanced capabilities of the mind, such as telepathy, and for evidence for what survives bodily death, such as poltergeists, that the conservative paradigm of psychology refuses to admit.

In searching the literature of parapsychology, Dr. Stevenson discovered a few isolated and scattered reports of children's spontaneous past life memories. Digging further, he garnered a total of forty-four such cases that had been published in newspapers, journals, or books over the last hundred years. All were reported as anomalies—fascinating stories of unusual occurrences that, when taken one at a time, were easy to write off as insignificant. But when he began to analyze and summarize these cases, he noticed that they had many similarities. The patterns convinced him that the cases were probably authentic and warranted further investigation. He saw an opportunity to consolidate these cases and offer powerful new evidence to the debate on reincarnation. A systematic study of children's past life memories had never been attempted before.

In 1961 he traveled to India to investigate a single new case and to validate some previously published cases himself. Shortly after he arrived, he encountered a surprise. Word had gotten around that an American professor was interested in past life memories of children, and people began to bring fresh cases to his attention. Within his first five weeks there, he had found no fewer than twenty-five new cases to investigate; within three years he had four hundred. This was the beginning of a project that would occupy him for the rest of his career. He began doggedly pursuing cases where he could find them, constantly innovating and improving his research methods. Soon other researchers began copying his methods and duplicating the results. Dr. Stevenson, now in his seventies, still sets the pace for this steadily growing field of research.[5]

His most brilliant innovation was to look to young children for evidence for reincarnation. When adults have past life memories, it is impossible to prove, beyond any doubt, that the subject has not somehow acquired the information from books, TV, or hearsay. Children's memories, on the other hand, are relatively pure, unsullied by worldly experience. It is possible with very young children to identify almost everything they have been exposed to, making it much easier to isolate memories that can be explained only by a past life.

And Dr. Stevenson limits his cases to only *spontaneous* memories in which the child began talking of a past life identity of his or her own volition, with no prompting from anyone. This eliminates hypnosis or any technique that would fish for memories, avoiding criticism that the researchers somehow directed or influenced the child.

The sheer volume of cases that Dr. Stevenson has investigated, cataloged, and published adds enormous weight and credibility to his proof. The composite strength of the body of cases compensates for any flaws in individual cases. A well-established principle of science is that general patterns from many cases are much more reliable than any one case taken separately, no matter how airtight that one case may be. When a growing volume of cases from other researchers shows the same patterns, the proof is almost indisputable.

In the thirty-five years since he first went to India, Dr. Stevenson has generated an impressive body of work. To date he and his colleagues have collected more than 2,600 cases[6] from a wide range of cultures and religions around the world. Most of the cases are from southern Asia, but many are also from the Middle East, Africa, Europe, and the United States. Sixty-five fully detailed cases have been published in books such as his four-volume set, *Cases of the Reincarnation Type;* more than two hundred new cases are on the way. He has also published more than 260 articles with catchy titles such as "The Belief in Reincarnation Among the Igbo of Southeastern Nigeria with Particular Reference to Connections Between the Ogbanje ("Repeater Babies") and Sickle Cell Anemia."[7]

Past Life Sleuth

Once I learned how to decipher Dr. Stevenson's abstruse writing style, I discovered the drama in his books. The cases are detective stories. He himself, of course, is the chief sleuth, aided by his sidekick research associates. He follows leads anywhere they take him, often down miles of muddy jeep roads to remote rural villages in Third World countries, never knowing what he will find. He runs into all sorts of colorful characters, many dead ends, and some danger. He's interested in just the facts but has developed a keen eye for the subtle details, the contextual clues that mark the difference between a mere investigator and a master detective.

Like a detective, his immediate goal is a solved case, which to Dr. Stevenson is a well-defined objective. A case is "solved" when he finds a child with spontaneous and detailed memories of a past life, and is able to match the child's memories to the life of one (and only one) deceased person. (He uses the term *previous personality* for this deceased person.) Finally, to be deemed "verified," he has to be satisfied, after rigorous investigation, that the child had no possible opportunity by normal means—no matter how improbable or absurd—to learn about the previous personality. (Normal is anything *other* than a past life connection; Dr. Stevenson even screens cases that could be explained by telepathy or spirit possession.)

In other words, a verified case is one where both sides of the equation match convincingly, and where the only explanation—beyond even an *unreasonable* doubt—is past life memory. Dr. Stevenson has more than eight hundred verified cases in his files.

Where do these cases come from? Because he is studying the natural phenomenon of spontaneous memories, they can't be created in a clinic or laboratory. Dr. Stevenson has to wait for the cases to come to him. He relies on a worldwide network of scouts and colleagues to collect reports and rumors of young children claiming to remember a past life. One of the reasons he has so many cases in India is because his network is more fully developed there than in any other country.

Each of these cases begins when a young child, usually two to four years old, without prompting from anyone, begins talking about a past life. The child will name people and places that nobody in the family has ever heard of before, or will exhibit odd behavior. In most cases he will describe intimate details of the death—often a violent one. In some extreme cases the child will tell his surprised parents that he is really someone else and that he has different parents or even a spouse and children who live in another village or city, and then insist that he be taken there.

The child usually persists in talking about his memories for months or years, despite the sometimes harsh attempts of the family to suppress the memory. (Dr. Stevenson reports that in over half of the cases the family tries to suppress the memory.) Stories about the child's past life memory leak out to the village and spread across districts, finally reaching the ears of a family who have a deceased relative that matches the description the child is giving. This family, upon hearing the news, seeks out the child, curious to see if this is really their deceased relative reborn; or the child's family finally gives in to his pleading and takes him to find his former home.

Typically on these first visits the child will lead the way unaided through the streets of the village to the homestead of the deceased, spontaneously recognize family and friends of the previous personality and call them by their pet names, comment on changes to the house, inquire about people and possessions that he finds missing, and reminisce about obscure events from the past—all from the unique perspective of the deceased. In some cases he will reveal knowledge of hiding places for the family gold, or of secret debts, or of family scandals that no one else knows about. Most amazingly, the child will know nothing about what happened after the previous personality died. The memory is frozen in time. Changes in buildings, in the rooms of the house, or in the appearance of family and friends since the death will strike the child as new, strange, and disorienting.

At some point one of Dr. Stevenson's scouts hears of the case, and the researchers rush to the scene while the memories of the child and witnesses are still fresh. When Dr. Stevenson arrives, he does everything he can to *disprove* the child's past life memories. Using interview techniques adopted from the field of law, he interviews the child, the family, relatives, and villagers, probing to test the validity of their statements, matching one against the other, and looking for patterns of inconsistency. He refuses to accept secondhand accounts and insists on interviewing only people who witnessed the child speak. Without the knowledge of the family, he discreetly finds and interviews villagers not directly involved with the case to get unbiased character references on the family. He makes surprise visits to the family months and years later to repeat the interviews.

Dr. Stevenson takes every precaution not to make mistakes himself. If he doesn't speak the native language (he knows five languages), he will use two interpreters, and sometimes three, for the interviews. In addition to the notes taken by the team of interviewers, the sessions are taped. He collects and photographs hard evidence, like written records and birthmarks. He transcribes and organizes his notes within days of the visit and carefully builds a chronology of the unfolding of the memories, looking for flaws and gaps.

With the same meticulous care he reconstructs from witnesses exactly what happened when the child met the previous personality's family for the first time and made the first recognitions. He probes especially to discover if any cues were inadvertently supplied to the child. He verifies every fact about the previous personality that the child remembered. On average, in all of his solved cases, 90 percent of these statements check out.[8] Then he investigates any contact the two families might have had, no matter how indirect or remote. He presses to find any other opportunity the child might have had to learn the facts he alleges to remember.

When Dr. Stevenson publishes a case, he includes every scrap of raw data that may have a bearing on its validity. Within the text he explores the pros and cons of every possible flaw in the case, every opportunity for normal communication, every way the case might be discredited. These issues are described and dissected in enormous detail. He wants to assure the reader that he has followed through on every possible way the child might have acquired the knowledge, no matter how farfetched. Some of these individual discussions continue for several pages, which make for slow reading.

Dr. Stevenson carries his strict, empirical attitude through to the end. I was amazed by the many direct hits the children make with their memories—these cases are full of them—but in his writing he never gets excited, never calls special attention to the extraordinary things these children say and do. These gleaming nuggets of past life evidence, along with some of the most profound and bizarre human stories I've ever read, are buried among the tailings of technical data and commentary.

––––––––––––––––

Sweet Swarnlata

The story of Swarnlata, from *Twenty Cases*,[9] is characteristic of Dr. Stevenson's cases. The girl's past life memories began when, at the age of three, she gave enough information to locate the family of the deceased person she remembered (the case was "solved"), and she gave more than fifty specific facts that were verified. But Swarnlata's case was different from most because her memories did not fade. And this is a sweet case, characterized by love and happy memories.

Swarnlata Mishra was born to a middle-class family in Pradesh in India in 1948. When she was just three years old and traveling with her father past the town of Katni, more than a hundred miles from her home, she suddenly pointed and asked the driver to turn down a road to "my house." She suggested they could get a better cup of tea there than they could on the road.

Soon after, she related more details of her life in Katni, and her father wrote them down. She said her name was Biya Pathak, and that she had two sons. She described her house inside and out and added that a girls' school was behind the house; visible from the front were a railway line and lime furnaces. Swarnlata said Biya died of a "pain in her throat" and was treated by Dr. S. C. Bhabrat in Jabalpur. She also remembered an incident at a wedding in another town where she and a friend had difficulty finding a latrine.

In the spring of 1959, when Swarnlata was ten years old, news of the case reached Professor Sri H. N. Banerjee, an Indian researcher and colleague of Dr. Stevenson. Banerjee traveled to Katni and, using nothing more than Swarnlata's description, found the house. The lime furnaces were on land adjoining the property; the girls' school was a hundred yards behind the Pathaks' property but not visible from the front.

The house belonged to the Pathaks, a wealthy family. Biya Pathak had died in 1939, leaving behind a husband, two young sons, and many younger brothers. Professor Banerjee interviewed the family and verified everything else that Swarnlata had said. These Pathaks had never heard of the Mishra family, who lived a hundred miles away; the Mishras had no knowledge of the Pathak family.

A few months later Biya's widower husband, one of her sons, and her eldest brother journeyed to Swarnlata's town to test her memory. They hid their identities and purpose, and employed nine townsmen to accompany them to the Mishra home, where they arrived unannounced. The next scene in this story sounds like a scene from a mystery novel, but it is all true, extracted from Dr. Stevenson's tabulations in Swarnlata's published case.

Swarnlata immediately recognized her brother and called him Babu, Biya's pet name for him. Dr. Stevenson gives only the barest facts, but emotions must have run high at this point. Then ten-year-old Swarnlata went around the room looking at each man in turn. Some she identified as men she knew from her town, some were strangers to her. Then she came to Sri Chintamini Pandey, Biya's husband. Swarnlata lowered her eyes and acted bashfully, as Hindu wives do in the presence of their husbands, and spoke his name. Dr. Stevenson says nothing of Sri Pandey's reaction at finding his wife reborn twenty years after she died.

Swarnlata also correctly identified Biya's son, Murli, who had been thirteen years old when Biya died. But Murli schemed to mislead her and insisted for the whole day that he was someone else and not Murli. He also tried to convince Swarnlata that a friend he had brought along was Naresh, Biya's other son. Swarnlata wasn't fooled by either trick. She insisted that Murli was her son and that the other was a stranger. Finally, Swarnlata reminded her former husband that he had purloined twelve hundred rupees from Biya before she died and that the money had been kept in a box. Surprised that Swarnlata remembered this secret that only he and Biya had shared, Sri Pandey conceded that what she said was true.

A few weeks later Swarnlata's father took her to Katni to visit the home and town where Biya had lived and died. Upon arriving she immediately remarked about changes to the house. She asked about a parapet, a veranda, and a neem tree that used to grow in the compound—all had been removed since Biya's death. She identified Biya's room and the room in which she had died. Then she correctly identified more than two dozen people Biya had known, reacting to each with emotions appropriate for Biya's relationship to each of them. Murli again set traps, but Swarnlata didn't fall for any of them.

This must have been quite a spectacle. Here was a ten-year-old stranger from far away—so far, in terms of Indian culture, that her dialect was distinctly different from that of the Pathaks—who acted confidently like a matron of the household, was familiar with intimate names and family secrets, and remembered even marriage relationships, old servants, and friends, re-marking and joking about how they had changed in twenty years. Most interesting, Swarnlata knew *nothing* about the Pathak family that had happened since 1939. Her memory was frozen at the time of Biya's death.

In the years that followed, Swarnlata visited the Pathak family at regular intervals. She developed a loving relationship with many of her past life family, who all accepted her as Biya reborn. Swarnlata's father also accepted the truth of Swarnlata's past identity. Years later, when it came time for Swarnlata to marry, he consulted with the Pathaks about the choice of a husband for her.

How did Swarnlata feel about all of this? Was it confusing for her to remember so completely the life of a grown woman? Dr. Stevenson corresponded and visited with her through the years, and he reported that she had grown up normally, matured into a beautiful young woman, gotten married, and earned an advanced degree at the university. She told him that sometimes when she reminisced about her happy life in Katni, her eyes brimmed with tears, and for a moment she wished she could return to the wealth and life of Biya. But she remained loyal to the Mishra family and accepted fully her station in this life.

Behaviors—Acting Out the Past

Dr. Stevenson records more than just the verbal statements of the children he investigates. He pays special attention to their behavior as well. Traits, skills, phobias, and preferences that are out of place for a child's natural family, but that match the life of the previous personality, reinforce the verbal memories and strengthen the evidence for reincarnation. This emphasis on observing behaviors is another of Stevenson's important innovations.

For example, children in India who remember a past life in a higher class may scold their lower-class parents for having uncouth habits and lifestyle, and they may refuse to eat the food of inferiors. Bishen Chand acted exactly like the spoiled rich man he remembered being. He contemptuously rebuked his parents for their poverty, demanded better food, and rejected the cheap clothes he was given, saying that they weren't good enough even for his servants.[10] On the other hand, some children who remember being from a lower caste than their parents may display the coarseness and survival instincts of the desperately poor and habits offensive to the new family. Some are grateful for their improved station and show great pleasure in eating good food and owning nice clothes. One girl who was born a Brahmin—the highest caste in India—remembered the life of a sweeper from the lowest or "untouchable" class. An otherwise sweet girl, she horrified her family with her repulsive habits and by her repeated requests for pork (the family was vegetarian). And "unlike the other members of the family, she willingly—almost eagerly—cleaned up the excrement of younger children."[11]

When a child with past life memories visits the family and friends of the previous personality, he will often discriminate in his behavior toward the individuals he recognizes. Stevenson cites a case of a young girl from Thailand who was overjoyed to be reunited with a beloved daughter from the past life, and at the same time, hostile to the former husband from a bitter marriage.[12] He cites another where a boy in Sri Lanka remembered a life as a girl and was happy to see his former sisters, but was cold toward his brother, who had been cruel to her in the past life.[13] In another he describes a young boy in India who reprimanded a woman he recognized as his former wife for wearing the white sari customarily worn by widows, rather than the colored sari of his wife. It would normally be a serious social offense for a small boy to make such a comment to an older woman.[14]

Dr. Stevenson admits that a lone example of unusual behavior in a child means nothing; the trait could be explained in many ways. But when many characteristics, all unusual and seemingly unrelated, form a syndrome of behavior that corresponds perfectly to the life of the previous personality, that offers convincing evidence for reincarnation. Dr. Stevenson documents clear correspondence of behavior in almost all of his solved cases.

Phobias are an impressive example of behavioral memory. They are common in these cases and almost always correspond to a past life death. The case of Shamlinie is a striking example because from the time she was born she had *two* seemingly unrelated phobias that made perfect sense when the details of the past life death became known.[15]

As a little baby, Shamlinie was terrified of water and resisted, with screaming and struggling, any attempt to bathe her. At the same time she had a severe phobia of buses. She cried hysterically when she rode one, and even when she saw one in the distance. Her parents were puzzled because they knew of no events in her short life that could have caused either one of these bizarre fears.

Then, soon after Shamlinie began talking, she told her parents that she had lived before, and gave full details of her life in a village not far away called Galtudawa. She also described how she had died. One morning she was on her way to buy some bread. Because the ground was flooded from heavy rains, she walked on the raised part of the road reserved for vehicles. A bus passed too close, splashing water on her and throwing her into a flooded paddy field. She threw up her arms and called, "Mother." After that, she said, she fell into a long sleep.

Later the family learned of an eleven-year-old girl, Hemaseelie, from the village of Galtudawa, who had died when she stepped back to avoid a passing bus, fell into a flooded rice paddy, and drowned. When Shamlinie was four she was taken to Galtudawa, recognized members of Hemaseelie's family, and in other ways convinced witnesses that she was, indeed, Hemaseelie reborn. Finally, her parents had an explanation for Shamlinie's two unrelated phobias, which faded soon after she was reacquainted with her Galtudawa life.

Ravi Shankar Confronts His Murderers

The case of Ravi Shankar[16] (not the musician) was one of the most celebrated cases of reincarnation from India even before Dr. Stevenson investigated it. It is a dramatic example of how cases of strong verbal memories are sometimes reinforced by physical marks on the body.

Ravi Shankar was born in July 1951. When he was barely two years old, he informed his parents that he really was Munna, the son of Jageshwar, a barber in the Chhipatti District of Kanauj. He told them, in great detail, how one day he had been enticed away from his play by two men, a washerman and a barber, who took him to an orchard near Chintamini Temple, slit his throat, and buried him in the sand.

Ravi repeated his story over the next two years to relatives, friends, and his schoolteacher. He asked his parents repeatedly for toys he said that he had owned in his previous life—a large wooden slate, a toy pistol, a wooden elephant, a watch, and a school bag. These were toys his present family could not afford; still, little Ravi rebuked them for not letting him claim them. He talked of his life as Munna so often that he was a bother to his family and friends, and he threatened to run away to this "other family." His schoolteacher, recognizing the significance of Ravi's statements, wrote them down and sent them to Professor B. L. Atreya, who was the first to investigate the case.

Ravi's insistence that he was the murdered boy spread through the village and eventually traveled to neighboring districts. This is how Sri Jageshwar Prasad learned of Ravi's story. On January 19, 1951, Prasad's only son, six-year-old Munna, had been murdered with a razor after being enticed away from his play. Some-one had seen Munna go off with Jawahar, a barber, and Chaturi, a washerman, which led to their arrest. One of the alleged murder-ers, a relative, had a motive for killing the child: it would put him in line to inherit Sri Jageshwar Prasad's property. When Munna's mutilated body and severed head were found buried in the sand, Chaturi, the washerman, unofficially confessed to the crime, but later retracted his statement. Since there were no wit-nesses, the case was dropped, and the barber and the washerman were freed.

Prasad was deeply aggrieved and angered by his son's murder. When he heard of Ravi Shankar's claim to have had his throat slit by a barber and a washerman, he went to visit Ravi to see if he was, in fact, his dead son reborn. But Ravi's father feared that Ravi might be taken from him by Prasad and violently refused to let his son meet with him. He also feared that the murderers, who were still at large, might avenge any attempt to open the case. But, a few days later, Ravi's mother disobeyed her husband and allowed Prasad to talk to the four-year-old boy.

Ravi immediately recognized his former father and identified the watch he was wearing as the watch he had bought for Munna in Bombay. He told details about the death of Munna, all of which matched the alleged murderer's confession and the mate-rial evidence of the crime. Prasad confirmed other details of Munna's life that only the family knew: Munna had taken some guavas to eat before he left the house before his murder, and he had possessed all the toys Ravi mentioned. Munna's murder had caused his mother to go insane, and she had carefully preserved all of Munna's toys in a closet, waiting for his return.

Ravi trembled with fear any time he saw a washerman or a barber. One day while attending a religious ceremony, he became suddenly terrified of a strange man in the crowd. He recognized the man as Chaturi, the washerman, one of Munna's murderers. Little Ravi angrily vowed he would avenge his death. When his mother saw her son's reaction to this unknown man, she made inquiries and confirmed that he was indeed one of the suspects in the murder of Munna.

But there's more to this case. Ravi was born with a birthmark that resembled a long knife wound across his neck. From the time he began telling his story at the age of two, he said that the mark was where the washerman and barber had slit his throat in his past life.

Dr. Stevenson saw Ravi in 1964 and examined the birthmark; Ravi was thirteen years old. He described the mark, which ran horizontally across Ravi's neck, as being one-eighth to one-quarter inch wide and "darker in pigment than the surrounding tissue and had the stippled quality of a scar. It looked much like an old scar of a healed knife wound."[17] According to witnesses, the birthmark had been longer when Ravi was a small child but had gradually faded as he grew older.

Dr. Stevenson met Ravi Shankar for a follow-up interview in 1969, when Ravi was eighteen years old and headed for college. Ravi said that his memories of the previous life as Munna had vanished; he knew the story only from what other people told him. All of his phobias—of barbers and razors—had vanished as well, though he still felt uneasy whenever he was in the area of Chintamini Temple, where Munna was murdered. The birthmark was still clearly visible across his neck.

Birthmarks and Birth Defects

The birthmark on Ravi Shankar that corresponded exactly to the fatal wound on Munna's neck is not an isolated instance. Dr. Stevenson found that in 35 percent of his verified cases (309 of 895), the children had birthmarks or birth defects that matched wounds from their previous lives. He has published recently a monumental set of books devoted exclusively to this phenomenon entitled *Reincarnation and Biology: A Contribution to the Etiology of Birthmarks and Birth Defects*. Its 2300 pages include 210 verified cases. The scale of this work—Dr. Stevenson's magnum opus—indicates how much importance he gives to these cases as evidence for reincarnation. They are important because they offer *physical* evidence for the link between past and present lives. No matter how strong the verbal and behavioral evidence is in a case, critics will find fault with the data. But birthmarks and birth defects—especially when they can be verified against medical records of the deceased—are undeniable, tangible evidence of a direct correspondence between a past and present life.

One of the stories in Stevenson's new volumes, previewed in an article in the *Journal of Scientific Exploration*,[18] is of an Indian boy who remembered being killed by a shotgun blast to his chest. On this boy's chest was an array of birthmarks that matched the pattern and location (verified by the autopsy report) of the fatal wounds.

Another shotgun victim was hit at point-blank range in the right side of the head (confirmed from the hospital report). The Turkish boy who remembered this life was born with "a diminished and malformed ear (unilateral microtia) . . . and underdevelopment of the right side of his face (hemifacial microsomia)."[19]

One woman had three separate linear scarlike birthmarks on her back. As a child, she remembered the life of a woman who was killed by three blows to her back with an ax.[20]

Another boy in India was born with stubs for fingers on only his right hand—an extremely rare condition. He remembered the life of a boy who had his fingers cut off by the blades of a fodder chopping machine.[21]

The birthmarks in most of Dr. Stevenson's cases are not the common molelike birthmarks that appear in most adults. They actually look like scars and wounds. They are distinct, large, and notable marks, "likely to be puckered and scarlike, sometimes depressed a little below the surrounding skin, areas of hairlessness, areas of markedly diminished pigmentation, or port-wine stains."[22] The same is true of birth defects—deformed limbs, for example. They, too, are unusual and rare specimens, not falling into the "recognizable patterns of human malformation" and looking like the result of injuries caused by an external implement.

Dr. Stevenson applied his usual rigorous methods to examining and recording the birthmarks and birth defects. He required that eyewitness reports verify that the marks were present at birth. He carefully measured and photographed the marks. He screened cases where the birth defect could have been genetic, caused by a family relationship between the subject and the deceased, or that could be explained by events during pregnancy. Then he documented the facts of the previous personality's life and death from eyewitness accounts, medical records, and autopsy reports. (Remember, Dr. Stevenson was trained as a medical doctor, so he knew what he was looking at.) Finally, he would compare the verified death wounds or marks on the previous personality with the marks on the child subject.

Dr. Stevenson was very careful to guard against cases where the past life memories were fabricated as a way of retroactively explaining the birthmark. He would accept only those solved cases where the child had sufficient verbal memories—the many facts and people that Swarnlata remembered, for example—to identify and locate the previous personality. In many instances this was a person the child or his family had never seen or known about. In other words, these cases had to stand on their own merits before the birthmarks and birth defects were admitted as further evidence.

Some critics might attribute these birthmarks to chance. But a significant number of Stevenson's birthmark cases involve *two or more* matching birthmarks—for example, the woman who had three scarlike marks on her back. Among the 210 cases in his volumes are eighteen cases of double birthmarks. Nine of these cases involve bullet wounds where not only do the marks match the exact site of entry and exit, but the mark corresponding to the entry wound is small and round, and the mark corresponding to the exit wound is large and irregular. This conforms perfectly to the ballistic fact that the exit wound from a bullet is always larger than the hole where the bullet entered the body.

What are the odds that two birthmarks would randomly correspond to *two* wounds? Stevenson did the calculation and determined that the odds are 1 in 25,600. The odds against this happening by chance eighteen times are astronomical.[23]

Credo

Does Dr. Stevenson prove reincarnation? He will never claim that he does. Stevenson maintains that he is providing *evidence* for reincarnation, but he stops short of saying reincarnation has been proved. He intentionally titled his first book *Twenty Cases Suggestive of Reincarnation.* As an empiricist, he believes he would be out of bounds to make any claims or final conclusions. His attitude is: here's the evidence, you decide for yourself.

This attitude is similar to that of Dr. Woolger, who says it doesn't matter if you believe in reincarnation or not, as long as the effects heal. He's interested only in the psychological truth of the memories. But as a healer, Woolger says it works best to *treat* these memories as if they originate in past lives.

Drs. Stevenson and Woolger both stop short of publicly saying they believe in reincarnation, despite being steeped in evidence for it every day. I'm not going to be so circumspect. I believe, from Dr. Stevenson's empirical evidence, Dr. Woolger's clinical results, and my own experience, that these memories derive from past lives. Past life memories are *really* from past lives.

The doctors' attitudes bring to mind the old saying, "If it walks like a duck, looks like a duck, and quacks like a duck, it's a duck." Well, if Dr. Stevenson wants to say only, "Here's evidence for a duck, but I'm not going to tell you what it is," and Dr. Woolger suggests, "Let's treat it like a duck," that's okay with me.

But I call it a duck.

After reading Dr. Stevenson carefully, following his logic, and absorbing the facts of these cases, how can anyone not be convinced that these memories are real? In his own words: "What evidence, if you had it, *would* convince you of reincarnation?"[24]

Proof Is *Not* the Point

To Dr. Stevenson, proof is the point. Thanks to him, for the rest of us, proof is *not* the point. He has prepared the way so we can go beyond the issue of proof. He has done the heavy lifting, freeing the rest of us to fly with the ideas, to soar with the implications, and to explore the finer points of healing.

To build his proof, Dr. Stevenson accepted only the rare and extreme cases, those with dozens of convincing details and where the previous personality could be identified. Now, we don't have to repeat his proof or duplicate his methods. We can accept the more common cases—those that fit the pattern of a past life memory but that do not have enough detail by themselves to prove anything—and work with them on their own terms.

So, for example, if a child is telling us of his life as a Civil War soldier, we don't have to greet every detail with skepticism, thinking, "Well, he could have learned that from TV," or "His imagination luckily hit on the right details." Because we know, thanks to Dr. Stevenson, that spontaneous past life memories do happen, and we can coast on the proof issue and focus instead on the significance of the memories to the child. We can advance to the more satisfying work of factoring past life memories into our theories of child development, psychology, and metaphysics.

Patterns from the Body of Data

From Dr. Stevenson's enormous body of verified cases we can identify the patterns of true past life memories and use the patterns, in turn, to help us understand *how* these memories operate. Some of the patterns confirmed what I had learned from past life therapists. Others explained features unique to children's memories.

The first of these is the remarkably young age at which children begin speaking of their past lives. Most of the memories appear for the first time when the child is between the ages of two and five. This pattern is universal, occurring in every country and culture. But it is not a rule: some children talk of their memories as soon as they can put words together.

Generally, the memories begin to fade around school age, between five and eight. They recede into the unconscious, fading like a dream in the morning. After they have faded, the child will typically deny he ever had them. In a small number of rare cases the memories remain intact into adulthood.

A second pattern is that many young children with verbal past life memories also have phobias relating to their past lives. Dr. Stevenson found that 36 percent of the children—more than one out of three—had a phobia that corresponded to the way they died.[25] If a child was killed by a truck, he could have a fear of large vehicles or trucks; if a child drowned in the past, he could have a fear of water, or of being bathed.

Past life therapists have found the same high correlation between phobias and the manner of death in their adult regression cases. But the "proof" in these regressions is subjective, since there is rarely verification of the memories. For the first time, thanks to Dr. Stevenson, we have many cases where the mode of death has been verified by witnesses and medical records, and the phobia documented by independent researchers. The direct correspondence between the past life death and the present phobia is clear; both sides of the equation balance. Dr. Stevenson's findings give objective credibility to what the past life therapists have presumed all along—that past life deaths cause present life phobias.

This is good news for past life therapy. It's significant for parents too. Many children have phobias that cannot be explained by anything that has happened to them in their present lives. If a parent sees an unexplainable fear in their child, they can now suspect a past life cause even if the child has made no statements about a past life. That is the way it happened with my children: the phobias appeared before they expressed any conscious memories of their past lives.

A third pattern is the importance of the moment of death. Dr. Stevenson found that 72 percent of the children remembered how they died, and more than half of these died violently.[26] This is significant when compared to the fact that far fewer children in his cases could remember their past life names. In other words, the death itself left a greater imprint on the transmigrating memory than the facts of the everyday life. *Most spontaneous past life memories in children involve memories of death—especially a violent one.*

In *Twenty Cases* Dr. Stevenson speculates why this is so: "It seems reasonable to suppose that the intensity of an experience such as a violent death can in some way strengthen or 'fixate' memories so that they are more readily preserved in consciousness."[27]

Dr. Woolger and the past life therapists were coming to the same conclusions in their study of adults' memories. Dr. Woolger suggests, and I repeat for comparison: "The heightened consciousness that occurs at death imprints with exaggerated intensity the dying thoughts, feelings, or sensations on whatever we call the vehicle that transfers our essence from one lifetime to another."[28]

Violent deaths are what children remember most often, Dr. Stevenson suggests, because they are sudden, unexpected, and involve strong emotions. They cut the natural life-span short, leaving the dying person in a state of incompleteness.[29] Even in the "natural" deaths recounted by the children, the lives remembered were in some way incomplete. They left with what Dr. Woolger calls "unfinished business of the soul."

The picture Dr. Stevenson draws with his cases and statistical analyses confirms another basic principle discovered by the therapists: dying burdened by unresolved emotions and issues, or dying incomplete, energizes the memories to influence subsequent lives. For children the memories can be particularly vivid, demanding closure. A part of the child is still "back there" with one foot in the past life, stuck in the web of unresolved feelings, still attached to a life left behind unexpectedly.

A Natural Phenomenon

I believe that the most important pattern in Dr. Stevenson's work is also the most obvious: *children's past life memories are a natural phenomenon.* They are just there, in the conscious awareness of some children. They emerge spontaneously, without prompting, with a volition and logic all their own.

A *natural phenomenon.* The words flashed like a neon sign in my mind. This means that any child, anywhere in the world, could have a spontaneous past life memory. But how many do? Is it a rare aberration of nature, or does it happen all the time in mild forms that we miss because we don't know what to look for? Dr. Stevenson doesn't answer this question; he doesn't do anything to compare the extreme cases he studies to the population as a whole. That question remains open.

I thought more about what this means. If past life memory in children is a natural phenomenon, what is the natural reason? Is it simply a cosmic parlor trick, a crack in the system that leaks memory into some children but has no purpose? Or is it a natural part of our soul's evolutionary development, an opportunity to clear issues from the past? This fits with the Hindu and Buddhist belief that each incarnation is an opportunity to learn and grow spiritually.

Past life therapists show that memories stemming from traumatic deaths create problems in adulthood. And Stevenson shows that most of the children's memories center on a death. Could the spontaneous appearance of these memories in childhood be nature's way of giving us a chance to reverse the effect of a traumatic death before it grows into more complex problems in adulthood?

If so, then what is the parents' role in this? Since the memories occur when children are so young and still totally dependent on us for their physical nurturing, maybe children's past life memories are a valuable opportunity to nurture our children spiritually too. Maybe we, as parents, are part of the plan for helping our children benefit from spontaneous past life memories.

CHAPTER 7

Children's Past Life Memories

Ian Stevenson's rigorous research proved that children's memories are real and natural. The past life therapists convinced me that these memories can heal. But where were the researchers and practitioners working with children? In several years of searching, I hadn't found them. So I decided to do my own research to confirm what I knew was true—children's past life memories can heal. Armed with the regression techniques I had learned from Norman Inge and Roger Woolger, and all that I had learned from my reading, I was ready to proceed. I decided to start regressing children myself to see what I could discover.

Young Explorers

Seven-year-old Chase, now a seasoned past life explorer, was my first subject. One afternoon, without fanfare, I asked him if he to try a regression with me. He said, "Sure, why not?" I had him lie down on his bed, close his eyes, and pay attention to his breathing. I was excited. But I was also nervous—not for what might happen, but for the event that *nothing* happened.

My apprehension disappeared as soon as I saw Chase's eyelids fluttering wildly. I asked, "What are you experiencing?"

Chase, with the now-familiar halting syntax of past life recall, told me of a life as a wood craftsman in fourteenth-century Russia. I was suspicious at first. Was this just a replay of the uneventful life as a woodcarver he had seen with Norman? No. Apparently, he had had this skill in another lifetime too. Chase described himself this time as a successful woodworker who was known throughout his district for his inventiveness and craftsmanship. He said that he had designed a corner shelf that was an innovation and became widely known, and because of that, his skills were in great demand. He mentioned that he had a family, and that he was happy. But his thoughts were focused on his achievement as a craftsman in this life, not on his relationships. He died a peaceful death as an old man, surrounded by his family.

Chase lay on the bed quietly, as I had seen him do previously after "dying" in a past life. "What did you learn from this lifetime?" I asked.

"If you have an idea and keep working at it, you will be successful." He continued, "Since I was successful, people came from all around to tell me their problems and ask my advice. It was easy for me to help them. It's good to share your wisdom freely." This was a startling nugget of philosophy coming from a seven-year-old.

Chase smiled and opened his eyes. I could tell he was back in the present. About fifteen minutes had elapsed. Chase said that his regression had been fun and that the images of his Russian town were perfectly clear, as if he were really there. I asked him to draw the shelf he had designed. Closing his eyes to recall what he had seen, he drew a small ornamental corner shelf, with a curved design on the top and on the sides. "That's it," he said proudly as he put the finishing touches on the tapers and rolls of the folk-art design. "Let's do that again," he added over his shoulder as he ran out of the room.

I had taken notes of Chase's regression. As I reread his words, I wondered if this lesson of perseverance would stay with him and guide him in his present life. Is wisdom from the past renewable through remembering? What a gift it would be, I thought, if Chase could start his life without having to relearn these lessons of focus and dedication.

A few days later I recruited Sarah to be my next subject. She went into trance quite easily with a suggestion to close her eyes, focus on her breathing, and go back to any past life. Sarah saw herself as a young girl in a hot, sunny landscape with clay buildings. She was an orphan who stayed alive by stealing food and hiding in whatever shelter she could find at night. Her survival depended on her stealth and speed. She said that she died young, killed for stealing food. Still in a trance, she did not seem to be sad or troubled by her untimely death. She felt relieved.

I asked her what her last thoughts were when she died: "I'm glad that life is over. It was too hard. I don't want to do *that* again."

I was curious about what she might be bringing with her into this lifetime, so I asked, "What did you learn from that life?"

"It's not enough just to run and steal to survive. That didn't work; I couldn't stay alive that way. I have to learn *other* skills to make a full life." When Sarah opened her eyes, she was surprised by what she had seen. "I'm glad I'm here now," she said with a relieved sigh.

How did this past life relate to present Sarah? I chuckled to myself as I realized that Sarah is very hardworking and practical, always saving and squirreling away her money. And she is fanatical about scouring the refrigerator for leftovers, because she can't stand to see any food wasted. Could her prudence have anything to do with this unconscious memory of deprivation? It will be interesting to see how this translates into her work and career choices later in life. As with Chase's regression, I wrote it down and tucked it away for future reference.

More Little Time-Travelers

Since I had run out of kids of my own to experiment with, it was time to find other children to regress. I wanted to see what would happen when I regressed children who had not been regressed before. Would they be able to access memories easily? And if so, what would their memories be like? Would they see gory images from the past, or sweet, uneventful lives?

I had a pool of about a dozen five-to-eleven-year-olds available to me among Sarah and Chase's friends. Their parents saw that Sarah and Chase were normal and well adjusted and hadn't turned psychotic from experiencing past life regressions, so they agreed to let me experiment with their children, as long as the kids were willing. Sarah's ten- and eleven-year-old friends were most curious about it and made excellent subjects.

First, I explained to each of my volunteers that I believed we have lived different lifetimes as different people, and that when we're relaxed, we can remember those lives. The children didn't have any trouble accepting the possibility of past lives; they were eager to see who they could have been. I also prepared them by saying that sometimes nothing happens when we try to remember, so they didn't have to say anything that wasn't true. If nothing happened, that was okay.

I also prepared them in the event that a traumatic life came up. I explained that we live many lifetimes, and some are happy and some are not. If they should remember anything that was painful or sad, it would be all right. It was like watching a sad or scary movie in a theater. When we get absorbed in a movie, we can laugh or cry; but when the movie is over and we step out of the theater into the light of day, we feel better and aren't sad or scared anymore. The regressions, I explained, worked in the same way.

Most of the children easily went into trance with a simple relaxation exercise. As with adults, as soon as they began getting images, I told them to focus on their bodies—what they had on their feet, the color of their skin and hair, their age, what they wore—so they could see themselves more clearly. I asked them to describe their surroundings—the landscape, the buildings—and to tell me what they were experiencing. I watched their eyelids flutter and their faces strain as they concentrated on these inner images and feelings. They told me about the vicissitudes of their lives and described their deaths.

In none of the stories these children encountered was there a major trauma or a violent, difficult death. They saw only normal lives and peaceful deaths. Even when the children had experienced the loss of a loved one or a catastrophic setback, they seemed to be at peace with it.

Accessing past lives was not difficult for most of the children, but I found it did not always work. When I tried the same regression techniques with younger children, five- and six-year-olds, nothing happened, except a lot of fidgeting and random images. Some came up with fragments of stories that sounded like pieces of dreams, TV adventure shows, or responses that they thought I wanted to hear. But I could always spot these ramblings right away. The children would tell these stories in a conversational, almost singsong way—not with the halting, starting-and-stopping style that I associated with true past life expression. When they were fantasizing, they weren't emotionally engaged with their stories, either. The easiest flaw to spot was that they lacked the consistent, realistic story line typical of past life memories.

One story, for example, sounded suspiciously like a video game. This little boy saw himself as a prince in a castle, walking through different corridors, entering different rooms, and battling dragons that lurched out from dark spaces. He was involved in the fantasy, as he would have been in a good video game. But it lacked realism. In each case like this, when I felt that they were fantasizing, I just let them go with it, and I joined in for fun. I didn't want them to feel that they had "failed" to do anything, because they hadn't. There was no harm done.

The Flower People

Sarah's friend, Amanda Dickey, was eleven when I regressed her.
She had particularly vivid recall of an Englishwoman by the
name of Elizabeth C. (she couldn't remember the last name) who
lived in London with her mother and brother in the mid-1800s.
Elizabeth would often sit in a garden near her townhouse and
talk to the "flower people," little spirits who came out from
behind the flowers and advised her whenever she had a problem
in her life. Elizabeth wrote stories about these "flower people,"
which were published in a London newspaper and became quite
popular as a serial. She married and had a son. Widowed at an
early age, she and her son emigrated to America. She continued
to support herself with her writing until she died of a disease
Amanda couldn't identify. Her life was marred only by an irrec-
oncilable quarrel she had with her brother.

I was curious about Elizabeth. Was she someone we could
trace? I asked Amanda if Elizabeth had published any books.
According to Amanda, her stories had only been serialized in
newspapers. That sounded authentic: I recalled that serializing
stories was very common in the nineteenth century because books
were too expensive for most people. Would Amanda have known
this as an eleven-year-old? The rest of Amanda's story rang true
as well; the details of her life as Elizabeth were realistic and came
to her readily. And it resonated with present-day Amanda, who
does have an uncanny facility with words.

But "flower people"—where had *that* come from? Amanda,
down-to-earth and sophisticated, was embarrassed by this seemingly incongruous embellishment to the story. I decided it was
probably a fantasy fragment. Norman Inge had taught me that
fragments of fantasy, or present-life experience, sometimes seep
into the stream of past life recall because, as he explained, past
life recall is filtered through the subconscious mind, the reposi-
tory of *all* stored memory from this and other lives. It is not
leakproof. But, he warned, don't let one inconsistency throw you
into thinking the whole thing is fantasy if the rest seems true.

Evaluate the story as a whole. With Amanda, the rest of the story felt and sounded genuine, so I accepted it as true, not wanting to throw out the baby with the bathwater.

Later that year Amanda won a writing contest in her school. When I congratulated her, I said, "See, you do have this talent from the past, don't you." Amanda just rolled her eyes at me and laughed nervously. She still wasn't sure about the regression, especially the "flower people."

Amanda and her family moved out of state the next year. She and Sarah stayed in touch, visiting each other during school vacations. This gave me the opportunity to follow her progress as a writer. She said she wrote short stories and poetry all the time and had joined the literary magazine at school. She admitted to me once that she still pondered her memory of Elizabeth, the writer in her past.

Almost five years after her regression, Amanda wrote to me with a most unusual epilogue:

"One of the strangest incidents happened to me about a year ago on my vacation in England. I had never been to England before. When my parents and I got off the plane at the London airport, we got a cab to our hotel. Our cab driver was extremely talkative and was willing to talk about anything. As we passed the first street of townhouses, my mother commented on all of the flower gardens. The driver told us that almost everyone in London had a garden. He said that Londoners used gardening as a way to escape from the pressures of their lives and that he, and other people he knew, *liked to talk to the flower people in their gardens.* My jaw dropped, and my eyes nearly popped out of my head when I heard that. Flower people, I thought. What a coincidence!"

Kids Remember Death

After regressing a dozen youngsters, I couldn't see that these random regressions had had any immediate value for them. The lifetimes they remembered were rich in story and fascinating to listen to, but what meaning did they have for the children? No traumas or unfinished business surfaced that needed to be resolved. Perhaps the past life stories they remembered would encourage them to build on talents and strengths they brought with them from past lives, or give them constructive life scripts or personal myths for guidance as they grew older, like Amanda's writer in her past. But would the children remember these insights as they grew up? I didn't know.

Although I hadn't seen any more dramatic healings like the ones my children had experienced, the experiment was successful in other ways. I learned that other children can easily be regressed to past lives. And I saw that the children showed no ill effects whatsoever from the regressions. If anything, they thought they were fun.

The process worked best with the older children—the eight-to-eleven-year-olds. It didn't work well with the few four-to-six-year-olds I tried. Yet I recalled that Chase had been only five when he had his first memories of the Civil War. So I couldn't draw any conclusions, one way or the other.

One question was answered with certainty, though. Young children *are* capable of reliving their deaths and visiting the after-death state. The death experiences were extraordinary. In fact, I had to remind myself that these were *children* describing death.

I hadn't prepared them in any way for their "remembered deaths." I didn't want to scare them. Yet at the end of each life, they naturally slipped into describing the death experience. All of these children remembered peaceful deaths, putting them in the 62 percent of Dr. Wambach's "natural deaths" category. And all the death experiences were similar. When they died, they described floating out of their bodies, lifting higher and higher into the sky, just as the adults had in regression. The transition seemed effortless.

Witnessing these kids go through past life deaths inspired me every time. It was always a sacred moment. I could feel a palpable shift of the energy in the room. At times I was sure that I saw light around the children as they lay there in absolute peace. I waited for these moments, these energetic peaks, to ask what they had learned from the lifetime they had just remembered. Each time the children delivered a gem of insight, more wise and mature than their few years of worldly experience could possibly render. It was in these moments that I was aware of being in the presence of wise and experienced souls. Only when the regression was over and they snapped back to their kid personalities could I accept how young they really were.

During one of Chase's regressions, after he passed through his death, I asked him, "What happens after we die?" Without hesitating, in a steady stream of words, and in a wise and knowing voice, he explained: "As you die, you have choices as to what you can do. You can go back to a scene from the life you left and get any information you want to answer questions to finish up your life there. You can see what happens with the people you left behind. You can go back while you're in spirit and say good-bye and see what happens to them in the future. If you see that all is well with them, this frees you to leave the Earth plane" (his words exactly).

I asked him what would happen if you saw that your loved ones were in trouble. He said, "You can come back into a body quickly to be back with that group. You do have this chance after death to move about quickly in your spirit body and fly above the scenes you left behind and see them in real time. You're in a different time than we have on Earth. Then you go to heaven before you come back in another body."

Chase's observations have been confirmed from reports of near death experiences, and from the descriptions by Eastern mystics of the after-death bardo states. If seven-year-old Chase knew this, do we all know it? Is our birth, as the poet Wordsworth wrote, but "a sleep and a forgetting" of these otherworldly states? Chase, it seemed, needed only a slight nudge to awaken this knowledge in him.

It was during this time of experimentation that Chase's Civil War anxieties were triggered by the Gulf War, and I regressed him again; he was eight years old by then. Three years after his first regression, he returned to that life with an urge to complete his death. He finally found peace with his memory and let go of the sad feelings from that lifetime. Again, I was reminded of the real power of this process: how lingering issues from the past could be put to rest by remembering them. That's where the real value is. That session was deep and engaging for both of us. Why couldn't I duplicate those deep experiences with these random regressions? Was it because my young volunteers had no specific problems to address? Or was it because the impulse to go into the past life originated with Chase and not me?

I had reached a dead end with my experiments with kids. I didn't feel that there was much more to learn from these regression sessions, and I wasn't sure if the children were gaining any insight or being helped by going back to past lives. What was the point? My enthusiasm was waning. I wasn't quite sure where to go next. So I waited. Then something happened to get me back on track.

Ninja Night

Chase had a problem we couldn't solve. On New Year's Eve he went to his first-ever slumber party at his karate school. It was during the days of the ubiquitous Ninja Turtles, so the kids were entertained with Ninja games, karate videos, and the favorite Ninja Turtle food—pizza. They made dark tunnels out of blankets to simulate the sewers the Turtles lived in. Chase appeared to be having a great time with the fun and games. But late in the night he became upset and couldn't sleep. My friend Amy McLaughlin, who was supervising the kids, couldn't comfort him. At dawn she put him in the car and brought an exhausted and tearful Chase home. He couldn't explain what had happened, except to say that he was trying to see how late he could stay up, then got very upset and couldn't fall asleep.

After that night Chase had anxiety attacks every evening at bedtime. He felt sick to his stomach, got very pale and quiet, and was anxious about not being able to get to sleep. We tried hot baths, relaxation exercises, music, and warm milk, but nothing worked. Talking to him didn't help either. I spoke with the adults who were at the party, and they assured me that nothing unusual had happened. So what was Chase's problem? This went on every night for six long weeks, and I was beginning to worry. We were at the point of calling a doctor for help, when Chase suggested that we try a regression.

I waited until bedtime when his anxiety started. Instead of doing a relaxation exercise, I decided to use the sick feeling in his stomach as a bridge back to the past, as Roger Woolger had taught me. I asked Chase to lie in his bed and describe the feeling in his stomach. He said that it felt like an emptiness, a spinning that would start in his stomach, travel to his throat, and flow back to his stomach. I asked him if he could see a color with this feeling, as a way to increase his focus; he reported that it was orange-yellow. He said that it was not a sick feeling (although he had vomited on several occasions) but a feeling of emptiness. I suggested that he "stay with the feeling of emptiness."

This worked. Chase saw an image of himself as an adult manacled in a dungeon, in what he described as "castle times." It was dark, and he was alone. His arms were stretched tightly above him, and they hurt. He continued to be aware of these sensations in his body as he told his story.

I suggested that he go back to an earlier time before he was put in the dungeon. He saw himself in a village square crowded with many people—a marketplace. He was planning a theft. He saw his hand reaching for something, when he was suddenly apprehended. The next thing he knew, he was in the dark dungeon.

I asked him to direct his attention to his emotions: "I feel guilty about what I did—sorry. It was a waste of a life to end up like this. I feel that sadness and guilt in my stomach. I *can't sleep* hanging in this position. I die here. I start swimming up into the air above the castle and the town. I see the town below. I know that I am supposed to go up. I feel better."

"Is there anything you need to say or do to those people you left?" I asked, probing for unfinished business from that lifetime, as Woolger would do in the after-life state with a patient.

"They know I was caught. That's enough." He was satisfied with his answer.

"What connection was there between Ninja Night and that lifetime?" I asked, to see if he could draw the parallels and find the reason for his symptoms. He said that he had been having fun at the slumber party seeing how late he could stay up, when suddenly he became anxious and scared about not being able to sleep. That was when the sick feeling in his stomach began. He said that the slumber party was "dark and unfamiliar like the dungeon," and that was why the sick feeling came up.

"How are you feeling now?" I asked, to make sure there was nothing more. Chase gave me a hug and said he felt better now. He was able to sleep soundly that night and was not bothered by the anxiety or sick feeling again.

This was what I needed; my enthusiasm was stoked. Chase gave me the opportunity to use past life memories for serious healing, and it worked. He had a real problem—physical symptoms—that we couldn't understand or cure. By using the awareness of his feelings, we traced his problem back to its *real* source, which was not anything that had happened at Ninja Night, but a past life memory that had been triggered by his feelings that night. It was really a very simple process. I followed Chase's lead and helped him articulate the cause of his problem in the past. Then, with only a little guidance from me, he knew what needed to be done to clear the memory. Any mother could have done the same.

English Tots Remember . . .

One day around the same time as Chase's Ninja Night regression, I was in the mall rushing to get some errands done before the kids got home from school. I ducked into a bookstore to check for new books on past lives, as was my habit. There, wedged tightly between the now-familiar titles on reincarnation, was a little paperback I had never seen before: *The Children That Time Forgot*. I tugged and pulled it down. On the cover was a sensationalized picture of children's faces in dark shadows, illuminated across the eyes. It reminded me of a movie poster for *Children of the Damned*. Ugh! Definitely not my style. But the subtitle grabbed me: *Shocking true accounts of children who remember their previous lives.* My heart raced in anticipation, hoping the "true accounts" would have some substance. I flipped it open and started reading.

The next thing I knew, a half hour had passed. I was so absorbed in the stories that I had forgotten about the time. I ran to the cash register, paid for the book, and made it home just as the school bus growled up the hill and released Sarah and Chase. I set out snacks on the kitchen table, said hi as they exploded through the door, and escaped to my reading chair. I was so eager to dig into my new treasure, I didn't even take the time to make a cup of tea.

The Children That Time Forgot reveals nothing about the authors, Peter and Mary Harrison, except that they're British. The cases they collected are well written and warmly told—not sensationalized and shallow, as I had feared from the cover photo. The book offers twenty-six cases of *spontaneous* past life memories of *English* children. In a chatty style full of British idioms, they recount stories of two- and three-year-olds who, out of the blue, tell their astonished parents about their past lives and deaths.

Sarah and Chase peeped around the doorway to see what I was reading that was so exciting, because every few minutes I let out an uncontrollable "Wow!" I was beside myself. These were spontaneous cases from an English-speaking, Judeo-Christian culture like my own. The book brought it all back home: it made the phenomenon less exotic, more familiar, comfortable.

These Western cases were as amazing and as rich in detail as some of Dr. Stevenson's cases, which were mostly from Asia. This book was the answer to critics who try to dismiss Dr. Stevenson's cases because they come from cultures that believe in reincarnation, claiming that because of the parents' beliefs, the children are unconsciously encouraged to speak of past lives. (A close reading of Dr. Stevenson, however, blows this criticism out of the water.)

But here in the Harrisons' book were Christian families, none of whom believed in reincarnation, testifying that their own children had past life memories. Most were baffled, if not shocked, when their young children started speaking of "when I lived before," and "when I died." As one father put it: "I've heard of odd things like this before, but I never thought it could happen in my own family."[1] These children certainly hadn't taken any cues from their parents or TV or storybooks that past life memories are normal. If anything, the opposite is true: the parents resisted believing that their little tykes were serious, and tried to "fob them off," hoping the strange behavior would go away. But their children's memories persisted despite this resistance. Eventually it was the parents who changed.

. . . and Mummies Listen

This book is as much about the parents as it is about the children. It's about the conflict between the parents' belief that "we only live once," and what they heard and saw coming from their own children. It documents the parents' initial doubt, their attempts to dissuade the children, and in many cases their long periods of bemused tolerance, until the mounting evidence convinced them to accept the truth of their toddler's utterings.

As I read each of the stories, I felt an inner gauge go off, saying, "Yes, this one rings true. And this one, and this one." I knew that I was treading familiar ground while reading these parents' confessions of their reactions to their own kids' spontaneous memories. I recalled the morning when Chase, in the middle of breakfast, surprised me with the news that he had been a black soldier, leaving me agape. It was reassuring to see this delicate and intimate interaction between parent and child described in a book. I hadn't seen it anywhere else.

Other things made these stories sound familiar and true. I was beginning to see many of the same patterns I saw in the Stevenson cases: the very young age when the children first talked about their past life memories and the fading of the memories by school age; children recognizing landmarks from the past; phobias relating to their deaths; and children being reborn into the same families.

In most of the Harrisons' cases, though, the children did *not* give enough specific information—names, dates, and locations—to establish the reality of their former identities. Dr. Stevenson would have screened out these cases because they lacked sufficient evidence that could be verified by outside sources. But the fact that the Harrison cases are not as scientifically rigorous as the Stevenson cases does not make them any less valid.

I realized, while reading through this book for the second time, that this is a very important point. The Harrisons are offering a different kind of proof. They document how the children's memories changed their parents' beliefs about reincarnation and death. These Christian parents had little to gain and a lot to lose by going on record about their kids' seemingly outlandish claims. Yet they were convinced. The past life memories reversed their deep-seated views and changed their lives. This is evidence that ordinary people can understand, and that is no less real than Stevenson's charts and corroborations.

After all, parents are in the best position to discern the truth and motivation behind what their own children are saying. They know what their children have been exposed to, what they know or don't know. Parents can sense when their kids are making things up and when they're serious. The Harrisons highlight nuances that a parent would notice, but an outsider looking only for objective evidence would have missed: the different tone of voice or the squeal of joy when remembering a pet from the past; the faraway look that passes over a child's face as he talks longingly of a loved one from another lifetime. It was these looks and sounds that gave the parents chills, or made them feel as though they had been "struck by an electric current," alerting them to pay closer attention to their child. It was this feeling that made one mother exclaim, "I just *know* that he is not making this up."

Tales from the Crib

Because the Harrison stories are reported from the point of view of the parents, they reveal subtle qualities and point to new aspects of the phenomenon that I hadn't seen before.

I wondered, for example, after reading some of the stories in

The Children That Time Forgot, if wee children ruminate about the past while still in their cribs, even before they can talk. Some of the children were so young when they first began talking about their memories, it seemed as if they had been just *waiting* for the words to come, frustrated that they could not tell their parents what they were thinking about. On the average, these toddlers were two years old, and many of them *still in diapers,* when they first began speaking of their memories. They were still babies.

One of the children, Elspeth, was only eighteen months old and had never put words together before—had never uttered a complete sentence. One evening when her mother was giving Elspeth her bath, the baby said, "I'm going to take my vows." Her astonished mother couldn't believe her ears. This was Elspeth's first complete sentence—did she say "vows"?

When she questioned Elspeth, the little one replied, "I'm not Elspeth now. I'm Rose, but I'm going to be Sister Teresa Gregory."[2] Now her mother was stunned. They were not Catholics: Elspeth could not possibly have known about nuns and vows. She was only a baby!

Elspeth went on to tell her mother that "when I was here before," she had been an old lady and wore a long black dress with a black cloth over her head. That was it. Then one day, two years later, Elspeth filled in the story about the nun's life, describing her jobs at the convent. Her day began when it was still dark; she milked goats, made cheese, and helped prepare the food. The nuns said prayers often, and when a certain bell was rung, they had to stop talking, no matter what they were doing. As an old woman, she fell over and died while saying prayers in her tiny room.

When she died, everything went black. She then woke up and found that she was with her friends—nuns who had also died. Elspeth said that they were still dressed in their nuns' habits and looked younger than they had when they were still alive. She too began to look younger after she died. Elspeth didn't remember anything else after that point. She never spoke of her nun's life again.

Several children remembered former lives as relatives who had died before they themselves were born. Dr. Stevenson also found that cases of reincarnation within the same family are common. The Harrison cases are most remarkable for how absolutely convinced the *family* members are that the young one is a relative reborn. Because the family knew the deceased relative and incidents in his or her life, they are in the best position to compare the child's behavior and statements with what they remember. They get goose bumps when the child's behavior mimics the dead relative, or when the child reminds them of obscure events that the family had forgotten or never talked about.

Desmond had been playing with his toy cars on the floor when he told his mother, without any prompting, "You know, Mummy, I went to Aunty Ruth before I came to you, but I didn't stay there very long." His mother was stunned to hear her three-and-a-half-year-old say this. Her sister-in-law, Ruth, had given birth to a stillborn son ten years before. But the family had a pact to never speak of it because it had been so traumatic for her. Desmond could never have overheard anyone discuss it.

Desmond remembered clearly what it was like in Aunty Ruth's womb: it was very warm and "quite bouncy." He was happy and comfortable and very wet. He used to turn "around and around all the time." It was always dark—but not scary. From time to time he would get sleepy. He said, "One time I went to sleep but when I woke up again I wasn't with Aunty Ruth any more."[3]

Over the next months, as Desmond spoke more and more of his memories, his parents gradually became convinced that their little boy was the child that Ruth had been expecting. But Desmond's mother never told Ruth. "She has no children of her own at all," she explained, "so I am afraid to tell her about Desmond in case she feels that he really belongs to her." Desmond's father stated, "How he could tell us that he went to his Aunt Ruth before he came to us is unbelievable. . . . There's no doubt in my mind that the kid must have experienced life before, and those memories stayed with him."[4]

Half of the children in the Harrison cases remembered how they died. Most were matter-of-fact about their deaths, and they talked about dying calmly, without sadness or fear. They seemed to be at peace with it, simply reviewing things that happened "when I was here before."

Little Mandy remembered being her sister who had died as a baby of a congenital heart disease. The death had wracked the family with grief, but Mandy's only problem with dying, she told her parents now, was that she didn't like it when everyone had cried so much for her. But, she added, "it was nice to come back."[5] Richard, a two-year-old who had thoroughly convinced his parents that he was his grandfather reborn, assured the adults that death was nothing to fear: "I'm not frightened of dying because it happened to me before. It was OK."[6]

Of the Harrison children who remembered violent or traumatic deaths, only a few suffered any negative feelings from them. In these few cases the children had phobias relating to their violent deaths. This conforms to the now-familiar pattern observed by all past life therapists and by Dr. Stevenson: traumatic deaths are usually at the root of otherwise unexplainable phobias.

One child, Dominic, had a phobia related to his traumatic death. As in Dr. Stevenson's most indisputable cases, he had a birthmark: a scar on his right thigh, "a raised white line of flesh which remains white when the rest of his body gets tanned."[7]

As an infant, Dominic was so terrified of being immersed in water that he screamed hysterically whenever his mother or grandmother tried to bathe him. Eventually they gave up and resorted to sponge baths. One day, around the time he was learning his first words, his grandmother, who had never mentioned the scar before, touched it gently. Dominic explained to the astonished woman, "Man on boat did that with big knife. Lots of blood everywhere. All covered with blood." He said he fell in the water and "got drowned."[8] His mother declared that her baby had never been on a boat, had no conception of killing with knives, and had never had a bloody injury. It was no random fantasy. Dominic's explanation jibed too well with both the birthmark scar on his thigh and his phobia of water. The adults had no choice but to believe him.

Did Dominic's hysterical fear of water diminish after he told his grandmother about his violent death? The Harrisons gave no clues. This lack of follow-up frustrated me. The Harrisons did a good job documenting the parents' reactions but, as far as I was concerned, they didn't go far enough. I wanted to know if Dominic had been cured of his phobia. I wished I had been the one interviewing these parents. I would have probed more about how they had responded to their children and what the result was.

Nicola's Catharsis

One story in particular sparked me the most. Of all of the Harrisons' great cases, the case of Nicola was the only one that described a catharsis and a healing.

On her second birthday Nicola was surprised with a gift from her parents, a little toy dog. She got very excited and told her mother the toy reminded her of her dog Muff, "the same as the other dog I had before."[9] Nicola's mother, Kathleen, thought her daughter's fantasy play was amusing but soon forgot it. But in the days that followed, she noticed that Nicola had regular conversations with the toy dog, asking if he remembered the fun they had shared in the past. Kathleen noticed because Nicola's persistence in this "fantasy" was most unusual.

One day Kathleen was taken completely off guard when Nicola asked her, in a gush, why she wasn't a boy this time like she was before when Mrs. Benson was her mommy and she played with Muff. This time Kathleen encouraged Nicola to tell her more. That was all Nicola needed for the story of her past life to pour out.

She said her family had lived in a gray stone house that was in the "middle of four houses joined together in a row" and next to railway tracks; her mother wore long skirts, the same Victorian-style clothing her dolly wore now, and the town they lived in was Haworth; she and her dog roamed the fields around her house and her "other Mummy" always warned her not to play near the railway tracks, but one day she was playing on the railway tracks when a train "came up fast and knocked me over." Men took her to a hospital where "I went to sleep and died and I saw God in

Heaven before I was born. But I didn't really die. I came to you instead and you got to be my other Mummy."[10]

This flood of detail couldn't be ignored. Little Nicola's story was so convincing that Kathleen took her to Haworth, a short drive away, to see if her daughter would recognize anything. Neither Nicola nor Kathleen had ever been to Haworth, but as soon as they got there, Nicola skipped down streets and unmarked lanes leading to the outskirts of town. She took her mother directly to the house she had described: one in the middle of four graystone townhouses. Everything matched Nicola's description perfectly, including the surrounding fields and the railway tracks.

Kathleen pursued her daughter's past life memory. Since she had a name and an address as leads, she decided to check the records of the parish church to see if she could verify the accuracy of Nicola's recollection. She opened the yellowed pages of the old census book and her heart "skipped a beat." She found the Benson family listed (an unusual name for that parish). They had one son, who was born in 1875. But the next census, taken six years later, listed the same Benson family with two young girls, aged three years and six months—but no son! Since the census required that each family member always be listed, Kathleen concluded that the little boy Nicola remembered must have died when he was between five and six years old.[11]

Nicola's was a remarkable case of spontaneous memory, with details that could be verified by her mother. But her story goes beyond mere recollection of details.

One night, soon after their expedition to Haworth, Nicola's family was sitting around the television watching a movie. On the screen appeared a train thundering down the tracks. Immediately Nicola went into hysterics, threw herself down on the floor, and thrashed about wildly, gasping for air. Kathleen ran to her, panicked, not knowing what had come over her little girl so suddenly. Nicola was inconsolable and started crying out repeatedly, "The train, the train!" Kathleen turned off the TV, and Nicola immediately stopped screaming, but continued to cry. Kathleen understood in an instant that the sight of the train had reminded Nicola of her death when she was the Benson boy. And she understood that Nicola was reliving that terrifying death. Because Kathleen knew what was happening, she let Nicola cry it out in her arms, not denying her fear of the train. After a while Nicola calmed down and was fine.

Nicola was never afraid of trains again. By the age of five she had forgotten almost everything about her life as the Benson boy—with one exception. She never forgot her pet dog, Muff.

What had happened with little Nicola? I was struck by what her mother did—and what she didn't do. Since Nicola's memory could be verified through historical records, Kathleen believed beyond a doubt that Nicola had lived before as the Benson boy and had been killed by a train. So when Nicola was reexperiencing her death on the living room floor, yelling hysterically about the train, Kathleen didn't mistake her daughter's fit for random hysteria. She knew without taking the time to think that it was a consequence of her daughter's past life memory. She immediately saw the connection, knew it was true, and gave Nicola her loving support. She didn't hamper the process with doubt. The memory ran its natural course, culminating in catharsis, giving Nicola a chance to finally vent the terror that had been trapped in her since the train ran her down so long ago. Then the memory faded and disappeared.

Parents Complete the Puzzle

Nicola's case was extraordinary because the entire process was spontaneous and natural. It came and went in its own time, at its own pace, without intervention from anyone. I hadn't seen this healing process in Stevenson. The Harrisons hadn't mentioned it either. In fact they didn't comment on any of the cases. They overlooked what I considered to be the significance of the Nicola case. But it jumped out at me. Why? Ever since Chase and Sarah met Norman Inge in my kitchen, I had been assembling pieces of the puzzle of children's past life memories. This piece from Nicola, this idea that *spontaneous* memories can heal naturally and on their own, was the last piece I was looking for to complete the puzzle. Now all the pieces fit together and made sense. I stepped back and admired the whole picture. It looked like this:

Any child, anywhere in the world, can have a past life memory, regardless of the cultural or religious beliefs of the parents. Most of these memories don't cause problems. They are benign and are useful to help explain a child's talents, temperament, behavioral quirks. And as the Harrisons showed, they can forever change the most fundamental beliefs of the parents about death and life. For, by sharing their memories with us, small children teach what we adults have forgotten: that life continues after death.

Sometimes, though, children have troubling memories from the past that create problems, such as phobias or physical ailments. These children may need help separating past from present—they may need to be told that the past life is over. Or if the memory is a sign that something from the past is unfinished, they may need help discovering what that unfinished business is in order to resolve it. They may need to examine their feelings and thoughts at the moment of death and be guided toward a resolution, à la Woolger.

For some children it's even simpler than that. I suspect that in some instances, all a parent needs to do is simply acknowledge the truth of the memory and not deny it. Then the memory will run its course. This was the important lesson from Nicola's case.

Whether these memories are benign or troubling, they offer an opportunity for parents to aid their children. The optimal time for acknowledging a child's past life memory is the moment it emerges, and parents are almost always on the scene when that happens. They are in the best position to support and encourage the child with their loving attention.

But they can help only if they recognize the past life memory for what it is soon enough to respond. If they're frozen by disbelief, they can't. The moment may be lost, or the child discouraged, and the evanescent memory may never surface again. Unfortunately, nothing in our culture prepares parents for this moment. On the contrary, everything in our culture teaches that children's past life memories are impossible. Parents are all alone, with no guidance to help them know what the memories look like, or what to do.

What can be done? Maybe the key to helping children with these memories is to educate parents. What if, I mused, parents knew how to recognize past life memories at the onset? Then instead of groping to figure out whether their child was babbling fantasy or remembering a real past life, they would have the tools to decide the question on the spot. And if parents understood the dynamics of past life memories—the idea of unfinished business, and the power of catharsis—they could choose the right questions to guide the child to resolution of a troubling memory. They would be prepared to respond in the best way in the moment. They would know what to do.

As I mulled this over, I became unsettled and a little excited. "Maybe I could write a book explaining these memories to parents," I allowed myself to imagine. But then another thought struck me: If these ideas were coming to me, had someone else already thought of them? Were others already on the trail currently doing the same research and preparing to write this book? If so, how could I find out?

I had a clue where I could look.

Roger Woolger had told me about a group that was the leading professional association and worldwide network for past life therapists. Surely if anyone was doing this research, the members of this group would know about it. They are the Association for Past Life Research and Therapies, known by the acronym APRT (pronounced *a-part*). I called and discovered that there was just enough time to sign up for the APRT spring conference in Florida. As a bonus, Dr. Elisabeth Kübler-Ross, famous for her book *On Death and Dying*, was to be the keynote speaker. For years I had admired Dr. Kübler-Ross's courage for breaking down our cultural taboo against speaking about death. Now here was my chance to see her in person.

My good friend Amy, who was working on a graduate degree in transpersonal psychology, succumbed to my enthusiasm for past life research and agreed to go with me. She wasn't hard to persuade: a trip to Florida at the end of a dreary Philadelphia winter sounded delightful. And why not go? It would be a chance to escape our routines and go on a wild and exotic adventure together. I couldn't wait!

APRT Adventureland

Amy and I arrived at the airport before sunrise. The dawn washed the jumbo jets in a soft pink light, making them look like giant pull toys, and the early morning mist softened the peculiar shapes of the terminal buildings and the odd machines servicing the planes. The airport had never looked so beautiful and fantastic. This was going to be a good trip. Pumped with coffee and anticipation, we boarded our flight for Fort Lauderdale.

Flying down the coast at 35,000 feet, I closed my eyes and let my mind drift with the droning of the plane's engines. I realized this was my first solo trip away from the family since Sarah was born. It was time, and I was more than ready. For the first time in thirteen years, I would be free from the responsibilities and distractions of home and family, a traveler in a world of ideas. I could concentrate exclusively on my quest for information. What joy!

I stared out the window at the barrier islands far below that looked like long bony fingers pointing south. I realized that this ride between Philadelphia and Florida marked a turning point in my research too. In the past years I had been alone searching for answers to my questions about children's past life memories. My only sources had been books and my improvised experiments. Now, for the first time, I would be mixing with other researchers, therapists, and past life professionals. The leaders and founders of the field of past life therapy would be there too—pioneers who counted as their peers Drs. Wambach, Fiore, and Woolger. I wondered apprehensively if they would accept me as a serious researcher—or would they see me as just a wacky housewife?

I knew that the people at this APRT conference were the central network for all of the serious work in the field. If any therapists anywhere were working with children's past life memories, or if research or books existed that I hadn't yet found, these people would know.

Amy and I arrived at our hotel early—hours before the conference was scheduled to begin. Our plan was to relax on the beach and get some color on our white winter skin before we were swept up in the action. Within an hour the blazing Florida sun—like nothing we ever see in Philadelphia—burned me as red as a tomato. When would I learn? Well, if nothing else, I would have something to show for my weekend in Florida.

I plastered myself with Solarcaine and changed into airy summer clothes, and we went down to register for the conference. People were arriving from all over the country, dressed in shirts and skirts as colorful and showy as the hibiscus in the hotel lobby. I quickly met, and was welcomed by, the "Matriarchs of APRT": Drs. Hazel Denning, Winafred Lucas, and Irene Hickman. These amazing ladies have been on the cutting edge of psychotherapy for the past forty years. In 1981, when they were in their sixties and seventies, they (along with Drs. Wambach, Fiore, and others) had started APRT to advance their vision of past life therapy as a legitimate healing tool. Now in their seventies and eighties, they were still organizing and training, still writing books, still vigorously pushing the frontier of psychotherapy, bucking the old psychological paradigms all the way. I admired their pluck.

By late afternoon a couple hundred people were milling around—psychotherapists, psychiatrists, clinical hypnotherapists, researchers, and like-minded nonprofessionals like me who had an intense interest in past life therapy. And they were all speaking my language. I could walk up to any group and be welcomed into a conversation about past life healing. I had found my tribe.

Even before the conference began, I had decided on my modus operandi. I had only limited time to canvass all the crowd in a search for people who knew more than I did about children's past life memories. In every workshop, every reception, and every intermission, I buzzed from person to person to introduce myself and, in the next breath, to ask if they had experience working with children: Did they know of children's past life cases? Could they recommend books on children's past life memories? Everyone was friendly and tried to help. I got leads to a few good cases. But in general I was surprised at how little these people knew about working with children. Most of their leads were to people or books I had already discovered on my own. Most had never worked with children, and they admitted they hadn't really thought about it, since they worked only with adult patients in their practices.

Almost everyone tried to refer me to Dr. Stevenson, admitting that all they knew about children and past lives came from reading *Twenty Cases Suggestive of Reincarnation.* "But," I countered, "Dr. Stevenson didn't say anything about the *healing* value of these memories."

Some even said they thought it was dangerous to tamper with the "fragile ego structures" of young children. This objection floored me. I thought of the many times I had regressed my own kids, and my experiments with other youngsters. Dangerous? Fragile ego structures? I described what I had already learned on my own, telling them that if anything, kids made better subjects than adults. Some admitted that this was news to them. They said they were interested and would watch for the results of my research.

After only a few hours of prospecting, I was getting the impression that past life regression with children was unexplored territory even for this sophisticated group. This was a surprise. I left the crowd and went into the lobby to sit and think. Was I the only person on this trail? Wasn't there anyone here I could compare notes with?

Just then Roger Woolger breezed through the front doors into the lobby. He wore a colorful Hawaiian shirt, looking every bit the dapper tourist. I was happy to see a familiar face. We chatted. He said he was here to teach a workshop, and I apprised him of my mission.

"Aha!" Roger said. "There's a woman here from Holland, Tineke Noordegraaf, who specializes in past life therapy with children. I met her in Europe recently, and I'm very impressed with her work." He told me to be alert for a woman with a thick Dutch accent, the tallest woman at the conference. Roger thought this could be the lead I had been looking for.

Tineke Noordegraaf

I watched above the crowd for Tineke and spotted her a few hours later gliding out of a workshop. Statuesque, standing at least six feet tall, she towered over me. She had a commanding presence, accentuated by her piercing eyes and thick crown of long brown curls. I introduced myself and asked if she had time to talk. She explained that she was on the run. Look for her later. She disappeared around the corner.

By the time Amy and I got to the banquet hall that evening, people were flowing in and the tables were filling up quickly. We hurried to the front to see if any seats were free—we wanted to be close to Dr. Kübler-Ross when she spoke. There were only two seats left—right next to Tineke Noordegraaf. She greeted me warmly as I sat down next to her. While the waiter negotiated around us to serve each course of our rubber chicken fare, Tineke told me as much as she could about her work. I plied her with question after question. Amy understood the importance of this moment and listened closely.

My last few years of questioning and searching culminated in those minutes between salad and dessert. Tineke confirmed what I had speculated about children's memories. Yes, they can heal—at deeper levels than I had imagined possible.

In her thickly accented English, Tineke talked with precision, choosing her words carefully. She told me that she had been using past life therapy successfully with children in Holland for seven years. She explained that in Holland, and in much of Western Europe, past life therapy was rapidly gaining acceptance as a legitimate form of psychotherapy. Yet she was one of the only therapists using past life therapy to help children overcome really serious problems such as palsy, phobias, diabetes, and sleep disorders. Because of her success, parents from all over Europe were bringing their children to her. And, since there was such a demand for this type of therapy, she and her colleague, Rob Bontenbal, had begun to train other therapists in Europe to work with children.

Tineke explained that she didn't use hypnotic induction with children. Instead, to help the children open up, to get them talking about their problems, she used toys, games, and, most often, drawing. These tools focused the children on their own feelings, images, body sensations, and key phrases as a bridge to the past life that was causing the problems.

Past life therapy with children is in many ways the same as with adults, Tineke explained, because the real work is done on a soul level. And the soul in a little body is the same as the soul in an adult body. In some ways it is easier with children because they are closer in time to their problems: it's usually the most recent incarnation, an incomplete death, that is the source of the problem. If the emotional charge of the recent past life experience is strong enough, the memory may come up spontaneously, driven by the soul's desire to finish what it couldn't before. The soul really wants to finish what it came here to finish. It's a natural drive. And, she stressed, children are amazing in therapy because they seem to know intuitively, if asked in the right way, what they need to do to complete the unfinished lifetime.

I tingled with excitement. This remarkable woman, perhaps the leading expert on children's past life therapy, was confirming what I had been formulating on my own.

I confessed to Tineke how glad I was to have found her and to hear that somebody was doing serious healing with children using past life therapy. I asked her if she knew anyone in the United States doing anything like her work. She said no. We both agreed that this was a big mystery. For some reason the acceptance of past life therapy in the United States lags behind Europe. It is still considered to be on the fringe here, and many past life therapists are secretive about their work, fearing for their professional credibility. I added that parents in the United States, from what I could tell, didn't have a clue that their children could have these memories, let alone that they could be valuable for healing.

Thinking of the thesis of the book I hoped to write someday, I asked Tineke, "Do you think *parents* can work with their own children's spontaneous memories?" She said, "Sure, why not?"

"Are you writing a book about working with children?" I asked her, feeling suddenly nervous.

"Yes," she said. "A book about past life therapy with children—a clinical book for therapists. And you?"

"Well, I guess I'm writing the *other* book," I blurted out. "The book for parents. To let them know what these memories are in case they run across them." Then I added, "But I'm not sure if I'm the best one to do it. That's why I came here, to . . ."

Tineke stopped me with a wave of her hand. She pierced my doubts with her cobra eyes and said, "Listen to me. You must start your book now. Just begin! No excuses!"

I knew she was right. After such a forceful proclamation, there was nothing more for me to say.

Butterflies and Oprah

In the next moment the tinkling of a knife on a water glass silenced the chattering crowd around us. Dr. Elisabeth Kübler-Ross, the featured guest speaker, was introduced. Dr. Kübler-Ross, a tiny woman dressed in plain pants, a shirt, and socks and sandals, looked as if she had just hiked in from the mountains. Although her appearance was modest, her words dazzled us.

She spoke of her own spontaneous past life recollections. Then she told us a story. Immediately after World War II, as a young Swiss doctor, she traveled across Europe to help treat the survivors in the recently liberated concentration camps. In one of the camps, in the bunkers that housed children, she saw something so amazing, she would ponder it for years to come. Above the children's bunks, on the beams, everywhere, were etchings of butterflies that the children had carved with their fingernails. The doomed children, surrounded by the stink of constant death, had left a final message of hope and liberation with their feeble scratchings. I heard sniffles all around the room.

Dr. Brian Weiss spoke next. The crowd was eager to hear his story because he, of all the APRT members, had the most visible success. His book *Many Lives, Many Masters* was a best-seller. He was the first prominent member of conservative mainstream medicine to endorse past life therapy. Everyone in the room knew how important that was for the widespread acceptance of their work.

Dr. Weiss retold the story of how he had discovered past life regression—the case history of Catherine, on which his book is based. His story is remarkable because his background was so traditional. He received his medical training at Columbia and Yale and had reached a position of influence and power in the medical establishment as the chairman of psychiatry at Miami's Mount Sinai Medical Center. His professional world regarded past life regression with the same esteem as voodoo and witchcraft, and Dr. Weiss had shared this opinion—until he encountered Catherine.

Catherine came to him plagued by a host of serious complaints, including panic attacks and multiple phobias. For eighteen months Dr. Weiss tried conventional therapy with no success. Then he hypnotized Catherine to probe for buried trauma in her childhood. When he instructed her to "go back to the time from which your symptoms arise," she recalled what appeared to be a vivid and coherent past life memory. While still in a trance, Catherine also spoke of spiritual insights about Dr. Weiss's personal life that were impossible for her to know. This was the stroke of grace that changed Dr. Weiss's beliefs about what is possible. And as further proof that something significant had happened during the session, Catherine's symptoms began to clear up immediately after this regression and disappeared after several months of intensive past life therapy.

It took eight years for Dr. Weiss to muster the courage to publish his account of Catherine's lengthy case. He knew he risked censure from his psychiatric colleagues for describing past life regression as a legitimate therapeutic modality. But instead of being ostracized from the medical community, he received letters and calls of gratitude from psychiatrists all over the country who had also discovered that past life therapy healed their patients. They were grateful that the eminent Dr. Weiss had gone public with his story, for now they could be more forthcoming with their own successes. Some of those therapists were sitting in the lecture room with me that evening, listening to Dr. Weiss tell his story.

Dr. Weiss's talk was fascinating, but I was itching for the question and answer period so I could ask him about children. Surely he had worked with some children in his practice. Had he regressed any? When the time came, I raised my hand like an eager schoolgirl. But each time he passed me by and picked someone else in the audience. Finally I sat back and gave up. I'd have to get his attention some other way, some other time.

I perked up again when questions led to a discussion about the TV talk show circuit. Dr. Weiss had appeared on almost every talk show in America. He knew the ropes. He warned other therapists that some talk shows would try to trap them with their "experts," attempting to discredit past life therapy for the sake of a sensational confrontation in front of the cameras. Dr. Hazel Denning, one of the APRT matriarchs, stood up to set the record straight about the Oprah Winfrey show. She said that Oprah and her staff had been truly interested in what she had to say and relied on getting to the heart of interesting subjects rather than staging cheap-shot sensationalism. Other APRT members, who had been on national TV, joined in the banter. They made appearing on TV sound so normal. I could see myself doing it.

With that thought a realization shot through my body. I knew in that instant that I was going to be on *Oprah* too.

What? Where was this coming from? I started giggling. Amy turned to me and arched her eyebrows in a "What?" position. I whispered in her ear, "I'm going to be on the Oprah Winfrey show." Amy gave a little snort of surprise, then looked me directly in the eye, and said with a straight face, "Oh, okay."

I sealed the premonition a week later by announcing to my hairdresser, Kathleen, that I was going to be on *Oprah*.

CHAPTER 8

Blake

Experienced Souls in Little Bodies

One day, soon after I returned from the APRT conference in Florida, I went to the elementary school to pick up Chase and take him to his dental appointment. It was early afternoon, and I knew that Chase wouldn't mind missing a few hours of school on this gorgeous spring day, even if it meant going to the dentist. I was early, so I found a spot on the lawn to sit and enjoy the radiant sun while I waited.

Children were everywhere on the playground, running around, playing tag, or just zooming for the fun of it. I spied one little girl on the swing set, arching way back on the swing, with her long brown hair almost dragging the ground behind her. She looked mesmerized by the motion of the swing. A few boys conspired on the edge of the playground, slinking into the shadows of the neighboring woods. What were they thinking?

Scanning the playground, I wondered how many of these fifty or so children had tried to tell a parent about when they had lived and died before. One? Two? Maybe a dozen? If they had, presumably the parent had no idea what their child was saying and completely missed it. But now I knew with certainty that it was possible for any of these children to have a spontaneous past life memory. Not all of them, I didn't think. But out of the fifty, I would be surprised if there wasn't *at least* one who, when younger, began to speak of "when I lived before."

Watching these kids, I realized that what I had learned about children's past life memories had changed the way I look at all children. Most adults unconsciously see children as something less than real people because the young haven't had enough life experience, haven't matured into adults yet. But if we all have had innumerable past lives, then these children zooming around in front of me could be very experienced souls, only in little bodies. I looked again at the kids on the playground, squinted my eyes, and imagined them as wise beings trapped temporarily in childhood. That made a difference. It made me want to ask each and every one of them: "Where have you been? What can you teach me?"

My mind drifted back to the APRT conference. Tineke's words, now a familiar mantra, chanted in my ears: "You must start your book now. Just begin. No excuses." I couldn't ignore the message because I knew she was right; there was no avoiding it. But . . . a book? A formidable job! I hadn't written anything longer than a letter since college. Strangely, though, I felt myself getting energized just thinking about it.

Chase tapped me on the shoulder and startled me out of the warm bubble of my thoughts. It was time to go to the dentist.

_____

Venture Outward

While I waited in the dentist's office, I thought about a plan. Where do I start to write a book on children's past life memories? I took stock: I had ideas and theories, but I didn't have any cases of spontaneous memories of my own (except for Chase and Sarah). I was sure they were out there, if only I could survey enough parents to find at least a few. How could I get the word out to hundreds and thousands of parents?

Leafing through an old issue of a parenting magazine that my dentist had preserved in the waiting room since last fall, I got an idea. I flipped to the back. Classifieds. That's it. I would advertise for cases. But not in this ad-factory baby-care magazine. I would put an ad in my favorite progressive parenting magazine, *Mothering,* which I had discovered before Chase was born. As soon as I got home, I juggled my household funds to create an advertising budget and placed an ad. I couldn't wait for the next issue to hit the stands.

Next, I needed to start writing. I had to get my feet wet, to get experience while I was waiting for the cases to pour in. Who would listen to me? I thought back to the APRT conference and how most of the members had never heard of the Harrisons' book, which I thought was so valuable. With one phone call to the APRT *Journal of Regression Therapy,* I had a writing assignment: a review of *The Children That Time Forgot* for their next issue. The editor was encouraging, but since I had never had anything published, he couldn't promise that my article would be accepted. The editorial board would have to approve it first.

I labored over that short article for weeks, with Steve's help as my editor. I nervously sent it off and waited for the verdict of the board. When I got a postcard from the editor a few weeks later, I danced in the middle of the street in front of my mailbox. All it said was "Yes." I was going to be published!

Now I was on a roll, looking for more targets for my writing and more sources for cases. A friend had given me a copy of

Venture Inward, the magazine of the Edgar Cayce Foundation. Edgar Cayce, the great psychic healer, was also one of the earliest past life counselors; *Venture Inward* regularly features articles on reincarnation and past lives. I called the editor. By the end of our conversation, I had agreed to write an article about Chase's and Sarah's past life memories for an audience of about 50,000. Ready or not, I was diving in. Headfirst.

Tiiu's Liia

Everywhere I went, I tactfully steered the discussion to the subject of children's past life memories. I was getting skilled at slipping it into almost any conversation. Just by bringing up the subject everywhere and often, I found the cases were there right in my own back yard.

I first met Tiiu at tea at a friend's house. She looked like a good fairy with her white-blond hair, sparkling, swimming pool—blue eyes, and puckish grin. I liked her immediately. She was fun to listen to and enlivened the conversation with her sharp views and quick retorts. When I had the opportunity to mention children's past life memories, she didn't hesitate a second.

"Oh," she said, "Liia had a past life recollection just last year. I'm sure that's what it was."

Tiiu told what happened:

When Liia was two years old, we were riding in the car together; Liia was in her car seat in the back looking out the window. We went over a bridge with aluminum guardrails that spanned a steep ravine, when suddenly she said in a clear, excited voice, "Mommy, this is just like where I died!" She was not upset, just very matter-of-fact.

I said, "Liia, what are you talking about?"

"I was in my car, and it fell off the bridge into the water, and I died."

I was shocked by what she said and pulled off the road so

I wouldn't have an accident. I then asked her, "Where was Mama?"

"You weren't with me *that* time."

I was amazed at what Liia was telling me. I wanted to find out more, so I ventured, "Well, who was driving the car then?"

"I was big. I could reach the pedals," Liia answered.

I wondered, how did Liia know that you drove the car with pedals? She always sat in the back in her car seat and couldn't see what my feet were doing.

I continued, trying not to lead her, "Then what happened?"

"I didn't have my seat belt on, and I fell out of the car and into the water." Then she put her hand up on the back of her head and continued, "Mommy, I was lying on the rocks. I could feel the rocks on my head." She moved her head back and forth to show me how her head was positioned on the rocks. And she added, "And I saw the shiny bridge." She then pointed up and tilted her head back and said, "I saw the shiny bridge and the bubbles going up." Her eyes gazed upward.

This floored me. How could she know about the bubbles? At this point in her life, she had never been underwater because she didn't swim. She doesn't put her face in the water in the tub. She had never watched television at all—I know because I'm her mother, and I didn't let her watch until she was older. Yet she said, "I could see the bubbles going up, and the sun on the bridge through the water."

For the next year and a half, she talked about this often, always with the same detail, never with any variation. She was always very cheerful and matter-of-fact; remembering dying didn't seem to bother her at all. And the amazing thing about all this is that Liia has always been a fanatic about wearing seat belts. Even before she could talk, she would always make sure that her seat belt was fastened before she rode in the car. And as soon as she knew enough ·ds to make demands, she insisted that everyone else in ·r wore a seat belt too, every time we drove anywhere.

Like so many of the Harrison cases, Liia's memory was benevolent. It didn't cause any problems. On the contrary, it helped Liia's parents better understand her by providing a logical explanation for her curious obsession with auto safety.

"Man Hit Me with Truck"

A couple of months after my ad in *Mothering* came out, in January 1993, I received a call from Colleen Hocken, a soft-spoken mother of three from the Midwest. Over the phone Colleen nervously related the story of her three-year-old son, Blake, who, she felt, was remembering a traumatic past life death.

Colleen told me that six months previously she had seen psychiatrist Brian Weiss, the author of *Many Lives, Many Masters,* discussing past life therapy on *Oprah.* Colleen had never thought about reincarnation before, but she was fascinated by what Dr. Weiss had said about using past life therapy with his patients. He mentioned that children sometimes tell adults about their own past life experiences, but that most parents think their children are making up a fantasy story. As she listened to Dr. Weiss, Colleen mulled it over and thought, "Gee, my kids never say anything unusual."

The very next day Blake, who had just turned three, was standing at the front door, watching his older brother, Trevor, wait for the school bus. Colleen, who was in the other room, heard Blake yell out the front door, "Get out of the street, the bus is coming!"

Colleen rushed to the front door to make sure Trevor was all right. She found Blake standing at the door with his hand to his left ear saying, "My ear hurts."

"Why does your ear hurt?" Colleen asked.

"A truck hit me," Blake answered.

Colleen, assuming that a child in play school had hit him with a toy truck, asked, "Who hit you with a toy truck?"

"A man did."

"A man hit you with a toy truck?"

"No," he insisted, "a *big* truck."

"A big truck like the ones driving down the street?"

"Yah," affirmed Blake.

Colleen, who was trying to make sense of what Blake was telling her, asked, "Where were you when you were hit?"

"In the street."

At this point Colleen immediately thought back to what Dr. Weiss had said on *Oprah* the previous day. Later she explained her state of mind: "I didn't want to dismiss what Blake was saying; I was real curious at this point as to what he was trying to tell me. But I didn't want to put words into his mouth either, so I asked, 'And then what happened?' "

Colleen listened carefully as Blake continued his story. He explained to his astonished mother how the truck had really hit him. She questioned him, "Where did you get hurt?"

"All over. I went under the wheels." Blake made sweeping motions with his arms over his left side, demonstrating how the wheels of the truck had run over him. Colleen could see the pain on his face as he showed her how badly he was hurt.

"Then what happened?" ventured Colleen.

"Man put me in the truck and took me to a school." Colleen commented that any large building was a "school" to three-year-old Blake. She interpreted this to mean that he had been taken to a hospital.

"Where were Mom and Dad when this happened?"

"Gone bye-bye at the store."

Colleen's mind raced to find an explanation for what Blake was telling her. First she wondered if he was imagining all this. Then she reasoned that he could not be making this up—how could a three-year-old envision a truck's wheels running over his body, as he so clearly described it? Then she thought that perhaps Blake had seen something like this on TV, something that his older brother was watching while she was out of the room. She suggested to Blake, "This happened on TV, right?"

"No!" he exclaimed. At this point Colleen saw that Blake was getting irritated with her for not remembering his accident. "No," he insisted, "it happened in the street."

She then asked, "Did you die?"

"Yes," he responded in a perfectly normal tone.

Colleen explained to me how amazing it was to hear Blake describe the entire incident in such a matter-of-fact way, as if she should already have known all about it. At no point did he indicate that he was joking or making it up. If anything, he was irritated with her for asking such stupid questions!

Nothing more was said until a week later, when a big garbage truck passed the house. Unsolicited, Blake told Colleen, "That was like the truck that hit me." She decided not to ask Blake anything more about the incident, hoping that he would forget it.

"I Love You, Then I Hate You."

Shortly after Blake told Colleen the story about the truck, he went into a depression that became more and more severe over the next few months. Colleen didn't notice the change right away. She only gradually realized that he wasn't playing as he used to and that his usual cheery disposition and sense of humor had disappeared. In fact, there were many days when Blake just sat and stared blankly at the TV screen, or out the window. This was very much out of character for him. He had always been a happy child who instinctively "rolled with the punches." The neighbors had even nicknamed him Smiley because of his cheerful nature.

Colleen felt guilty about his dismal state. In addition to Blake she had a demanding one-year-old baby and six-year-old Trevor to care for. She thought that maybe Blake was play-acting to get more attention. Middle children sometimes get left out, she reasoned; perhaps Blake was beginning to feel that way. She was reluctant to ask family and friends for help in dealing with his depression, fearing they would blame her for not being a good mother. After all, she was feeling bad enough about it already.

But Colleen knew she couldn't ignore it either. There was something very puzzling about Blake's gradual personality change. Something was happening with him, something she could not understand.

She tried different ways to cheer him up and give him more attention. She played his favorite musical tapes, but after he got up and danced for a short time, he would just go back to the couch and resume staring vacantly into space. One day he was watching his favorite TV program, *Mister Rogers,* and there were many balloons on the show. Knowing how much Blake enjoyed balloons, Colleen encouraged, "Aren't balloons fun?" He just looked at her blankly and said, "No, balloons are bad." This really worried her: what was wrong with Blake? He was seriously troubled. She tried spending more time with him, reading to him, playing with puzzles. But his response now was "Go away."

Blake began having physical symptoms too. Every day he complained that an arm hurt, a leg hurt, and even an eye hurt—always on the left side of his body. "Would you like me to rub it for you?" Colleen offered, thinking that Blake would like the extra attention and cuddling. But he would say, "No, go away." She suggested that he draw pictures of how he felt. Perhaps, she reasoned, if he couldn't tell her directly what was troubling him, he could reveal the source of his problem nonverbally, through pictures. But he simply drew a flurry of lines and marks and told her, "These are my ouches."

Colleen responded with an attempted hug, saying, "Maybe I can help you. You know, Blake, I love you very much." And Blake announced emphatically, "I love you, then I hate you."

Later Colleen explained to me, "He seemed to love me and hate me at the same time, and he didn't know why." And neither did she.

She considered taking him to a therapist but doubted that a therapist could do any more with him than she had already done. Still, she couldn't stop blaming herself for his condition. She felt that she could not tell her husband how concerned she was, because he might blame her too.

Three months later, when the family went to London for Christmas, a terrifying incident gave Colleen a clue to the cause of Blake's mysterious change in personality.

She tells her story: "One day, while in London, which was very busy with Christmas shoppers, we were waiting on a center island in the middle of the street. The traffic cop blew her whistle for the pedestrians to stop. We were all crammed together like sardines on the sidewalk, unable to move. Blake was in an umbrella stroller, which was a real treat for him, since it was usually occupied by his younger brother. The stroller was at the edge of the curb. No one was moving. But just as a large truck came around the corner, Blake jumped out of his stroller and into the path of the oncoming truck. I cried out to Blake to get back, but he just stood there, as if he were frozen. I couldn't grab him because I was behind the stroller. Instantly my husband grabbed him and pulled him back to the curb. The truck driver slammed on his brakes, got out of his truck, and yelled at us for not watching our child. It was so terrifying for all of us.

"This started me wondering if Blake's depression could have anything to do with what he had told me a few months earlier about being hit by the truck. Could he be thinking, in some twisted way, that he *needed* to be hit by a truck again? This really scared me."

Two weeks after Colleen returned from England, she saw my ad in *Mothering* and immediately called me and told me Blake's story. I felt her distress and heard the fear in her voice as she posed her urgent question: "If this is a past life memory, does it mean that Blake has to repeat the experience again?"

She was terrified that Blake might try again to run under a moving truck. I too considered his behavior to be potentially dangerous. He needed immediate attention. I knew that Colleen was describing what Freud called repetition compulsion, the compulsive drive to repeat earlier traumatic experiences, regardless of the consequences. In Blake's case, the original trauma he felt compelled to repeat on that London street was not a present-childhood memory. It extended further back than that, to a past life.

I assured Colleen that if Blake were truly experiencing a past life memory, there were steps she could take to ensure his safety. But first I wanted to establish beyond any doubt that we were dealing with a past life memory, not a fantasy. I compared the signs in his case with the patterns I had seen in other cases. For starters I knew that Blake, who had just turned three when he first described being hit by a truck, was at the optimal age for expressing a past life memory.

He had been matter-of-fact when he told his mother that he had been hit by a truck. By the way he spoke, she knew that he was making what he believed were statements of fact; it was clear in *his* mind what had happened. And his story didn't change, despite Colleen's questioning and probing.

His vision of the accident was graphically accurate—from a convincing perspective *under* the truck. This first-person perspective is quite different from what he would have learned by watching toy trucks hitting toy persons or a fictionalized accident on television. How could a three-year-old have that perspective?

Blake's reported aches and pains on the left side of his body, where he claimed the truck had hit him, and his personality change were the most convincing indications to me that his memory was authentic, that it wasn't a fantasy or daydream.

I hesitated to recommend that Colleen take Blake to a traditional therapist, because I truly believed that her son's problems were rooted in a past life trauma. I imagined that most therapists, even if they took Colleen's claim seriously, would not know what to do with a past life memory. And neither Colleen nor I knew of any past life therapists in the Chicago area who worked with children.

We agreed that the best strategy would be for her to try to help Blake herself. I knew that nothing she did would hurt Blake. And if she couldn't help him, we would try something else. But before Colleen could help Blake, she needed to understand the basic principles of how past life memories can affect children in the present.

To illustrate to Colleen how emotions from the time of death carry over into the present lifetime, I used Sarah's regression as an example. I described how Sarah, who had mistakenly believed that her past life parents had not tried to save her from the fire, had brought anger toward those parents with her into her present life.

As I talked about Sarah, Colleen felt something inside her click with recognition. Could Blake still be angry with his past life parents for not watching him and protecting him from the truck in the street? When Blake told Colleen, "I love you, then I hate you," could he be confusing his feelings for his past and present parents? Intuitively Colleen recognized that he was.

I then explained to her that young children sometimes have difficulty distinguishing between past life events and the present. Sometimes events and feelings of the past are as vivid and real as anything that happened recently. Blake was confused and hurt by his memories of the accident and by his resentment toward his parents. He needed clarification that these painful events had happened in another life and that he was now safe.

I suggested some strategies that Colleen could try. First, I assured her that her love for Blake was the most powerful tool she had, more important than any words or techniques she could learn from me. I trusted her motherly intuition to find the right words and to convey feelings of love and safety to her son. I told her to talk to Blake when he was relaxed—just before bedtime or at bath time—when he would be quiet and receptive.

Then she needed to acknowledge that what he remembered was true and let him know that she understood what had happened to him—that she believed him. Finally he needed the assurance that he was now safe in a new body and that Colleen and her husband were different parents from those who had gone to the store and left him to be hit by the truck. This, I suspected, was the clarification between past and present that Blake needed.

"We Got Our Blake Back"

A week later I received another call from a very excited and happy Colleen. She told me what happened:

"I followed your advice. I tucked Blake into bed and gave him a back scratch and then asked him, 'Blake, were you hit by a truck?'

"He told me, 'Yah.'

"I then explained to him that he was hit by the truck in a different life, not this life. I told him he had a different body then and that he had a different mommy too. I thought that I'd get another blank look like he had been giving me for the past several months, and that he wouldn't understand what I was saying.

"But the look on Blake's face was worth a thousand words! His eyes lit up with surprise and he said, 'Really, that was a different body? I had a different mommy?' I answered yes to both questions and explained to him how much everybody in this life loves him. I then named all the people—his Nanna, Dad, his brothers, and all the other people he knows—who love him and care for him.

"It was like I had told him that Santa Claus was coming! He was happy for the first time in a long time. He smiled from ear to ear and lit up like a Christmas tree. The sparkle came back to his eyes. You could just feel this incredible weight lift off him."

Colleen continued, "I was amazed that he immediately understood; I really didn't expect my words to have such an impact on him. I thought that it was going to be a long process, that we would have to talk over and over again. But to my amazement, the next morning he was playing and laughing and running around. He's playing all the time now. He's back to using his wonderful sense of humor to the fullest. He's back to being full of happy mischief. I thought he wouldn't understand. But as you know, children are full of surprises!

"Also, Blake's physical symptoms have completely disappeared. My husband and I can't believe the difference in him. We feared that we had lost our Blake for good. But his depression was resolved overnight with those few words that I told him. We got our Blake back."

CHAPTER 9
Presto, Chicago

Colleen and I concluded our telephone conversation by marveling together at how simple, how instantaneous, how direct Blake's cure was. What a miracle to see that he could change back into his former, smiley self simply by understanding that his past life was over.

Colleen said, "More people need to know that children can have troubling past life memories and that their parents can help." She added, "I'm going to write to Oprah Winfrey to tell her about this."

I chuckled to myself, thinking that Oprah probably gets thousands of letters a week. But I humored Colleen: "Sure. If you want to write to Oprah, go ahead. But wait until I write the book first!"

My Plan to Conquer Fear

I was elated that those simple techniques had worked with Blake and that the Hockens "got their Blake back." What a joy to be able to make such a positive difference in people's lives just by sharing what I had learned about children's past life memories.

Blake's story was very important to me in another way too. This jewel of a case crowned my healing model. It was the culmination of all my questioning and searching. It confirmed my theory that children can be healed if their parents understand the principles of children's past life memories. And because it so dramatically illustrated these principles, it was a case I could use to show other parents what to do with their own children.

Now, with this validation I had the confidence to push ahead with my book. But I needed more cases. I renewed my ad in *Mothering.* Cases trickled in from that ad, and in response to my article in *Venture Inward,* and from my network. With Steve's help I wrote another, more comprehensive article for the APRT *Journal,* incorporating the new cases and, of course, the Blake case. I took another big leap: I enrolled as a graduate student in the counseling program at Villanova University. I wanted to expand my counseling skills and to see what the academics could teach me about doing rigorous research.

I dreaded the next part of my plan. I knew that I couldn't rely on articles alone to communicate what I was finding or to attract more cases. I had to go out and personally share my discoveries. I had to begin public speaking. There was only one problem. I had *never* done any public speaking in my life. And for a very good reason: speaking in front of any group, no matter how small, absolutely terrified me. I had recurring nightmares about it. For years I had sidestepped all situations that might require me to speak or perform in front of a group. Ever since I was young, even in school in the most innocuous classroom situations, when called upon to speak, I stepped into a white fog. My mind would go blank, my heart would beat wildly, and I'd break out in a sweat.

I felt as if I were blindfolded, waiting for the executioner's bullets, my terror was so great.

But now I was determined to overcome this demon fear. My vision was too compelling to let it get in the way. My friend Amy, who understood this dilemma, organized an audience of eight people for me to address in my own living room. She assured me that I could do it, and I agreed, thinking I could start small and build gradually to larger audiences. Much to my surprise, after the first terrifying ten minutes, I was able to relax and speak. My need to share the stories was stronger than my fear. I was so encouraged by this success, I told Amy I was ready for a bigger group next time—maybe twenty people.

Lightning Strikes Ice

But the progress I was making with the research, the writing, and the campaign to conquer my fear of public speaking would soon freeze to a halt. Nineteen ninety-three was a rough year for our family. The year before, Steve had been "downsized" out of his corporate job, and the consulting business he was running out of our home barely made enough money to sustain us. I knew I had to be realistic and devote more of my time to making money.

In the first week of 1994, matters got much worse. The Philadelphia area was paralyzed by a series of ice storms and severe cold that never let up. One night during the worst ice storm of all, we trembled in our beds as trees and limbs came crashing down around the house. It sounded like a battle zone outside. One giant limb just missed hitting the roof over Chase's bedroom. The next morning when we ventured outside, *everything,* even the delirious tangle of fallen trees and branches, was resplendent with an inch-thick coating of prismatic ice. The sun angling through the trees blinded us with a blaze of rainbows and diamonds. Surrounded by such surreal beauty, we forgot our problems for the day and reveled in this epiphany of light.

The extreme weather continued for weeks, one terrible ice storm after another. The roads were covered with black ice, and the road crews gave up when they ran out of salt. School was canceled for almost a month. Time stopped. Commerce ceased, and so did Steve's consulting income. With no money coming in, our fortunes were looking bleak.

Nothing was happening with my research either. I couldn't afford even a small advertising budget to solicit cases. My plan was as frozen as the water in the birdbath, and my lucky stars and auspicious planets seemed to have lost my forwarding address.

In mid-February, on a somber, cloudy day between ice storms, I took a walk around the neighborhood and had an honest talk with myself. I decided that I needed to get my graduate degree as quickly as possible so I could get a *real* job. I accepted this course as a dire necessity, although it pained me to abandon my dream of writing a book to share my discoveries. I conceded to the sullen sky that if I were meant to write the book on children's past life memories, I would need a miracle to make it happen. In the meantime I had to do what I could to keep my family from skidding into a ditch.

When I got back to the house, I poured myself a cup of tea and sat outside on the porch. I studied the steam from my cup as it rose in chaotic whorls and disappeared into the air, like my plans. When my cup was empty, I sat numbly staring into the cold. I was finally and painfully resigned to letting the book go indefinitely.

Blowing aside my doldrums, Steve burst out the door with the portable telephone in his hand. He looked pale. Shocked. "*Now* what's wrong?" I asked. My stomach sank into my boots.

He coolly punched a key on the telephone to replay the voice-mail message, stuck it up to my ear, and said, "This is the call you've been waiting for."

The voice on the telephone said: "*This is the Oprah Winfrey show in Chicago calling for Carol Bowman. Could you please call me back right away?*"

I cried. Steve cried. In a flash I grasped the full meaning of this call. I had gotten my miracle.

In a File Abiding

Suddenly energized by this bolt of good news, I took a deep breath and dialed Chicago. The woman who had called introduced herself as a producer for HARPO, Oprah's production company. She told me that she had been doing research for a program on children's phobias when Colleen Hocken's letter—the one she had sent to Oprah almost a year before—fell out of the file. It had been *misfiled* a year ago: it should have been filed under "past lives," not "phobias." She explained that for a long time they had wanted to do a show on children's past lives but couldn't find any material or experts on the subject. So when she read Colleen's letter, she called me immediately.

"Do you have any more information on your research that you can send me?" she asked. "I want to see if there's enough material to do a whole show on this topic." I assured her there was, and faxed her my latest, most comprehensive article, which I had written in the year while Colleen's letter was abiding in the wrong file.

Minutes later she called back. She hadn't even read the article all the way through—she just couldn't wait to tell me how excited she was by what she had read. She asked one question after another, and we talked for a long time. I surprised myself, not only by having answers for all of her questions, but also by how much I had to say. And I was flattered that this woman who had, as she said, "seen it all," was so excited to learn about my work. I told her that I was excited to finally have an audience—I had been barking alone in the wind long enough.

There was still a lot of work to be done, she explained, before she could get the go-ahead to do the show. She wanted Sarah and Chase and other mothers with their children to appear. She had many questions—and a few immediate requests. She wanted copies of Sarah's and Chase's birth certificates (they took nothing for granted) and copies of Chase's medical records from North Carolina to prove that he really had suffered from eczema. I was amazed at their thoroughness.

Two days later it was official: the show was approved. The whole family would fly to Chicago the next Tuesday for the taping on Wednesday. We would be Oprah's guests, stay in a fine hotel on Chicago's North Side, and be conveyed from place to place in a limousine. What a contrast to our stuck-in-the-snow lives of just a few days before!

——————————————

Mind Working Overtime

The headlong tempo accelerated. The producer and her staff at HARPO seemed to be working around the clock. Early in the morning till late at night, they called and faxed. Didn't they ever sleep? Each day as they shaped the show, we had more in-depth discussions of my research. It was becoming clear that they were relying on me for most of their information.

While Chicago worked overtime, so did we: shopping for new jeans for the kids and an outfit for me; fielding calls from amazed friends and astounded relatives. Haircuts all around. Kathleen, my hairdresser, when I told her the news, screamed, "Oh my God, you predicted it!"

Another little matter: nobody in our family had ever seen Oprah on TV. So Steve hooked up the antenna to our old television, and we watched the show every afternoon that week, trying to visualize what it would be like when it was our turn on that stage. Watching Oprah at work, I saw how incisive her questions were and how she kept the ideas moving at a fast pace. I realized that when it was my turn, I wouldn't have the leisure to sit back and wait for Oprah to ask the right questions. I had to be thoroughly prepared to push the ideas I wanted viewers to remember. I knew that if I wasn't confident and clear, my ideas would get garbled in the fray. Over the last few years, I had pondered constantly the meaning of my growing file of cases. But I had never forced myself to collate and order my ideas because, I thought, I would have months to deliberate these questions as I wrote my book. Now, I had to process all my material in one week. My mind was working overtime every day, every moment, until the minute I walked onto the set to begin the show. Even while I tried to sleep, my mind buzzed with ideas. Could my brain take a week of this?

During one of my conversations with Chicago, I asked how many people would see our show. The producer said about twenty million, all over the world. Twenty *million*?! I maintained composure on the phone—but inside I screamed.

I hadn't let on to the producer that I suffered from serious stage fright. She had no way of detecting it because I was relaxed and confident talking one-on-one over the phone. But what would happen when I faced a studio audience of more than eight and cameras with the eyes of twenty million? Would I seize up when I walked onto the set? Would I faint or get sick? I could picture them picking me up off the floor while everybody watched. It could happen.

Up to this point, by keeping focused on the material, I had avoided thinking about my fear. But the taping was only a few days away. There was no going back now; too many people were depending on me.

During this phone call I realized for the first time that the conflict between my personal demon and my life's work had taken on mythic proportions. This was bigger than just me now. I believe that the unseen forces that govern my life had opened all these doors for me; it wasn't by coincidence or luck that I had this opportunity. But I couldn't complete the mission I was given until I conquered the terrible dagger-eyed demon blocking the door. If I failed, I would never get another chance, and I would be worse off than before. This was *do or die.* I prayed for help, for strength, for victory.

Names and Dates

The format for the show was almost set. Chase, Sarah, and I would begin on stage with Oprah, then other mothers and children would join us as the show progressed. Tiiu Lutter and Colleen Hocken would be there, and Mary Fleming, another lovely mother who had contacted me through *Mothering,* would be there too with her three children. This was the best possible setup—mothers and children telling their own stories to the camera. There wouldn't be any tricks, I was assured; no traps to make us look foolish. There might be other mothers and children I didn't know: the producers were working to find more children with past life memories. And there would be a psychologist, a woman, with an opposing view to balance out the show. That was fine with me, I told them, as long as the psychologist didn't intimidate or challenge the children directly.

The producers in Chicago were fascinated with the idea of verifying Chase's Civil War memories on the show. They hired a Civil War historian and a private investigator to check out the facts of Chase's memory. I was delighted to hear this. I had always been curious to see if Chase's memory could be traced to a real person, yet I had never had the resources to do it properly. But since they had only a few details from Chase's story to work with, and no names, I wasn't sure how far they would get.

Then the producer had an idea: would I regress Chase and Sarah again to see if they could remember names and dates from their lifetimes? The session could be taped and shown during the show. That might work, I agreed. But I suggested it would be more credible to have someone other than their mother do it. I offered the name of a psychiatrist I knew who I thought could do the regressions. It was arranged.

The next day a film crew came and filled our home with microphone booms, lights, a big video camera, monitors, and cables running everywhere. The psychiatrist arrived bearing a fax he had received from Chicago that directed him to probe for names, dates, locations—anything that might help verify the memories. Wasting no time, he regressed Chase first, using a hypnotic induction. He instructed him to go back to the Civil War lifetime he had remembered before.

Chase went into a light trance quickly. But after a few minutes, I regretted not having done the regression myself. The doctor, who had taken time off from his busy practice, was rushing Chase through the regression, with the sole objective of digging up facts. Since the doctor had his own agenda, he was not completely tuning in to Chase or following his lead. I could tell Chase was really back in his Civil War lifetime again, but every time he appeared to sink more deeply into the images and feelings, the doctor would interrupt and ask, "What's your name? Do you remember your name? What year is it?" and Chase would lose his concentration. Chase strained and got a name—Henry Johnson. But he wasn't sure about it.

When Sarah was regressed, she experienced the same frustration. After the doctor left, both Sarah and Chase confirmed that each time he had asked them for factual information, it had interrupted the flow of their memories. They both admitted that they might have been making up the names just to satisfy the doctor's prodding. They were worried about this. I assured them that it wasn't important.

Sarah added: "That's not what regression is really about anyway. It's about what you experience and feel, and how the feelings follow you into your present life. That's what makes it real—not names and dates." I heartily agreed. As it turned out, much to our relief, HARPO decided not to use the tape on the show.

To Chicago, Pronto!

We were scheduled to fly to Chicago on Tuesday, but on Monday afternoon HARPO called with a change of plan. They had arranged for the kids to meet with a sketch artist Tuesday morning. Could we fly to Chicago—right now? The next flight was leaving in three hours.

I sped to school and picked up Chase; Steve got Sarah. I threw clothes into suitcases and everybody into the car. Blowing down Interstate 95 to the airport with just enough time to catch the plane, we ran over a piece of debris on the highway. A minute later Steve reported that we might have a flat tire. On the exit ramp to the airport, we could all feel the tire beginning to rumble. Would we make it? Steve ran a red light to keep going. We rolled up to the terminal door just as the tire started to flop like clown shoes. I grabbed the kids and luggage. Steve negotiated with a sky cap for a can of compressed air (he wouldn't tell me how much he had to pay), pumped up the tire, and took off down the tunnel to the parking garage. He made it to the gate in the nick of time, just as they were closing the doors. We rushed onto the plane, collapsed into our seats, and tried not to think how close we had come to being stranded on the gritty interstate.

Chase and I watched out the window as the plane followed the winter sunset west. The clouds above us were still tipped with pink and orange, while the land below was already flooded with black night. The twinkling grids of midwestern cities spread flat beneath our plane. Chase wanted to know where all the electricity came from. I could only think of all those televisions glowing below and wonder how many of the people we were flying over would be watching my family on *Oprah* in a few weeks. The thought made my knees quiver. I took a deep breath—and picked up a mindless magazine to zero out my thoughts.

When we arrived at the gate, the fun began. In the limousine Chase pushed every button in sight, controlling the stereo, the TV, the windows; Sarah helped herself to a soda from the bar. The hotel had more gadgets—Sarah couldn't get over the telephone in the bathroom; Chase was fascinated by the electronic exercise machines in the fitness room. Since Oprah's guests always stayed in this hotel, the staff was curious to know what *our* topic was. Answering their questions gave me a chance to practice explaining my ideas in concise sound bites.

Drawn from Memory

All the next morning we were sequestered in the conference room at HARPO with Sally, the artist, and a mound of catered food. Sally's job was to make sketches of Chase's and Sarah's past lives to be flashed on the screen when they told their stories on the show. Sally, a mother herself, knew how to make Chase and Sarah feel comfortable. They opened up to her. She began by asking for a detailed description of what they had looked like in the past. As they talked, she sketched, then showed them what she had drawn to get their feedback, then drew some more. With each iteration, Sarah and Chase focused more deeply on their internal images, entering a light trance. They were actually regressed back to those lifetimes. With eyes open they were seeing the scenes more clearly than ever, feeding more and more details to Sally's pencil, including some I had never heard before. She literally drew the memories out of them.

We finished with Sally by early afternoon, and the limo took us back to the hotel. We were free until the taping the next morning. "Relax," the producer said, "and rest up for the show." Relax? I wished! Sarah was getting a sore throat and losing her voice. A blizzard was forecast to hit Chicago that night—would Tiiu make it in from Philadelphia, and would the others, especially Colleen, who were driving from out of town, get stuck somewhere? And what curve balls would the psychologist be throwing me tomorrow?

I decided that the most constructive thing I could do would be to try to get some sleep and not think. And not worry. So Sarah and I went to bed, while Steve and Chase ventured out into the howling windy streets in search of a virtual reality machine that Chase was dying to try. I curled up under the covers in a fetal position and battled the reality of my fear. I busied my mind by rehearsing the points I wanted to make, and by imagining dialogues between me and Oprah: "Yes, Oprah, it's the healing power of these memories that is most important." "No, Oprah, the memories don't hurt the children in any way." Still, I felt as if I were going to jump out of my skin.

A call from Colleen brought me back. She was calling from within the hotel; HARPO had brought her downtown early to beat the blizzard. We met for the first time at dinner that night and she was as sweet and genuine in person as she had been on the phone. She was really nervous too. "Remember," we told each other, "we're doing it for the kids." That calmed us down a little.

Snowy Reception

The next morning we looked out the hotel window and saw that while we had slept, the streets below had been magically transformed. Yesterday's noisy Chicago was now muffled and rounded by deep mounds of snow. Heavy snowflakes floated in the spaces between the office towers. But was the show still on? Had Tiiu arrived?

When we got to the studio, the green room was filled with jittery parents and pale, lost-looking kids. I met Mary Fleming and her three children. Who were all these other people that I didn't know? What surprises would I face in front of the camera? But there's Tiiu! She told me in a torrent of her odyssey through snowy airports that finally delivered her to the hotel at four in the morning and she only got two hours of sleep but don't worry she's fine she's had plenty of coffee to keep her going. There was a family with two girls about Sarah's age; the girls had luxuriant hair that they repeatedly brushed back with gloved hands. This made Sarah suddenly anxious.

We all took turns getting made up and blasted with hair spray. I bumped around the room, trying to remember everything I knew about staying calm: deep breathing, visualizing a successful performance, repeating to myself that in just a couple of hours the taping would be over. It wasn't working, though.

Then, minutes before we were to walk on stage, Sarah panicked and refused to go on. She realized that what she was about to say in front of the TV cameras was too personal for all of her friends to see. My nerves were stretched to a frazzle already; I couldn't reason with her. I imposed parental authority and insisted that she go on, that it was too late to back out. That only made it worse. A kindly assistant producer took her out of the room to talk to her.

It was time. Everyone else was ushered into the studio to be seated in the audience; Chase and I were told to wait backstage. Once the audience was seated (Steve reported later), a peppy, well-dressed woman came out to warm up the audience. With a rhetorical flourish she revealed that the topic for today's taping was "Children Who Remember Past Lives." She asked for a show of hands from people who believed in past lives, and more than half of the people raised their hands. She encouraged people to walk up to the microphone to speak. Some ladies wearing hats complained that reincarnation wasn't sanctioned in the Bible; a gentleman with a beard countered that reincarnation had been deleted from the Bible centuries ago by the Church.

Most interesting, a lady in a halter top and mustard-colored jacket spoke up to tell of a past life memory she had when she was a child. She said it was so vivid, she *never* forgot it. When she was a little girl, she heard a single airplane flying high overhead, but had a vision of the sky filled with squadrons of planes coming to attack. She ran to her grandfather, screaming, "Run to the cellar, the bombers are coming!" Hmmm. . . . If one person in this group of about a hundred had a memory, how many of the millions of viewers would be triggered to remember too?

Meanwhile Chase and I waited backstage. I paced. Chase helped himself to another Coke. I was white with fear. And Sarah was still missing, which didn't help one bit! At the last minute she strolled in. Somehow the assistant producer had charmed her into going on stage and telling her story. What a pro.

The time had come. We were ushered down the wide hall to the open door of the studio.

A Recapitulation of Grace

The moment I was led through the door and first saw the studio audience, my knees turned to jelly and my head started to spin. I feared I might lose control and faint. My body pumped adrenaline, screaming "Run! Go hide!" But my rational brain, still functioning somewhere, told me not to run and worked to remind me of the reasons why I had to carry on. I must, my brain argued, summon the steel to continue walking toward the stage. Again I had that feeling that I was going to jump out of my skin.

From this vantage point, slightly outside of myself and outside of time, I suddenly saw a vision of the nineteenth-century pianist I had remembered being. I saw him, full of grace and command, on a stage performing for an enraptured audience. He and the audience were one. I could hear the round tones of the piano; I could see his arms and body moving effortlessly with the music; I could feel his joy and confidence. As this vision absorbed me, a gust of energy threaded through the top of my head and down my spine to the bottoms of my feet, grounding me to the concrete reality of the moment. The energy braced my knees and snapped me back into my body. Then, as suddenly as the image had appeared, it vanished, leaving in its wake a calm strength that diffused throughout my body and flushed my fear. The words came to me: "I know I can do this. *I've done it before.*"

Suddenly I was keenly aware of everything around me. My mind was sharp. My legs stopped shaking, and my breathing was calm. I felt centered and ready for anything. I knew what I had to do. I stepped onto the stage and sat down.

Oprah walked in, filling the air with her awesome voltage, which sparked and arced, lacing through everyone in the room. The audience instantly came under her spell and exploded with adoring applause and cheers. She smiled and waved, then came directly to the stage and sat down across from Chase and me. She chatted and joked to put us at ease. Technicians adjusted our mikes, and big cameras rolled into position on the floor.

Sitting knee to knee with Oprah, I could feel her high spirits and expansive energy. She seemed to be genuinely happy to see us and eager to hear what we had to say.

On the Air with Flying Ideas

Oprah began with Chase. She encouraged him to tell his story and to trace on Sally's drawing his movements around the battlefield. He surprised me with how clearly he spoke and how well he handled himself. He was relaxed and jamming with Oprah just as though it were no big deal. Then Oprah turned to the historian and asked his opinion on the authenticity of Chase's memory.

(This I was waiting to hear.) He admitted that he was skeptical about past lives, but he confirmed that Chase had accurately described and drawn a Civil War mortar, and he conceded that "Everything he [Chase] says is consistent with things that could have happened."

Sarah joined us on stage for the next segment and told her story, accompanied by Sally's drawings of her running through the burning house. As Sarah spoke, I realized that Oprah had switched away from Chase before I had gotten a chance to mention that his past life memory had healed him. I waited for the right moment, then jumped in and made my point.

Oprah asked each of my kids in turn what it was like to die. With authority and confidence they both answered that death is quick and painless and, as Chase put it, "the next thing you know, you're floating above." Sarah added, "I'm not afraid of death, if that's what it's like."

The show was beautifully orchestrated, with one story flowing into another. One at a time, sweet and sincere Colleen, wired and sparkling Tiiu, and Mary with her three doe-eyed artist children, joined our lineup and told their stories with heart and conviction. No one fainted, no one faltered. Everyone did a great job.

Oprah never let the energy flag. She pounced on any opportunity to bring out a new idea. I had to think fast to keep up with her, to keep track of what had been said and what needed to be added or clarified. I was in a game of mental Ping-Pong, constantly alert and waiting for my chance to hit a flying idea and make a point. I worked hard to shift the emphasis from simple wonder that children can have past life memories at all, to the progressive idea that this is a psychological phenomenon with the potential to heal.

I was relieved to see that the other children—the cases that the producers had found on their own—complemented my cases and reinforced the points I was making. The first girl, Erin, had a terrifying phobia of natural disasters—especially fires and floods. The tape was shown of her regression by a therapist a few days before. She remembered drowning in a flood: "I see people drowning and flames going into the air. The water is rising, and I can't swim. . . . I'm trying to get as high as I can away from the water." She described standing on a table until the water rose over her head. Then she "just died."

Another girl, Shannon (one of the girls with the luxuriant hair) was convinced she was the reincarnation of her own grandfather. When younger, she had told her parents details of her grandfather's life that she couldn't have known. Then in a regression she saw herself as her grandfather, and she saw him fatally shot through the neck by two men. Interestingly, she had a birth deformity—a severely protruding muscle in her neck that had required surgery—in precisely the spot where her grandfather had been shot. I was excited: here was a Stevenson-type birthmark case standing right in front of me and the cameras.

The sophisticated art produced by Mary Fleming's young children got a big response from Oprah. She was impressed! She said, "If I could draw like that, I wouldn't be doing this talk show, I'll tell you that right now."

While the cameras were pointed at somebody in the audience, Chase leaned over and whispered to me, "I have to go to the bathroom." I gave him my sternest mother look and hissed, "Hold it!"

Clinging to the Old Paradigm of Psychology

After the mothers and kids told their stories, the psychotherapist, Isabelle, was brought on to give the obligatory "opposing view." I waited to see what she would say. Had she listened to us? Had she read my articles? Even if she didn't agree with us, would she at least be open to the wonder of these children's experiences? I was hoping that we could have an intelligent debate about the meaning of the memories.

Or would this psychologist simply not believe any of it? In spite of our evidence, would she explain these memories away with a psychological catchall concept such as fantasy, wish fulfillment, or projection? I've heard other critics do this all too often.

They're stuck on their belief that "we only live once" and close their minds to any other conclusion the evidence might be pointing to. Instead of building a theory to fit the evidence (as scientists are supposed to do), they work backward to squeeze the evidence into existing psychological categories from the old paradigm.

With Isabelle's first remark I knew her mind was made up before she came. She admitted: "I don't believe that there is another life, that we die and come back, no." Case closed. This wasn't going to be a discussion of the evidence. It was going to be a defense of her beliefs and psychological training.

She hadn't been listening. She made no effort to respond to all of the amazing stories that had preceded her on that stage. Instead, she began spouting jargon to give Oprah a rational explanation for past life memories. One after another she offered that they were "metaphors," "manifestations of conflict," "expressions of repressed spiritual quests," and "cries to be acknowledged as persons," or they come from "in utero experience." She intoned the word *unconscious* several times, as if that settled the matter.

I knew it would be worthless for me to argue with a person whose mind was made up. But I wasn't quite sure how to approach her. The others jumped in. Oprah led the charge and nicely challenged the psychologist each step of the way. When Isabelle suggested that past life memories were an expression of a spiritual quest, Oprah asked how this explained all that two-year-old Liia had remembered about dying after crashing off a bridge. Tiiu, who was getting visibly impatient, burst in to remind everyone of the evidence: "She had a multisensory recollection—five senses—of something that could not have possibly been mimicked in her experience at any time." Tiiu gave Isabelle a look that said, "Cut the bullshit."

Isabelle responded by pointing out that Liia had described an underwater experience. "Water or the ocean is a symbol of the unconscious. . . . These children have very powerful unconscious drives. And that's what they're responding to."

Without missing a beat, Tiiu exploded: "She could have Jungian symbolism but no past life?"

Isabelle's jaw dropped, and she fumbled for a second. She

seemed surprised to hear such an astute remark, especially one couched in her own psychological jargon, coming from this pretty blond mother. Then she responded, not with an answer, but by repeating her belief that past lives are impossible.

To this, Oprah said, "I certainly hope you're wrong. We need another chance someplace else."

A minute later Oprah asked a question of her own: "Isabelle—I'm trying to get you to come over to our side—what do you say when you see these children who, quote, 'seem to have been here before'? There's a sort of light in their eyes. And people look into that child, and they say, 'That child's an old soul.' What do you think that is?"

And Isabelle answered, "Well, I think we have to consider what happens with the *unconscious*."

Oprah pleaded, "But *what* is the unconscious? What is that?" Yay, Oprah! She was not going to let these kids' amazing experiences be explained away in a single word.

Sarah, who was listening closely the whole time, looked at me and rolled her eyes at the psychologist's twaddle. Then she got Oprah's attention and addressed Isabelle: "I say it doesn't matter what it is. Maybe it's not a religious—whatever you said that was. What matters is that I was afraid of fires and I'm not anymore. And Chase had problems with his wrist and he had a fear, and he's over that. What matters is that it helped me." Touché, Sarah! I was so proud of her. Isabelle had ignored the healing altogether, and Sarah brought the idea back in.

Then a man in the audience stood up to challenge Isabelle. He asked her, referring to the masterful art of little Michael Fleming: "How do you explain the five-year-old child's exceptional artwork, which is tangible? He's not fantasizing that he's a great artist. He has something on paper that demonstrates his ability, that he had no previous training in whatsoever. Now how would you explain that?"

Isabelle's answer was predictable. She used another high-minded word that gave it a name but explained nothing: "I would look at that as great *talent*."

Oprah caught her: "That came from *where*?"

Isabelle had the answer—more imperial words: *"Creative genius."*

Oprah wouldn't let up: "But where does that come from?" Isabelle changed the subject.

Before the final wrap-up, a mother in the audience gave a beautiful explanation of why reincarnation is logically consistent with the laws of nature. She said, "When you realize that energy is neither created nor destroyed, and our soul is energy, and the life force is energy, you have to expect reincarnation. Because no other energy is destroyed, why wouldn't we, too, continue to change and transform?"

To which Oprah added, looking straight into the camera: "We'll be right back."

March 1, 1994

On the first day of March, across the great water in Ireland, Cathy Sky, my friend from Asheville, was relaxing with a friend. Suddenly, out of the corner of her eye, she saw a familiar face on the telly across the room. Cathy jumped up and shouted, "That's Carol Bowman! That's my friend. Carol's on *Oprah*!"

Cathy called me the next day. "You made it, girl! Sitting in your kitchen a few years ago, who would have believed you'd end up on *Oprah* with your ideas!"

"Yeah," I said. "But this isn't the end. It's just the beginning."

PART TWO

A Practical Guide to Children's Past Life Memories

CHAPTER 10

The Four Signs

When I talk to people about children's past life memories, invariably the first question they ask is: "How can you distinguish past life stories from fantasies?"

At first I could answer by saying only, "Well, the parent just *knows.*" Not a very satisfactory answer, I admit. But as I studied the cases that came in, I began to see and hear the same comments over and over, almost word for word. These comments were becoming very familiar. I found I could rely on them as a test of past life memories. When parents described their experiences to me for the first time, I found myself going down a mental checklist to help me decide if the memories they were describing were real or fantasy. This checklist evolved into the Four Signs.

(When I say "parents," I don't mean to exclude other adults. These signs can be just as useful to grandparents, aunts and uncles, day care providers, teachers—anyone who spends a lot of time with children.)

The more I spoke to parents and compared cases, the more I understood why these signs work. Past life memories sound, look, act, and feel distinctly different from fantasies because they issue from a different source. Fantasies are the mind at play. Past life memories, on the other hand, are full-bodied images of real events. The difference can be discerned by any sensitive observer who understands the signs.

I discovered more than a dozen signs of past life memory, especially if I tallied all the nuances that parents notice as they struggle to judge for themselves if their child is really remembering a past life. But to keep it simple—to make it easier to remember how to recognize a past life memory—I've bundled and organized all these secondary signs and nuances into four primary signs.

The four signs of children's past life memory are:

1. Matter-of-fact tone

2. Consistency over time

3. Knowledge beyond experience

4. Corresponding behavior and traits

Not all past life memories show all four signs. The memories come in an infinite variety, and they emerge in different ways and to different degrees for different children. But as far as I've seen, the signs always appear in combination: some cases have as few as two, some have all four. I have yet to see a case with only one sign. Whatever the combination, no matter how rich or sparse the case, the signs always outline a coherent past life story. The best way to understand how they work together is to practice looking for them in the cases in this book. Even in cases where I highlight only one sign, others are usually visible in the story as well.

These four signs are for parents to use with their own children. They point to subtle clues that only a person who knows the child well would be sensitive to. They depend on being able to spot changes of countenance and tone of voice that a stranger would miss; on an awareness of what a young child has or hasn't been exposed to; and on having watched the child over a period of time, detecting small changes, remarkable consistencies, or unusual behaviors for that child.

The four signs have nothing to do with the scientific proof of past life memories or reincarnation. They are tools for private assurance and recognition, not public proof. When the memories emerge, the questions you ask, the clues you listen for, should have nothing to do with proving the case to outsiders who don't know your child—even to neighbors or skeptical relatives. In fact, worrying about proof can bend your perception and block the flow of the memory in the child. *Proof is not the point.* Healing and growth and understanding are the point.

Do not confuse the four signs with the methods of researchers like Dr. Stevenson. This is important. His methods are designed to verify the memories of children who are strangers to him. And his cases are not typical: they are rare cases of extreme past life memory. The four signs are appropriate for the more common cases, those where the child has only fragments and traces of memory.

Of course, not all unusual statements or stories that children blurt out are past life memories. Children often say things that make their parents wonder, "Where did he get that?" I caution you not to overreact to every intriguing remark your child makes. You *may* be witnessing a past life memory. But the odds are you are not. Children's minds are so wonderfully loose and alive, they come out with startling and fresh statements all the time. Fantasy and imagination are the natural occupations of young minds, and most of the time this torrent of wonder has nothing to do with past lives. Children often make believe they are living in the past, imitating storybooks, TV, or movies.

But sometimes the veil does lift, and a child does speak of a genuine past life. If you know the signs, you can catch this magic moment when it happens.

This is totally unfamiliar territory for most people. When a child suddenly starts talking about a past life, most parents are unnerved and confused. They feel their hearts pulling them one way, their minds the other. Past lives just don't fit into their worldview, and their rational mind would rather believe that the strange behavior has some logical explanation, somehow. At the same time their hearts feel the sincerity of the child, their bodies tingle with profound energy, and their intuition signals that something special and timeless is happening. This confusion is normal. I offer these four signs as compass points to orient heart and head both—to help you find your bearings within the different reality that rushes in and spins you around when your little one solemnly says, "I remember when I died."

Sign 1: Matter-of-Fact Tone

Most past life memories are first communicated in statements of fact from the child. Quite spontaneously, while riding in a car or playing on the kitchen floor, a young child will say very matter-of-factly, "This is just like where I died," or, "My *other* mother used to make that." Kids babble all the time, so remarks such as these would slip past a busy parent unnoticed as simply more patter—*except* for the sudden change in the child's tone of voice. This switch to a matter-of-fact tone imparts a significance to the child's words that suddenly commands attention.

When I questioned parents as to how their children described their past life experiences, they would always report that children sounded different. I would hear comments like "He was very *matter-of-fact* about the whole thing" or "She was direct and *matter-of-fact*." I heard this phrase so often, it was uncanny.

Usually, when children are telling a made-up story, there is a singsong, lilting, drifting quality to the voice. The voice modulates, rising and falling, as the fantasy story is conceived and developed. The language and tone sail along, buffeted by the shifting breeze of imagination. You can almost sing along to a fantasy.

This is not at all the case with past life memories. One mother, Charlotte Swenson, says:

When four-year-old Jerry speaks of dying along with all of his friends in 1945, his voice suddenly changes. He speaks in a grief-stricken, very serious way. You can just feel the change. He becomes very intense, he sounds older. This tone really gets my attention. When he tells my friends these things too, they all notice that he doesn't sound like a four-year-old anymore.

Ed Durbin's three-year-old son spontaneously began talking of a Civil War memory when he saw an image of Abe Lincoln on TV. Ed tried to explain this mysterious difference in tone:

It was suddenly like talking to a grown-up. The way he spoke was like a man relating his own experience. It wasn't that his voice deepened; it was the *way* he said it. He was giving me a factual account of his experience as a soldier. He was aware that he was talking to me, factually recounting something he had seen. Yet the feeling I had was more like talking to someone else—someone older than my three-year-old son.

The *mood* can be serious, happy, concerned, excited, or sad; but the tone and the intent are always direct and matter-of-fact. You can hear that the child is not playing games or joking. Tiiu described Liia's tone of voice not as serious but as excited: "Suddenly she said in a clear, excited voice, 'Mommy, this is just like where I died!' She was not upset, not unhappy, just very matter-of-fact."

Lisa, a child psychologist and mother, is well practiced in this art of detection since her daughter, Courtney, has had many past life recollections. She explains that this directness of communication is one way she distinguishes these memories from fantasy.

In my experience as a counselor and as a mother, when children tell fanciful tales, they are told to get a reaction from me. They are told as a story: they want me to laugh, challenge them, tell them how silly they are, or whatever it is they're up to. Fantasy stories are told to me as the *audience*. It is interactive communication.

But Courtney is not interactive when she tells me of her past life memories. She is making statements. If you said nothing, that would be fine with her. She is making statements of fact. It's like if I said to you, "The sky is blue," I would not expect you to argue with me on this because I know and you know with certainty that the sky is blue. That is not interactive communication. Courtney is not saying these past life things to me waiting for a response or for me to prod her. And if I ask her questions like "What color is the dress?" or "What time of the year is it?" she doesn't usually answer these questions. She's not asking questions, and she doesn't expect *me* to.

Children are matter-of-fact when speaking of their memories, because they are reporting what they remember, just as they would report something that happened last week or last month. The memories of the incidents they relate are just as real and vivid to them as memories of their last birthday party, or a vacation at the beach last summer.

Because children are making statements of fact and not fantasizing, they are puzzled if we don't immediately grasp what they are saying. If we question them, asking them to repeat their remarks so we can make some sense out of them, they may become indignant. They may put us off by saying, "I already told you." Some children simply don't understand that *we* don't remember their past lives; they assume that if it's so clear in their minds, we must remember it too. After all, parents know everything, right? When we meet them with a blank, uncomprehending look, they may think that we're joking with them or playing a game when they're trying to be serious. They may give us an irritated and exasperated look that says, "You know what I'm talking about—don't play dumb!" When we insist that we don't remember, they may get confused.

If you follow the dialogue in Blake's story, you can see this progression. Blake showed his irritation with Colleen when she probed to understand his statement that he was hit by a truck.

He explained to her many times that he had been hit by a truck and that it wasn't something that happened on TV. He seemed truly upset and frustrated when Colleen didn't understand him. It was clear in *his* mind.

One nuance of the sign, Matter-of-Fact Tone, is when a child achieves a sudden breakthrough in language. While expressing a past life memory, the child may, for the first time, speak in full sentences or use words outside his vocabulary. A child who already speaks in full sentences may suddenly speak with a more mature syntax and with more confidence and fluency than ever before. Some children begin speaking of a past life when very young, sometimes as soon as they can talk. These babies stretch themselves to be understood and persist until they succeed. Their need to communicate their previous experiences overpowers their frustration with the language. This is why in many cases children doubly surprise their parents with a language breakthrough while simultaneously making their first statements about a past life.

As Pat Carroll, the mother of two-year-old Billy, puts it:

He was using words that were too big for a such little kid. I remember thinking that he was talking like he was an adult or an older kid. He used full sentences, which was very unusual for him. He didn't pause, he didn't search for words, and he didn't struggle to describe things, like he usually does. He was very fluent. The words just came out.

Phyllis Elkins describes how her two-year-old daughter's diction changed when she spoke of her memory:

In that moment Natalie was more articulate than she's ever been. Her words were deliberate and crystal clear. All of her answers were immediate, without hesitation. Her tone was older, more mature, serious, and unbelievably matter-of-fact.

Not only do children sound different when they speak of memories, they *look* different. Their expression changes; sometimes an unusual peace or calm appears on the child's face. They glow. Pat Carroll noticed this change when Billy began speaking of his memory:

> It was really strange. It's hard to explain. His face was the same, but he looked so deep and calm. His shoulders dropped—I can't really describe it, but suddenly he looked much older than his age. I knew something had happened to him, but I didn't know what. And each time he talks about his memories, that is what happens.

Other mothers say that the difference is easy to spot. They say that their children look as though they are in a trance, losing touch with their surroundings as they focus inward. They may stare off into space while speaking of their memories and appear "wide-eyed," or their eyes may become "glazed over," as they report seeing and sensing something outside their ordinary range of perception. One mother says her daughter "stays very serious in her face" and maintains eye contact the whole time while speaking of a memory.

When the remembering is over, you'll know it. The eyes and face will snap back to a normal little-boy or little-girl countenance. And the transition is quick: they will immediately change the subject, resume playing, or dance out of the room. The bounce and bubble return to their little bodies. They are back to their two- or three-year-old selves and act as if nothing unusual has happened. Whatever that state was, it disappears as quickly as it appeared. You can't bring it back if you try.

Another telling sign of past life memory is what I call the *goose bumps effect*. Odd as it may sound, almost all parents I have talked to describe the same chills, goose bumps, or energized feeling that runs through their own bodies—sometimes all three at the same time—when their child speaks of a past life. Practically everyone describes these feelings in the same way.

Charlotte Swenson sums it up well:

> When kids are pretending something, you know it's a story. But this *feels* different. I feel my spine tingling. I get chills.

You can feel the energy of the memory—my whole body tingles, like pins and needles, but it doesn't hurt; your whole body is energized. This *doesn't* happen when he tells me a fantasy story. Even though this past life incident didn't last long, maybe a few minutes, my son and I were both feeling it. Then it was gone.

I have felt this sensation too. When my children first spoke of their memories, the hair on my arms stood on end, a charge of electricity ran along my shoulders and down my back, and a surge of energy rushed through the top of my head. I interpreted these feelings as my body's recognition of the truth of the memory.

What is this feeling? It is a scientific fact that our bodies are surrounded by energy fields. I suspect that when a child is remembering a past life and enters a different state of consciousness, something shifts within the energy field around the child's body. Perhaps when we tune in to what the child is saying, we are doing more than just listening—we are reacting to this change in energy. We can actually feel the change as it registers in our own energy fields as well as in our brains.

Whatever the explanation for this feeling, it can be quite unnerving. Some parents are shocked both by what the child is saying and by their own bodily reaction. They feel disoriented, unbalanced, as if they were in free fall, slipping through a crack in reality. Don't worry. This is normal. It cannot hurt you or your child.

Sign 2: Consistency over Time

The second sign of past life memory is consistency. Children will retell a past life experience repeatedly over a period of days, weeks, months, or years without making significant changes in the story or details.

This consistency over time marks a major difference between past life memory and fantasy. With fantasy, a child will fabricate a story—even an elaborate story—but rarely can he repeat it with the same details the next week, the next day, or even the next minute. Fantasies spout from the imagination of the child; they are volatile and are soon embellished, changed, or forgotten altogether. But past life memories are a mental movie of real and personally significant events that actually happened. They are stable, like memories of crucial events from this life. Each time the story is told, the child looks inward and describes the same coherent images residing in his mind.

The story and details remain constant, but the child may *add* details or episodes as their use of language improves or as things they see and hear in the outside world remind them of the past. These additional details serve to flesh out and animate the skeleton of a story that, in many cases, began as fragments.

I first recognized and was surprised by this characteristic when Chase did his second regression to the Civil War lifetime, three years after his first regression with Norman at age five. We hadn't discussed the details of his memory at all in the intervening years. Yet in his second regression, Chase's story was totally consistent with the first regression, down to the most mundane details: chickens walking along a dusty road beside the cannon, the description of the field hospital. He was able to describe more of the story, since he had a greater vocabulary at his command, but the core of the story remained intact, including the sequence of events. This consistency was extraordinary, because so much had happened to Chase since then. In fact, Chase remembered the details of his past life memory better than he did some of the particulars of his life in Asheville before we moved.

Phyllis Elkins explains how Natalie's past life story was different from the fantasy stories she often tells:

> With these memories she comes up with the same story consistently. When she tells a fantasy story, she will add pieces from other stories, from her imagination, and from fairy tales, mixing it all together with the story she's making up. I can identify these easily: she alters them and the stories always change. But in this past life story, there is no fantasy about it. She is very matter-of-fact and is very clear

about the details. She has told this at least three times, and it's always consistent.

Victoria Bragg was working in a nursery when she met four-year-old Mark, who remembered a lifetime they had shared before as husband and wife. He repeated the same story four times, over a period of a few weeks.

> I grew up in the Church as a pastor's daughter and I've taught many kids of all different ages. I know that kids always forget the stories they make up. They can't be consistent because their little minds don't remember exactly what comes out of their imaginations. When they make up stories while we are talking and pretending, they have to write it down if they want to remember it.
>
> But Mark was completely consistent. He was also consistent with what he told his mother too—he was telling her exactly the same things. He never changed the details—never.
>
> Mark didn't act upset when he told me that I died first; he was very nonchalant about it. But he was very adamant and got aggravated when *I* didn't remember it. I asked him the same questions every time I saw him to see if I got the same answers, questions like "When did this happen?" He got very upset and would say, "I told you already."

Sign 3: Knowledge Beyond Experience

If you hear your young child speak of things that you *know* he or she hasn't learned yet or could not have been exposed to, it is likely you are hearing a past life memory. Remember, when evaluating this sign, *you* are the judge of what is beyond the experience of your own child.

Obviously it is easier to know what your child could or could not know if he is very young and hasn't been far out of your range. You know what he has been exposed to through conversation, radio, TV, movies, and books. So, for example, when your one-, two-, or three-year-old accurately describes the daily routine of a sailor and correctly names the types of masts his ship had, and you know that this is something that he never learned (*you* don't even know these details), this could be a sign of past life memory.

With older, more worldly children, it may be more difficult to discern how they know things that appear to be beyond their range, especially if they go to school. But follow your intuition. Probe. If you suspect your child is speaking from past life experience, try asking a direct question: "How do you know that?" If they say, "I just do," continue probing—you may be on to something. They may open up and tell you about "when I was here before, but you weren't my mommy."

Sometimes a memory can be indicated by a single remark. But a remark conveying information you know is beyond your child's experience can knock you off your feet and light up the heavens in an instant.

Silver Tooth

Karen Greene, who lives in rural Illinois, was driving three-year-old Lauren home from the dentist.

> Lauren had six clunky silver crowns put on her back teeth. She had been a really good patient, not crying and very cooperative. Then on the way home she said, with great concern in her voice:
> *"I don't like having silver teeth, because remember when we died together and those bad guys took our silver teeth?"*
> When she said that, my heart began pounding wildly and my body began to shake. I pulled to the side of the road for a minute, so I wouldn't have an accident. Since we are Jewish, I knew immediately that she was talking about the Holocaust. [The Nazis extracted the gold and silver out of the mouths of many of their victims.] I knew that I had not misunderstood her words; I knew that she was not playing a game. I honestly didn't think it could have been anything

else. I could feel the truth of what she was saying. I truly believed that she was remembering that she and I were somewhere together and that someone took our silver teeth.

Lauren said this without any fear. She wasn't complaining, or carrying on, or kicking her feet saying that she didn't want to have these silver teeth. She said it like, "Don't you hate it when you want to ride your bike but you can't because it's raining?" She said it as if she knew I would understand exactly what she was talking about. She said it like she was recalling something she expected me to recognize because we had shared it together. There wasn't anxiety attached to it, just concern that the bad guys might still want her silver teeth.

The chances that Lauren could have known this detail are absolutely zero. Even my ten-year-old, who now knows what the Holocaust is, would not know such a detail as having teeth taken out of your mouth. They certainly haven't watched anything on TV about this; I haven't read anything to them about the Holocaust. I would never want to scare them about such things; this was something that just was not necessary for them to know.

In that moment, I felt a great love for Lauren and absolutely believed what she was saying. And I thought how wonderful that she is having such a good life after that horrible tragedy in her last life.

With Lauren's one remark, Karen had known exactly what she was talking about. Lauren's concerned tone, the peculiar knowledge of what the bad guys had done to her, and Karen's own immediate body reaction left no doubt in her mind that Lauren's memory was real—even though reincarnation was something that she herself had never considered before.

Justin

Justin's parents were stunned when their baby told them how he had died in a past life. His mother Linda explains:

Justin was extremely precocious in language; he began speaking in sentences when he was only one year old. One day, out of the blue, he told us that he had gone ice skating, fell and hit his head, and then died. He went on to say that his parents were named Harry and Bobbie Colomby and that he lived in Carson, California.

He was very matter-of-fact about it: "Well, I fell on the ice and died, and they were my parents." He described what happened like it was just something else that happened to him, like "I bumped my knee" or "I dropped my cookie."

He had absolutely no way of knowing there was a Carson, California, because we didn't even know of it, since we live in Brooklyn, and he was just one year old. We looked it up, and sure enough, there is one. He also had no way of knowing that Bobbie could be a woman's nickname, and we didn't know anyone with that last name either. We tried to look up the Colomby family in Carson, California, but we couldn't find anyone by that name. And we don't know how long ago it happened.

He talked about it for about a year, because we reinforced it by asking him. When Justin went ice skating for the first time when he was six, we were a little concerned and asked him if he remembered what happened the last time he went skating. By that time, though, he had completely forgotten it.

One detail about Justin's story troubled me, and I asked Linda about it. Carson, California, is in metropolitan Los Angeles, where it's warm all year. How could there be ice skating there? Linda didn't know. But she and her husband were so convinced by the power of Justin's out-of-the-ordinary statements that this apparent discrepancy didn't faze them. His tone was so matter-of-fact, and the rest of the details so coherent, that they figured that there must be an explanation for this one inconsistency. They speculated that he could have been at an indoor rink or vacationing somewhere else where there was ice when the accident happened. Or maybe part of the memory was distorted and, for example, he was actually roller skating when he fell.

Distortions in memory do appear in past life memories, just as they do in present-day memories. We've all had the experience of describing something that happened to us in the past, only to be corrected on some detail by someone else who had been there too. We don't abandon the memory and say, "Never mind, since I didn't get all the details right, I guess it never happened." Instead, we continue with the gist of the story and pass over the disputed detail. Treat past life memories the same way: discern the story as a whole, especially if other signs of past life memory are present too.

One statement that convinced Linda that Justin wasn't making up a story was his remark that he had died because he hit his head on the ice. Would a one-year-old know that you can die from hitting your head on ice? Unlikely.

In general, these matter-of-fact "when I died" statements are the single best indicator that very young children are talking about a past life memory. For one thing, as Dr. Stevenson showed, the death is the most common event that children remember from a past life. And a violent death is often the reason why these memories come up in the first place. The details of dying are not something that a toddler jokes about or even thinks about, beyond the usual "bang, bang, you're dead" fantasy play, which is easy to spot. And when these little ones describe a past life death, they will throw in telling details, including what they saw or thought as they lay dying—details that you know are too realistic to be from a video game or action show. How many two- or three-year-olds know, or can imagine, the particulars of dying from drowning, suffocation, or fire?

Another form of knowledge beyond experience is the ability of small children to speak in an unknown language that they could not possibly have learned through ordinary means. This phenomenon is called xenoglossy. Since language requires months and years of repetition and practice to learn, science is at a loss to explain how anyone, especially a young child, could speak a language that he has never been exposed to. In the context of past lives, however, xenoglossy is simply another example of something learned in the past that carries over to the present life.

The following documented case, published in *Reincarnation: The Phoenix Fire Mystery,* is a striking example of xenoglossy:

> To the mystification of Dr. Marshall McDuffie, a prominent New York physician, and his wife, Wilhelmina, their twin baby boys were found to be conversing among themselves in some unknown vernacular. The children were eventually taken to the foreign language department of Columbia University, but none of the professors present could identify their speech. However, a professor of ancient languages happened to pass by and was amazed to discover that the babies were speaking Aramaic, a language current at the time of Christ![1]

This is a clear case of xenoglossy because there was no question that the children could have learned Aramaic through hearing it in their own home, or anywhere else, since no one speaks that language anymore. And the boys weren't just mimicking a few words: they were conversing with enough proper Aramaic syntax and vocabulary for the expert to be able to recognize the language.

Full cases of xenoglossy are rare, but they demonstrate the extent to which language can seep through from a past life. If your child shows xenoglossy at all, you are more likely to hear only a few isolated words or phrases. You might hear words from a foreign language, but be alert as well for obscure English words or jargon that you know your child has never been exposed to.

For example, in a Harrison case, the parents of two-year-old Simon were convinced that he was remembering the life of a nineteenth-century sailor. Once, in describing his days at sea, he referred to the "spanker" sail—the correct term for the aftmost sail of a fully rigged ship. Another time, when he accidentally knocked a jelly jar onto the floor, he nervously asked his mother if he would have to do "haze." When she asked him what he meant, he said it was what happened if a sailor did something "naughty," and he would have to scrub the decks and do hard work. His parents were astounded when they researched the word and found that *haze* is vintage sailor slang for extra work assigned for punishment. When Chase told me of his medieval life, he used the word *betrothed*, a word rarely used now but perfectly fitting for the time he was remembering.

The child's perspective in the story is also a clue to real past life memory. Is he speaking as someone who is actually there in the situation he is describing—seeing, sensing, and feeling from another's perspective? This is a fine but revealing point. The visual perspective may be chillingly realistic, as when Blake saw himself being run over by a truck from *under* the wheels; or as Liia saw the bubbles flowing *up above her* as she lay dying underwater, gazing up at the silvery bridge. Such an accurate perspective is not something that two-year-olds can fabricate, imagine, or assimilate from TV or movies. Most scenes in TV and movies in which a person dies are filmed from the perspective of an outside observer.

Two-and-a-half-year-old Philip, from the Harrison book, described an assassination (and used the word correctly) from the perspective of a six-year-old child crushed in a crowd. He couldn't see the murder itself because of the "big people" in front of him, but he knew something bad had happened because immediately everybody was screaming and jostling. If this had been a fantasy or derived from TV, Philip would have described an unobstructed view of the murder.[2]

These visual descriptions are so precisely tuned because the children are actually seeing from the perspective of their other bodies. Momentarily they are looking through the eyes of the person they were before. When two-year-old Natalie Elkins was telling Phyllis, her mother, about drowning in a swimming pool, she had her eyes fixed on her mother's eyes. But when Phyllis, probing for more of the story, wisely asked if she was wearing a bathing suit at the time, "Natalie *looked down at herself* and answered yes." She was seeing herself in that other body.

Another nuance of perspective to watch for is the emotions your child is describing. If he is remembering the past life of an adult, he may report mature emotions and concerns that are beyond the comprehension of a preschooler. Chase described his utter fear and confusion on the battlefield, and he was preoccupied with longing for his wife and children. Swarnlata lowered her eyes at the sight of her former husband and related to her former sons as a mother would, despite the fact that they were grown men and she was now a girl of ten. These are hardly the sentiments of young children, and even if they could mimic the words, they do not have enough experience to know what the appropriate emotions would be for the situations they are describing.

Some children who remember their past lives and deaths also have knowledge of what happened to them immediately *after* they died. Occasionally they speak from the perspective of an omniscient observer outside the body they just left behind, still seeing and hearing what is going on around them.

Blake, after being fatally run over by a large truck, remembered being taken to a hospital. Nicola, after being hit by a train, also described her trip to the hospital and how she tried to communicate with those around her but couldn't. It is likely that both children were either unconscious or dead at the time, yet still aware of what was happening around their bodies. Ravi Shankar, who remembered being murdered, told his parents exactly where his murderers had left the dismembered body; police records later confirmed that he was correct. One of the Harrisons' cases, two-year-old Mandy, who was verified to be her older sister reborn, recognized the cemetery where she had been buried and shocked her parents with an accurate description of her own funeral—complete with details of how her mother fainted and almost fell into the grave, and of a toy her surviving sister had sneaked into her coffin. Her funeral had never been discussed in their home.[3] These reports of out-of-body perceptions are consistent with those of thousands of adults and children who have had near death experiences.

Because consciousness is an unbroken continuum that stretches from death to birth, children may remember and describe events that happened anywhere along the continuum. Don't be surprised if your child describes the routine in heaven, visits from "shining ladies" or deceased relatives, or how they chose *you* as parents, with the same clarity and matter-of-fact tone they use to describe events in the past life. Or you may be blessed to hear your child casually describe events that happened to *you* months or years before his own conception—events that you never talk about or have forgotten.

The Little Red Car

This is one of many stories that I've heard of children who tell of hovering near their parents long before conception. It was sent to me by Judy, a mother from Washington state. It happened when her two-year-old, Jessica, had asked for the first time why mommy was always in a wheelchair and couldn't walk like other people. Using words her two-year-old could understand, Judy described the car accident that had left her crippled. Then Jessica said:

"I was there."

"No, honey, I was just a young woman then," Judy said. "It was before you were born."

"I was there," she repeated with calm sureness, and I knew I had to listen.

"Where were you, Jessica? I didn't see you."

"Oh, I was just sitting there watching . . . until the car that went 'URRR, URR' came and got you."

Stunned, I asked, "So you were making sure they took good care of me?"

"Uh-huh," she said, as she turned loose her grip of my wheelchair and ran off to play.

Jessica's words stuck with me for days, not just because of *what* she had said but because of the serious *way* she had said it. I told my mother what she said, feeling a sense of the incredible and, at the same time, a sense of a larger Truth. "I knew you had a guardian angel," Mother said, "I just didn't know that it was this one."

A couple of weeks later, something even more astounding happened. Jessica, out of the blue, came into the room and said, "When you had your wreck, the little red car threw you out and you hurt yourself."

"Oh," I answered her, "I was thrown out of the car, yes, but I don't remember a red car."

Jessica repeated confidently, "The little red car threw you out, and you hurt yourself."

I gasped and sat there with my mouth open looking at my little angel. Yes, I do remember now. Yes, yes! That car was a little red Volkswagen!

Courtney

Some children will make many statements about a past life, any one of which, taken in isolation, is not convincing enough to indicate a past life memory. But if all the statements taken together outline a coherent story, you can trust them as a sign of knowledge beyond experience. Very young children do not have the sophistication to fabricate a story with a realistic plot. They have no conception of how to keep details consistent and, at the same time, historically appropriate for the time and place they are describing. But past life stories are always realistic (even if bizarre), and the plot and details are always consistent.

The case of Courtney shows how this works. Repeatedly, over several years, Courtney surprised her mother, Lisa, with sweet recollections of a lifetime in what sounded to be nineteenth-century America. None of her statements alone would have proven the memory. But taken together, her statements were coherent and plausible, convincing her parents that she was remembering a past life. In a telephone conversation and a letter quoting from her journal, Lisa told me what happened:

My husband and I have three children; Courtney is our middle child and is now five, our oldest daughter is seven, and we have a son, three. There is something special about Courtney that is different from my other two children—you can see it in her eyes.

Courtney's first recollection, when she was three, came on the first day of the ground invasion of Desert Storm in Iraq. Our family was very reflective that day because my husband was a pilot with a Medevac detachment for the army reserve. He had already been put on alert, and we were simply awaiting "the call." It was late afternoon. My older daughter was at dance lessons, and my son, then age one, was napping. I was a nervous wreck, waiting for the phone to ring. In typical fashion I was cooking—my source of anxiety reduction.

The house was quiet, and Courtney was in the kitchen with me, doodling on an old calendar. She was softly chattering away to herself, and I was so wrapped up in my own thoughts that I wasn't paying a lot of attention to her. I started listening when I heard her talking about missing Grandma Alice. She kept on and on about missing her. So finally I said to Courtney, "Who is Grandma Alice?" She said, "Grandma Alice is my grandma." I explained to her that she had three grandmas, and I named them, but none of them was named Alice.

She looked right at me, and in a serious and matter-of-fact tone said, "I know that. She was my grandma before I was Courtney." When she said this, I got chills all over.

I was a little unnerved, but I probed anyway, not really knowing where this conversation was going. I asked her what she did with this grandmother and what she looked like, thinking that I could identify which of her "real" grandmothers she was talking about. Courtney went on to tell me all about Grandma Alice, whom she said she loved very much. After her parents died, Courtney said, she lived with her grandma and grandpa. She talked about how much Grandma Alice loved her. Giggling, she told how Grandma Alice played games with her and let her win. She described a game they played that sounded like Parcheesi, a board game we do not have in our house but that I played as a child.

During most of this conversation, Courtney did not look at me. She sat quietly (very out of character for our lively Courtney), continued to doodle on the calendar, and talked in a stream-of-consciousness kind of way. She didn't cry, even when she talked about being sad; but she was very subdued and reflective. I did not interrupt much or ask many questions. She wasn't talking to me—she was just spilling all of this out. *Catharsis* is the word that comes to mind.

She said that she was young, about sixteen [an odd thing for a three-year-old to say], when Grandma died. Another odd detail: she talked about her grandma getting fat right before she died—so fat that she couldn't put her arms all the way around her grandma anymore to hug her. Courtney seemed really sad about this.

Courtney ended the story with a deep sigh, saying, "I really miss Grandma Alice." I said that I was sorry that she missed her, but I was really glad that she was part of our family. Courtney's response left me chilled for hours: she looked up at me for the first time and said, "I know you love me—that's why I chose you to be my mother." She added that she and Grandma Alice had picked me out to be her next mother. Grandma Alice had recommended me.

Courtney spoke of her days with Grandma Alice often. Again, no single detail alone shows irrefutable knowledge beyond experience. But together they paint a consistent and authentic picture of rural life long before Courtney was born.

When Courtney first started talking about these past life things, I would always get completely unnerved and get goose bumps and freeze up. I would try to brush her off, saying, "Well, Courtney, we'll have to talk about that later," because I didn't know how to deal with it. Now, after more than two years of hearing Courtney say these things, I respond as well as I can, calmly and acceptingly. It still isn't easy, because these recollections raise my hair and leave me with gooseflesh for hours.

Since that day in the kitchen, Courtney has given more details of that life. For example, she mentioned that they lived where there were hills and trees that lose their leaves, and they had long, cold winters. Courtney has never experienced any of these things where we live in southern Louisiana.

One night all three children were bathing together.

Courtney was washing her older sister's, Aubrey's, back and began talking: "I miss taking a bath with Grandma Alice." Aubrey, who is very analytical and thinks this Grandma Alice story is a bunch of garbage, says, "Oh, no, here we go with this Grandma Alice stuff again!" (Now, a few years later, Aubrey asks, "Momma, how does Courtney *know* those things?")

Courtney looks right at her and says, "When I lived with Grandma Alice, we didn't take baths. We didn't even have a toilet!"

I probed a little here and joked, "My, you all must have been pretty stinky, never taking a bath or going potty in the toilet." Courtney then proceeded to tell me how they would heat water in a large pot and use cloths, and she gave an excellent description of a sponge bath—something she has never seen or heard about. She then described, with perfect detail, an outhouse. Interestingly, she never used the word *outhouse* and didn't know what I meant when I called it one. She also talked about remembering the day when her grandpa came home with a toilet. He had gone to a city far away to get it. He left early in the morning and didn't come back until the next day. The whole family had been very excited to get their first real toilet.

The fact that her other family didn't have a toilet could theoretically be the product of Courtney's imagination. But how would a three-year-old know that getting indoor plumbing for the first time would be such an exciting occasion? Nor would she be likely to know that it was common to travel two days to the nearest city for special purchases.

Once when Courtney recognized a common household implement from another time, she was so surprised that she "stopped dead in her tracks"—and so did Lisa.

I am very embarrassed to repeat how this next story came about, especially since I have a degree in family counseling. But the truth is the truth: my ultimate disciplinary weapon is the pancake turner.

It was very late one night, and Courtney and Aubrey, who share a room, would not settle down. I asked several times for them to quiet down, and they didn't. I fussed at them and scolded them to no avail. Courtney was especially worked up, squealing and jumping on the bed. I was tired and afraid they would wake up the baby. My husband was away, so out came the ultimate weapon—the pancake turner. I usually use a plastic one, in the event that I lose my mind and actually hit them with it. But I couldn't find that one, so I grabbed an old one—a very old one with the middle carved out, a wooden handle, and rust on it. I went into the bedroom and hit Courtney's mattress a few times and said that if they didn't settle down immediately, I would have no choice but to use this on their fannies.

Well, Courtney, who is usually openly defiant to this type of discipline, so I rarely use it, stopped dead in her tracks and turned white as a sheet with a very funny look on her face. She said, "Mom, if you hit me with that, you'll burn me."

I really didn't know what to say but continued the threat. "It won't burn you, but it *will* hurt you. So lie down and go to sleep!" I slapped the pancake turner on the bed a few more times for emphasis.

Courtney continued, "Mom, that will burn me, I know it will. You are supposed to use that to warm the sheets, not hit the children."

Well, *I* stopped dead in my tracks this time, frozen, looking at this old-fashioned pancake turner in my hand. I have no doubt in my mind that she thought it was a bed warmer. She was only four and had never been exposed to the concept of a bed warmer.

I hugged and reassured Courtney and let her touch the pancake turner, and we put it away together.

Sign 4: Corresponding Behavior and Traits

If you hear statements from your child that you suspect are describing a past life, look for behavior and physical traits that might be explained by the story. Think of any phobia, unusual mannerism, unlearned skill, or pronounced talent that would otherwise have no explanation or would be out of place for your family. The same is true of physical traits: if your child tells you a story of a past life injury or death and has a birthmark, a birth defect, or a chronic physical condition that matches the past life incident, it may be evidence that the story is a real past life memory and not fantasy.

Conversely, if your child has an unexplainable behavior that baffles you, ask yourself if you recall anything your child has said that might be related to the unusual behavior. Be alert for snatches of conversation, or odd remarks. Or, as Tommy's mother did in the case that follows, wait for the right opportunity and simply ask the child directly. But if no story emerges, don't force it. There may be another explanation, or your child simply may not remember.

We can rely on behavior as a sign of past life memory because Dr. Stevenson has provided the proof. He considered behavior to be such important evidence that he took special care in each of his cases to observe and record how the child's behavior compared with the life of the deceased person the child remembered being. In his best and most complete cases, the correlation is undeniable.

Not all past life memories have corresponding behavior or traits. Your child may have a recollection, like Lauren's, that manifests in only one powerful remark. Or you might have a child like Courtney, who makes many consistent statements about her past life but doesn't appear to have any corresponding behavior or traits. Both children had true past life memories, despite the lack of this fourth sign.

Carl, a case from the Harrisons, is an example of a child whose past life story neatly explains his temperament and physical appearance. His parents became convinced, by observing the other three signs, that Carl was truly remembering the past life of a Nazi pilot who had crashed his plane into a building. Then they realized that some of Carl's uncharacteristic behavior was a carryover from that strict military lifetime. He had "a perfectionist streak that belied his years."[4] He was extremely precise in everything he did and unusually clean and particular about his dress—imagine a young boy who insists on having his collars ironed! His physical appearance, too, was curiously consistent with his past life as a German. Both of his siblings were stocky with dark hair and tan complexions. Carl, though, was slight with a fair Aryan complexion and blond hair.[5]

Tommy the Sailor Man

Four-year-old Tommy Hibbert from California is an example of a child who had unusual skill and behavior but no verbal memories. He had knowledge far beyond his years of airplanes and flying. When his mother Bernice got curious, though, and asked him how he knew so much about planes, Tommy promptly told her about two past lives that corresponded perfectly to his baffling abilities.

> When my oldest son, Tommy, who is now twenty-six, was four years old, he had an inordinate interest in propeller planes. He was not interested in jets at all. He was in a cooperative preschool at the time, and one of our field trips was to a small airfield where they had small airplanes with propellers. A pilot there was willing to let Tommy climb into his airplane and look around. So Tommy got into the airplane, sat in the pilot's seat, looked at all the controls, pressed on the pedals, and demonstrated to the pilot that he knew exactly what to do to fly that airplane. The pilot was astounded. He said that if the key had been in the ignition, Tommy would have taken off!
>
> Two or three months after that, Tommy found a picture book of airplanes of the Second World War. And what airplanes did he immediately go for? The Japanese Zeros. He

was fascinated by them—he refused to look at any of the other planes. So I asked him, "I wonder if you ever flew any of those."

He replied, "Oh, yes," and then started telling me what it was like to fly and what he could see when he looked out of the cockpit of his airplane. He described the metal window frames and drew a picture of looking out of the window of the plane while flying high in the sky.

I then asked him, "If you were in a Japanese lifetime, I wonder how you died."

"I crashed my plane into a ship," he answered, very matter-of-factly.

I thought of the kamikaze pilots during the Second World War who had done just that. Tommy didn't seem to be bothered by his death at all. He seemed most involved in the memory when he was talking about flying the airplane. He loved the flying, and his face lit up—he absolutely beamed—whenever he talked about it.

At the time I believed he was talking about a past life, but I didn't know much about it and didn't have the presence of mind to question him more.

Despite her regrets Bernice did very well. She encouraged Tommy to talk by sharing his enthusiasm and asking him direct questions. And she got good answers.

Tommy gave her a second opportunity to follow the trail from behavior to past life memory:

Around the same age, when Tommy was four or five, he lost a button from his pants, and I didn't get around to sewing it on right away. So Tommy went and got a needle and thread, threaded the needle, and sewed that button on so expertly that I couldn't believe it. I had never taught him to sew, and he had never even seen me do it. Amazed, I asked him, "Where on earth did you learn to sew buttons on like this?"

"Well, we used to do it on my ship all the time," he answered.

"You were a sailor?"

"Oh, yes." And then he told me about how his ship would creak in the night while he was lying in his bunk in what he described as an old sailing ship with tall masts and many ropes. This memory proved to be very important to his life because when he grew up he joined the navy and went to sea for four years, hardly ever on land that whole time, and loved it. And guess where he was stationed—Japan!

Tommy's amazing unlearned ability to sew a button also points to a past life. Sewing a button is a complex skill that requires training and practice—especially to get the needle through the tiny holes. Most four-year-olds can't even lace their shoes. Bernice knew this, but the skill would have been nothing more than a mystery without the past life story. By simply asking, though, she triggered Tommy to explain where he had learned how to sew and to describe his life as a sailor on a wooden ship.

Gordon, a father from Vermont, saw my ad in *Mothering* and called me because he believed that he had solved the puzzle of his son's phobia and unusual play activity.

Since he was a baby, Sam would become terrified and scream uncontrollably every time he was in a bathtub that was filling with water. It wasn't water that scared him—it was the water *filling into the tub* that triggered his hysterics.

Sam also had a favorite play activity that left his father wondering. He frequently played in a knocked-over, empty metal trash barrel, and he would talk to his imaginary friend Carl. Gordon heard him say repeatedly to Carl, "Don't worry, I will take care of things."

One day when Sam and Gordon turned on the TV, they happened to see a World War II documentary. Little Sam got very excited when he saw the newsreels of Nazi Germany, especially those of a Hitler rally. He announced to Gordon how proud he was of the Germans. At first Gordon was shocked by Sam's admiration of the Nazis, and he explained that Hitler was not a nice man and that he had caused a great many people to be very sad, to be hurt, and to die. But Sam was not convinced and continued to identify proudly with Hitler and the Nazis.

Then it suddenly all clicked for Gordon. He believed that Sam had been on a doomed German submarine during World War II. He started putting it together: Sam's favorable reaction to the Nazis in the newsreel, his fear of the water *running into the tub.* The last thing many submarine sailors would see when their vessel suffered a fatal hit would be water rushing in to drown them. Gordon thought too of Sam's conversations with Carl inside the metal barrel. He guessed that Sam felt guilty about disappointing Carl when the sub sank after he had assured him, "Don't worry, I will take care of things."

I agreed with Gordon's hunch. Although Sam never said anything directly about remembering a past life, Sam's unusual behaviors, added together, suggest a coherent and plausible past life story. The strange phobia of water running into a tub is what gives the most strength to Gordon's conclusion. Nothing else in Sam's short life would account for such a specific fear—he had been born with it. But if he had in fact died by drowning in a submarine, it made perfect sense.

Phobias like this one are often a strong behavioral clue to a past life memory. Dr. Stevenson's data give a measure of how common it is: one of every three of his children who remembered dying in a past life had a phobia relating to the way they died. And phobias are often easy to spot because they sometimes are very specific and strange.

Another clue in Sam's case was his earnest play activity. Not all child's play is fantasy. Any obsessive or repetitive play activity could be a reenactment of a scene from a past life, an attempt to gain closure on unresolved feelings or unfinished business. If your child shows a persistent play pattern, look more closely for evidence of a real memory. Listen to play dialogues: is your daughter carrying on an unusually coherent conversation with a doll, making references to situations that are beyond her experience? If so, ask her who she's talking to. Or is she accurately imitating wiring a machine, although she has never seen an adult do it? If so, ask her how she knows how to wire machines. In either case you may be surprised to hear a coherent past life story that corresponds perfectly to the play activity.

Another type of behavior that could point to a past life is a strong affinity toward a different culture or time period. This affinity may manifest in a preference for a type of food, a distinctive style of dress, or manners that are out of place in the family. Perhaps your child is fixated on pictures or movies about another culture and time—just as Tommy was on pictures of Japanese fighter planes from World War II. Or the affinity could show as a strong attraction to people of another culture. Cody, a child from California, remembered dying in Vietnam. His mother believes that Cody had been a *black* soldier in that life because of his inexplicable attraction to the few black people in their mostly white community. He is immediately drawn to any black child playing on a playground. One day he met a black man fishing at the local pier and brought him home to meet the family.

If some children have affinities, the opposite can be true too: aversions can point to a past life. A child who has a strong dislike for a person or thing may be reflecting a past life trauma. Children may resist eating foods that remind them of that experience, cry when they hear a particular foreign language, or express disgust for a culture or time in history. If these dislikes are not anything they learned at home but are idiosyncratic to the child, it may be a sign.

John Van Dyk

A boy from Connecticut, John Van Dyk, recalled a lifetime that prejudiced his opinion of American Indians, at least while he was young. His mother Alison tells the story:

> On one occasion, three-year-old John was sitting in the back seat of the car playing with his box of Matchbox cars and trucks. He spontaneously began this conversation:
> "I remember when I was an Indian. I was young, but older than I am now. We all had ponies, and we kids did a

lot of riding and shooting animals. Then, one day they said we had to fight. We didn't want to because that was a man's job and we weren't big enough. But they made us do it anyway. It was awful. All my friends died, and so did I. It wasn't fair. We were just killed off like animals. It was disgusting. I hate Indians. I hate them."

Later, when John was five or six, I read to him from library books that we chose together. He was very interested in the cowboy and Indian times of the early Southwest. But I could never convince him to read books about the Indians. I tried repeatedly to interest him in my favorite subject, Native American people, figuring that if I was going to do all this reading, at least I could sneak in one book that I wanted to read. However, he remained steadfast in his refusal to have anything to do with the subject. Instead, he memorized the cattle trails, names of towns, and famous cowboys.

Alison notes that her son's anger has been transformed over the years. John Van Dyk, now in his twenties, has joined Christian missionaries to work among Native Americans.

Any exceptional talent can be a sign of past life memory, especially if supported by corresponding statements. Precocious ability in music, art, mathematics, and the sciences is a mystery that has baffled thinking people for centuries. History is full of examples of young children who master a difficult skill with such lightning speed that it seems they are merely remembering what they already knew. The traditional explanation has been to assign the word *genius* to these children, letting the word stand for a real explanation. But now that we know that skills and knowledge do carry forward from past lives, we can finally concede that these prodigies are literally remembering skills they honed in a past life. These children are picking up, more or less, where they left off. A child remembering previous skills need not have the prodigious talent of a Mozart. If your child learns with unnatural speed any discipline that ordinarily requires a great deal of training and study, it may be a sign.

Mary Fleming called me from Illinois in response to my ad in

Mothering. When her twins, Michael and Alan, were four years old and in preschool, their teachers began commenting on their artistic abilities.

Michael's preschool teacher told me that he was drawing at the level of a talented twelve-year-old. Curiously, at this time both boys were having difficulties learning and identifying the alphabet: they didn't have it down until they were almost six. But they both were producing this amazing artwork.

I was tucking Michael into bed one night—he was about four—when he started talking about his art. He said, "I'm so glad I remember my art, Mom. I was so worried I wouldn't remember. It's coming back all at once. I was so worried that I'd forgotten it. I am so happy that I remember my art." He went on and on like this for months, talking about remembering his art and how worried he was that he had forgotten it.

It sent me into shock. I can't remember what I said to him—past lives and reincarnation really weren't in my frame of reference. I'd read about it—I'd read Shirley MacLaine—and it was interesting. But it's one thing to read about it, and another thing entirely to have your own children say things like this.

They all had mentioned past life and prebirth memories before, in some detail. When they said these things, I didn't know how to respond. I usually mumbled something like "Oh" or "That's nice," not knowing what to make of it. But I was keeping an open mind about anything the children said on this topic.

This art is a different story entirely. When they said it was from a past life, I had to listen. Here was tangible proof. This couldn't be ignored or brushed off.

When Alan and Michael were five, I found an art teacher for them. She has been working with them for almost two years now. She says that Michael is exceptional. He approaches his work like a seasoned professional: once he starts a piece, he wants no feedback, suggestions, or interruptions until the work is completed. When she introduces a new concept to him, he learns it immediately as though he were being reminded of something he already knows. While most kids his age are drawing stick figures, Michael is drawing with perspective and shading. The teacher said she usually spends about ten weeks teaching perspective to adults, but with Alan and Michael she only had to show them once and they got it.

Billy

Pat Carroll called from Virginia and told me of a lifetime her son, Billy, remembered and talked about often. As she told me her story, I could see that the first three signs were clearly present. When I questioned her about any unusual behavior Billy might have relating to the memory, we both made a surprising discovery.

When Billy was less than two and a half years old, we were baking and using powdered sugar. I hate powdered sugar, so I had never used it before with him. But he wanted me to make a certain kind of cookie that his aunt made, so I had to get some and use it for the frosting.

I sat Billy up on top of the counter next to me so he could "help" me mix things. When it was time to make the frosting, I opened up the yellow box of powdered sugar. Billy said, "What's that?" I told him that it was some kind of sugar that wasn't very good, and he asked if he could taste some. I said, "Sure." He put his little finger in the box and got a tiny bit of it on his finger and tasted it.

Suddenly the expression on his face changed. It was really strange. It's hard to explain—his face was the same, but he looked so deep and calm. His shoulders dropped—I can't really describe it, but suddenly he looked much older than his age. I knew something had happened to him, but I didn't know what.

He said, "Oh, that's what my grandmother used to use."

I didn't know what Billy meant, because I know that my

mother never baked, so it wasn't her. I asked him if it was his other grandmother. He said, "No, no, my *other* grandmother." Again, I questioned him. "No," he insisted, "my other grandmother."

"Well," I asked, "which grandmother are you talking about?"

"My olden-days grandmother."

Getting more curious, I asked, "Who is your olden-days grandmother? What do you mean?"

He then told me that this grandmother used to bake all of the time and loved to use this kind of sugar. He was smiling and very happy as he explained to me how she loved him so much and how he really loved her.

"Do you have a mother?" I asked, thinking this must be a dream or something.

"Yeah, I did have a mom."

"Did you have a father?"

He looked like he was searching for an answer and just couldn't remember. Then he said, "There were a couple of guys who lived there sometimes, but I don't think they were my dad. I don't know who they were. They were my mommy's friends."

I was quite surprised when Billy told me these things. At first I thought that he had had a dream, but at the same time I knew there was something more because his face was different. And besides, this wasn't the kind of dream a two-year-old would have. I knew that he hadn't seen this on TV because I *always* watched with him. At that point I really didn't know what to think. I started getting this feeling—not a chill exactly, but something that told me to listen, to watch. So I stopped my baking and gave him all of my attention.

He was using words that were too big for a such little kid. I remember thinking that he was talking like he was an adult or an older kid. He used full sentences, which was very unusual for him. He didn't pause, he didn't search for words, and he didn't struggle to describe things, like he usually does. He was very fluent. The words just came out. I was shocked—he had never talked like this before!

I started thinking that he had more to tell. I tried to press for more information without leading him. I wanted him to tell me things.

He got real happy and told me how he and his grandmother for fun would sit on their back porch and look across big, big fields and watch trains go by in the distance. He and his grandmother loved to watch the trains. This is odd, because we live in an apartment. There aren't any trains around here at all.

I then asked Billy what happened to his family and his grandmother. He got very sad—a really deep sad. You know how when you're really sad, you don't sob, but it's deeper than that, with rolling tears? He looked melancholy and went on to tell me how his family didn't have any money and they couldn't keep him.

I asked, "Well, where did you go?"

He didn't answer right away. Then he said, "They didn't have money to buy food, Mom. We used to go to the grocery store, and the man at the store used to give us bread. And then one day he told us that he couldn't do that anymore unless we paid him. And we didn't have any money so we couldn't pay him. My olden-days grandmother used to make me cakes." Then he talked about watching the trains again.

I persisted and asked him what happened. He repeated: "They didn't have any money, and they couldn't take care of me, so they had to let me go."

I asked if he went to live with someone else. At that point he got frustrated and annoyed at my questioning, gave me an exasperated look, and said, "No, they had to let me go, Mom."

I told him that I didn't understand and asked him where he went. Then he looked deep into my eyes and said, "Mom, they gave me to you."

I got big chills throughout my body. I felt very stupid for not understanding what he was saying. But not having any knowledge of this kind of thing, I didn't know what to expect. I didn't want to say anything, I wanted him to explain it to me. I asked, "How did Daddy and I get you?"

"They had to let me die. I was seven years old when I died."

"That must have been very hard for your mother," I offered.

"Yes, they were very sad, but they knew that they had to let me go because they couldn't take care of me anymore."

"How did you die?"

"In a car crash in front of a Toyota dealership when I was seven years old."

Billy's statement stunned me. There was no way he could have known what a Toyota dealership was. *Dealership* was one of those words that was totally out of his vocabulary. And the way he described his death—he was so serious—sent shivers down my spine.

I asked Billy if he knew when this was or where he lived. He looked around and said, "Hollywood."

I said, "Hollywood, California?"

"No," he said, "the other one—Hollywood, Texas." Then he added, "This happened in 1987." That too was strange coming from a two-year-old. I now have a four-and-a-half-year-old who still doesn't understand years—they don't understand the time line yet.

I worked at a research firm that had one of those very detailed atlases, and I found a small town or subdivision in Texas called Hollywood or Hollywood Heights—Hollywood was in the name. But I've looked at other big atlases, and I didn't see it. Another woman who worked in the firm was with me at the time when I found it. We both saw it; it was actually there.

This first episode with Billy lasted only a few minutes. Then he was out of it. When I asked him to tell me more about his grandmother, he was back to being a two-year-old kid and had no interest in telling me anything more. That's fine. After that, I never tried to get him to bring it back again, because I didn't want to put anything into his head.

But every couple of months for about a year, he would bring it up on his own. Each time he would tell more of the story—mostly about his grandmother. He seemed to be close to his mother too, but his grandmother was the big link. He would continue to tell me different stories about his mother and grandmother, but he always came back to telling me about being on his back porch watching the trains. He would smile so big and start laughing a little while remembering this. These were happy memories for him.

He also seemed to be very hung up on the big man in the grocery store who had told them that they couldn't have any more bread. Billy would say things like "He just doesn't understand—he doesn't understand. They just can't take care of me anymore." He told me that specific story at least three times over the year without changing any of the details. Anytime he ever talked of this, he always described a very strong love: his grandmother's love, and how much they loved each other.

Then, just as quickly as the memories came, they went. There was nothing I could do to get them back.

Intrigued by Billy's story—his sadness about his poverty and lack of food, and the way he died "in front of the Toyota dealership"—I asked Pat if he had any unusual behaviors or fears that could be related to this past life.

Now that you mention it—I never really thought about this before—but he did. When he was little enough to ride in his car seat, anytime my husband or I would drive with only one hand on the wheel, which I still do all of the time, he would yell, "Hold two hands, hold two hands!" over and over until we held on to the wheel with both hands. This was particularly annoying when driving long distances, so I would say, "No, I want to hold with one hand." But he was adamant about it and repeated, "Hold two hands, hold two hands." He really got upset about it. I would have to wait until he wasn't looking and slip my hand back down again.

He did this when he was two to three and a half years old, the same time he was remembering the past life experience. He never said it before then or after then.

Billy also eats a lot. Now seven, he is four foot ten and weighs a hundred pounds. He is clearly a head taller than any other kid at school. When he gets home from school he eats at least two peanut butter and jelly sandwiches. He loves to eat—anything, anytime. I remember the pediatrician saying that I was feeding him too much, but I told him that I knew when my baby was hungry and needed food. My mother, who is a pediatrician too, agreed with me, and said to let him eat what he wanted. I used to give him lots of formula. He started eating solid food at six months, when he didn't have his teeth yet. He used to get very wild when he was hungry.

One more thing. Billy was so excited when he was finally old enough to go to kindergarten. I was excited too, and on his first day of school, I went to pick him up, eager to hear how his day went. But as soon as he got in the car, he threw his bag down in disgust and cried, "I hate it! They didn't let me do anything I wanted to do. Don't they know that I'm supposed to be in *second grade*!"

Now I understand why he said this. He died when he was seven, the age that he would have been in second grade!

CHAPTER 11

Triggers

What triggers spontaneous past life memories? What prompts these young children to start talking about "when I died" or "when I lived before"?

Anything.

Any sight, sound, taste, smell, person, place, or event that reminds the child of a former life can trigger a spontaneous memory. The moment Billy tasted powdered sugar, he was reminded of his past life grandmother's baking, and the memory poured forth. Liia saw the sun reflecting on the metallic guardrail of a bridge—the last image she had seen before she died was the sun reflecting on the silvery bridge above her. When Lauren had silver caps put on her teeth, she was reminded of her own death and the "bad guys" who had taken her silver teeth.

In that moment of recognition when a child sees an object, meets a person, or sees a place that resonates with the past experience, the switch is flipped, the circuit between past and present is completed, the eyes light up, and the images and feelings rush into the conscious mind.

There is nothing inherent in the trigger itself that switches on the memory. Each trigger is specific to the child's experience depending on what sight, sound, smell, or taste remains charged with significance from the past life.

An antiquated object—like an oil lamp, spinning wheel, out-house, or icebox, when seen for the first time in a museum or at Grandma's house—has the power to trigger an entire memory. Personal items like a locket or monocle may spark a child to say, "I had one just like that." In special cases, the child recognizes the selfsame object he knew in the past life. Heirloom gold watches figure in several cases that I know of, and it's not uncommon for a child to point to an old family photograph and say, "That's me!"

Children do not have to come in direct contact with the object. A picture in a book or an image or sound from a movie or TV can trigger a memory just as well. One father, Ed Durbin, from New York, was watching TV when his three-year-old son, David, passed by on his way upstairs to bed. David, looking over his shoulder at the TV, said, "That's Abe Lincoln, isn't it? I fought for him in the war." David proceeded to describe his life as a Civil War soldier with enough accurate detail, and in such a mature tone of voice, that Ed was convinced that David was remembering a real past life.

Sometimes a child will be familiar with images of an object from TV or books, but memories will not be triggered until coming face-to-face with the real thing. For example, the volume of gunshots on TV is nothing like the actual sound; when a child hears a real gun go off at close range, the intensity and realism of the noise may trigger the memory. A train may look cute as a toy or in a picture book, but a real train can be monstrous to a wee child, and the impact of seeing one for the first time may evoke memories of trains that were once a regular part of his life.

Anything that comes from an exotic culture or climate could trigger a memory when a child sees it for the first time: palm trees, terraced fields, a pagoda, an African mask, or an Egyptian statue covered with hieroglyphics. But the trigger doesn't have to be exotic. While watching her apron-clad mother baking in the kitchen, a two-year-old commented, "My black mother used to wear an apron too."

Any sound can trigger a past life. Chopping firewood, the chatter of a foreign language, the squeak of a gate hinge, or footfalls on creaky old floorboards can echo sounds heard in another time and place. Music is especially evocative: hearing for the first time reed flutes, a marching band, tribal drums, or a choir singing sacred polyphony may strike a dormant chord of memory. When I was four, I was triggered by the sound of classical piano music.

Smells and tastes, because they bypass the rational mind, can be strong triggers. The first whiff of saddle leather, temple incense, or smoke from a coal furnace—or the first time a child tastes sorghum, curried rice, or sassafras—may suddenly evoke another time and place.

An activity or event such as a traumatic separation from parents—the first day of school, going to camp, being left with a strange baby-sitter—can bring back separation anxiety from a trauma in the past, when the separation was tragically permanent.

The sight of blood, knives, ropes, lightning, violent wind, or water rushing in, or the sight of someone wounded and lying on the ground, might remind a child of the cause or setting of a past life death. Being accidentally locked in a closet, playing under blankets, or getting lost at night could bring back a trauma of death in the dark or by entrapment. Anything associated with war could trigger a memory of death in battle: loud booms, explosions, and heavy machinery are some of the sounds of war. Bright flashes, the rumble of airplanes, billowing black smoke, the smell of gunpowder, or spilled gasoline may remind a child of being bombed. Helicopters flying overhead may trigger a child whose previous personality died in a recent conflict, such as Vietnam. Of course, these triggers may set off a phobia only and no explicit memory—you might have a frightened child, but no words to explain the fear.

Rabbi Yonassan Gershom has counseled hundreds of adults who remembered dying in the Holocaust. In most cases these memories began surfacing in early childhood as phobias, night-mares, or recurring images. In his book *Beyond the Ashes,* he lists the common phobias associated with dying in the Holocaust: gas, sirens, explosions, airplanes, barbed wire. More than one child was terrified of black boots. Another was terrified of all uniforms, including her father's trucker's cap. Children also had fears of starvation, suffocation, or being buried or burned alive. All of these images and feelings triggered memories of the trauma of war and death, although most of the children in Gershom's book were not able to articulate these memories until they were adults.[1]

Some children may not be triggered until several fac-tors—sights, sounds, smells, lighting, atmospheric conditions, or perspective—converge in just the right combination to re-create a scene that matches one from a past life. Chase's Civil War memory was triggered most obviously by the loud booms of the Fourth of July fireworks. But there may have been more to the triggering than the sounds alone. From his vantage point on top of the hill, Chase had been looking down on dozens of people sitting or lying on the ground. The light was growing dim in the sky, and clouds of smoke from firecrackers and small fireworks were floating in the air. The whole experience was reminiscent of the scene where Chase stood with his cannon on the rim of a valley and watched the smoke and confusion of the battlefield below. When the big fireworks show began, the tremendous sounds of their exploding overhead and echoing in the hills was probably very close to the intensity of real cannon fire and the reverberations in the valley during the battle. The actual trigger of Chase's phobia, then, was not just the booms but everything together.

Landmark Memories

Any place or location—a building, a street corner, a vista—that the child has known in a past life, or that reminds him of a location from the past, can trigger a memory. Ian Stevenson has documented many cases of children who, when put to the test, successfully located the homes or shops from their former lives. A number of the children in the Harrisons' cases did the same.

In one Harrison case, three-and-a-half-year-old Jonathan was traveling on a city bus with his mother when he pointed to the intersection they were passing and suddenly got very sad. "That's where my daughter got killed," he said. He explained to his mother that when he was a big man his little girl, Angela, had been hit by a car at that corner. After that, every time they rode the bus past that intersection, he said the same thing. The trauma had been so intense that it had seared his memory, and seeing the intersection again conjured up the tragedy of his daughter's death.[2]

Pierce Hall

JoAnne Hall took her two young children with her on a business trip to Hampton, Virginia, about an hour from their home. The children had never been to this city before. They were driving down a street heading home when six-year-old Pierce seemed to know exactly where they were.

> Pierce said, in an excited voice, "Oh! Go down this street, Mommy. I want to see the water and the boats."
>
> Even though I couldn't see any evidence of the waterfront, I was so surprised by his command, I turned where he was pointing. We went down the street and found ourselves in an old part of town with grand, hundred-year-old homes. He excitedly cried out, "Mom, look!" Something about the way he said it made my skin crawl.
>
> "What am I looking at?" I said.
>
> "That house over there. That big house. Don't you remember it?"
>
> When he said that, I froze. I pulled over to the side of the road and stopped the car. "Pierce, I don't remember it. Why should I remember it?"
>
> "Well, we used to live there when you were my mother before," he said. Pierce has a good imagination, and I'm

used to him making things up. But this was different. I started trembling and got goose bumps all over my body. I don't remember ever feeling like that before. It felt as if cold air had suddenly flooded the whole car.

I collected myself. "Do you remember living there?"

"Yes, it was a long time ago."

He excitedly recalled people who lived in the different houses and told me about his friends. He said he didn't have any brothers and sisters and that he got very old, "but I never got grumpy."

Then Pierce gave me a funny look, and just as quickly as all this started, he changed the subject and said, "Mom, go down there. That's where the boats are. I really want to see the boats." Something in the car changed too. The chill drained away. Whatever had me frozen or cold for a few minutes seemed to pass. There was something about this whole thing that *felt* real. I wish I had thought faster and asked for his name, but I didn't.

The feeling had passed, but Pierce still knew his way around. I turned down the road he pointed to and went two blocks. Suddenly we were at the waterfront. I was surprised, but Pierce wasn't. He pointed to another beautiful large white house and said, "That was always your favorite house."

I answered, "I'm sure it was." The house really was beautiful.

It seems unlikely that, in such a big world, we would incarnate in the same locale to travel the same roads and see the same sites as in previous lives. But the cases give evidence that we do. In fact, the locations where we reincarnate are not as random as we might think. Both Stevenson and the Harrisons found that some children reincarnated within a hundred kilometers of their last life, often closer. If we are likely to be reborn in the same territory where we spent one or more past lives, then happening onto a familiar landmark is not unlikely. We do, literally, travel the same roads again.

Hello. I Love You. Good-bye.

Just as we are likely to cover the same ground, we encounter the same people we've known in past incarnations. When a child sees someone he knew in a past life, it can trigger a past life memory. If the past life was a recent one, the child could be recognizing a person he actually knew in his last life, a person who is still alive, as Swarnlata did. Or if many years and generations have passed, the child may recognize the essence, the soul of the person. How this works, I do not know. But I do know that souls come together again to complete unfinished business or to renew bonds of love.

Most of us have had the experience, when meeting someone for the first time, of looking into their eyes and knowing, without a doubt, that we've been together before. It is sometimes love at first sight, sometimes instant dread. But adults rarely remember a past life story to explain the connection.

Some children, however, do remember. And if they haven't yet been taught that recognizing someone from a past life is "impossible," they may walk up to an adult, look deep into his or her eyes, and innocently ask, "Don't you remember me?" This can have a powerful effect on the adult, especially if the child proceeds to unwind a convincing story of the past life they shared together. It can also trigger profound emotions *in the adult*. This is exactly what happened to Victoria Bragg.

Victoria Bragg

An attractive young minister's daughter, Victoria Bragg, was working in a nursery in Georgia when a child recognized her from another lifetime. Her deep feelings toward this four-year-old stranger turned her life upside down and led her on a quest to understand who this child was and why he had come into her life. She told me her story in a phone conversation.

* * *

About ten years ago I worked at a health spa, in the nursery. One day a little towheaded boy came in with his mother and sister. His name was Mark, and he was four years old. When Mark first came running into the nursery, he seemed distracted. Then he saw me and ran over and started hugging me around the legs. I thought, "What a friendly little kid!"

Then Mark looked up at me with his little round face. "Remember when you came to my shop and I was sweeping up and we went for a ride in my car and we had so much fun?"

I said, "What did you say?"

Mark repeated his question word for word.

I asked him, "When was this, Mark?"

"You know . . . before."

I was shocked into silence. I was confused. My mind tried to dismiss this little boy as just a kid with a vivid imagination. But his words sent chills down my spine, and I knew I couldn't ignore him. I urgently needed to find out more. By the time I got over the shock, though, he had run off and joined some kids playing on the rug.

I couldn't get Mark out of my head. That evening I talked to a friend and told her how obsessed I was about what this little four-year-old had said. She suggested I might have been with him before in another lifetime, and that I should ask him more questions and see what happens.

Mark came back to the nursery a few days later. Again he ran up to me and asked if I remembered riding in the car with him. Again I told him I didn't. He repeated the story in exactly the same way with the same details. He added that we had been friends at first and then later we got married.

When I asked him his name, he said, "They called me Painter."

"Were you an artist? Did you paint pictures?"

"No, I painted buildings."

"Did we have children?"

"Yes," he replied, "a daughter." Then he added that I had died first, and that he missed me so much and he loved me.

I saw Mark two more times. With each visit I felt stronger and stronger emotions toward him that I couldn't understand. I had a hard time sleeping at night. I cried for him. I know it sounds silly, but I wanted to be with him. I didn't see Mark as a little boy—I saw him almost as a different person, a grown-up. It was scary to feel these emotions toward a four-year-old. I wondered if there was something wrong with me. I felt very, very sad.

The last time his mother brought him to the nursery, I asked her if Mark had said anything unusual to her. She told me that Mark talked about me all the time and said that he loved me and missed me. He also mentioned that he wanted to take me for a ride in his car again, like he had done before. She said Mark used to hate coming to the spa, but now he couldn't wait to come so he could see me. She admitted she was as baffled as I was. I confessed that it was all a bit scary for me, because what we were really talking about was reincarnation. Then we got distracted and didn't have a chance to talk again. Soon after, I left my job at the spa and moved on, so I lost touch with Mark and never saw him again.

This wasn't the end of it for me, though. For years I was haunted by this experience. I couldn't stop thinking about Mark, wondering what it all meant. Why had he run up to me and told me those things? Finally I sought out a therapist who could help me with a past life regression. I immediately went back to that lifetime and saw clearly that everything Mark had said was true. I also saw that I was in a car accident with my little girl at my side. She survived, but I died. My husband never got over my death and became an alcoholic.

The regression helped me understand the meaning of our encounter. But it didn't help the sorrow. I felt I'd been cheated of love. Why couldn't Mark and I be together again? I'm starting to cry again as I tell you this, the emotions are so deep. I want so much to tell him that I'm sorry

I had to leave him when I died. I couldn't tell him when I saw him in the nursery because at the time I didn't know I had died and left him so sad. I regret not having asked him more questions.

But I believe I know why he came back to me. He wanted me to know he was okay. He wanted to tell me that we *do* come back and live again, and that the bonds of love are stronger than death. I believe a part of him knew that we're not supposed to be together in this life, and he just wanted to see me once more because he missed me. And to say "I love you" one more time.

The State of the Child

Some parents told me that their children began speaking of a past life without any prompting and without any specific trigger. This didn't surprise me. The logic of a child's mind is unfathomable. Young kids often blurt out bits of conversation, recollections, information, and fantasy that have no relevance to the topic at hand. That's part of the fun of having kids around. When Chase and Sarah were little, Steve and I often joked that random generators built into their brains determined what came out of their mouths. So it makes sense that past life memories, which mingle in the unconscious along with everything else, would also be subject to random generation and pop out for no discernible reason.

But as more stories came to me, I started to see a pattern in these seemingly random cases. Parents told me so often, "We were riding in the car when my child began to tell me about his past life," that I began to joke that the automobile is a past life time machine. But seriously, I wondered—what do cars have to do with it?

Then I was struck by the obvious. The motion of a car lulls children into a trance state. We mothers know we can usually rely on the hypnotic motion of a car to ease a child to sleep. A person of any age, just before falling asleep, passes through the border regions of the unconscious mind—a brief twilight zone of images and intuitive impressions—called a hypnagogic state. In this trance state, just before consciousness is drowned in sleep, psychic impressions, including past life memories, well to the surface. If the child floats in this zone without falling all the way into sleep, he will be in an opportune state to begin experiencing past life memories.

I thought about this some more and realized that the child's state of mind itself is a trigger. Anything—not only riding in a car—that induces a trance or relaxed state in a child can trigger a memory. Blake's mother used a back rub to bring up his past life memory again, and I've heard of other mothers who did exactly the same. Other children speak of their memories while in the bath or just before bedtime. Baby Elspeth was in the bath when she blurted, "I'm going to take my vows."[3] The motion of a rocking chair or a swing can sway a child into an altered state of consciousness as easily as the proverbial hypnotist's watch.

Children can also go into a mild trance while engaged in any creative activity like drawing, painting, or playing make-believe. These activities engage the right brain, the source of creative and unconscious images, while loosening the grip of the logical left brain. Past life therapists who work with children use drawing as a reliable clinical technique for accessing children's past life memories. Courtney first began speaking of her past life while doodling on a calendar in the kitchen.

The Mind of the Mother

After that Fourth of July when Chase became hysterical from the fireworks, I found myself asking, "Why didn't this happen before?" Chase had seen fireworks and heard loud booming noises on other occasions. But the memory hadn't surfaced (in the form of the phobia) until he was five. Were there other factors at work? I wondered if my own regression months before, and my new awareness of past lives, could have unconsciously triggered his memory, and Sarah's too. Perhaps their subconscious minds had gotten the signal that I would now be receptive, that the psychic climate was right for their own memories to come out. Intuitively I sensed this was true. But without more evidence, telepathic cause and effect is tough to prove. So I tucked this intuition away in my mental "unsolved" file, as yet another mystery that I hoped to answer someday.

Then I began to hear from other mothers. Colleen Hocken told me that she had heard Dr. Brian Weiss mention children's past lives on the *Oprah* show *the day before* Blake first spoke of his memory. I questioned her about this: "Before that day, could Blake have said anything that you missed because you weren't aware that past lives were possible?" "No," she assured me. She was positive that neither of her children had ever said anything that hinted at a past life. But once Colleen had been alerted to the possibility, Blake's memory broke through the very next day.

Another mother, Sharon Benedetto, did a past life regression with her therapist to a lifetime in Russia. She saw that her present son, Joey, had been her child in that lifetime too. A few days after her regression, five-year-old Joey began having nightmares—his first ever—about that same lifetime in Russia. Sharon was sure that her regression had unconsciously triggered his memory because she hadn't discussed her regression with anyone. (The full case is in Chapter 13.)

I was beginning to see a pattern, a cause-and-effect relationship between mothers' acceptance of past life memories and their children's first breakthrough with their own memories. Does this mean that a parent's awareness is required before a child's past life memory can be triggered? Clearly not. For in the majority of cases from the Harrisons, and even in some of Dr. Stevenson's cases from India, the parents were either totally unaware of past lives or hostile to the idea. The children had spontaneous memories anyway—the parents' awareness was not a prerequisite.

Sandy

Nevertheless, I was finding that in other cases awareness may be a factor, part of the unseen formula that determines when and where a past life memory will emerge.

This was getting more and more interesting. I heard from Sandy, a therapist and mother in New Jersey, who was struggling to understand her relationship with her seven-year-old son, David. Sandy told me, "He was acting as if I were the enemy, as if he needed to protect himself from me. Could I be such a bad mother? Could I be so far off in my perception of love and good intention?"

Sandy regularly uses writing in her journal as a form of meditation—a method to invoke her inner voice and solve personal problems. Her practice is to sit down and meditate until she is in a light trance. Then, with questions in mind, she writes freely until answers emerge in her writing.

That day I felt a sense of calm and safety that I always feel when I sit down to write. The question in my heart and mind was "What is going on with David? Why does he treat me like the enemy?" As I began writing, I was surprised at the words that came to me: "David's behavior can only be understood in light of his many previous lifetimes of persecution, slavery, and oppression."

No wonder he acts this way! I realized I could let go of the burden—my worry that "I'm not a good mother"—that I was carrying. I could focus now on finding ways to comfort and help David. I felt better and began to relax.

Just at that moment David walked into the room. He asked, "Mom, what are you writing about?" I was very surprised, because in the year and a half that I'd been doing this kind of writing, he'd never walked into the room and never asked me about it. I told him I wrote about different things, and that this writing was about him. I asked if he wanted to hear it, and he enthusiastically said, "Yeah!"

I read it. He listened intently. As I finished, I looked at his face. He looked different—serious, pondering, with a faraway look. And then, as if someone had flipped a switch inside him, he began to talk in a steady stream about his past lives. I had never heard him talk like this before. He was clear, involved, and certain about the information he was presenting. I sat quietly and listened.

David told me about five different lives. He told me in
detail about the persecution, fear, frustration, and hardship
he had endured in the past. He remembered scenes from
those lives vividly and painted pictures of people he loved
and hated. The last life he described was totally unlike the
others: it was a lifetime of reward, full of wonderful tran-
quillity and peace.

Since that time David and I have spoken casually about
other lifetimes, but never with the fluency and certainty of
that special afternoon.

Why had David walked into the room at that moment? Had he
intuitively sensed that his mother was writing and asking about
him? Had he unconsciously felt a change in Sandy's attitude—her acceptance of him and her openness to his past life
difficulties? Sandy and I both believe this was *not* coincidence,
but rather the result of a direct unconscious communication between mother and child. David was actually triggered twice:
once to walk into the room at that very moment, and again to
begin speaking of the memories. The psychic space was prepared
by Sandy's meditative state and awareness of David's past life
history—this was the first trigger. Then all she needed to do was
to mention past lives to David, and the switch was flipped—his
memories became conscious and poured forth.

Mother and Child Telepathy

When I heard Sandy's story, I began to take seriously my theory
that telepathy between mother and child is a powerful trigger of
past life memories. Her story reminded me of the many accounts
I have heard about the everyday telepathic link that mothers have
with their children. This link, from what I can tell, is common
knowledge among mothers, but it is rarely acknowledged in
books. Many mothers have had the experience of waking in the
middle of the night, moments *before* their baby stirs. The telepathy is most striking when a young child is in danger, when the

mother senses an accident about to happen and responds without thinking. She looks up at the very moment a toddler is headed toward the pool, or glances out the window just as the child wanders too close to a busy street. This is a form of telepathy.

A few researchers have studied telepathy between parents and children. Not surprisingly, it is more common between mother and child than between father and child. Mothers are naturally attuned to their young children. After all, they carry them inside their bodies for nine months. During pregnancy, psychologists believe, there is a fusion of consciousness between mother and child. To some extent the mother's thoughts and emotions are shared by the baby in utero. This deep connection is not severed completely when the umbilical cord is cut.

In Thomas Armstrong's book *The Radiant Child*, he quotes psychiatrist Jan Ehrenwald, who has studied this phenomenon. "ESP represents a natural symbiotic link between mother and child in the child's earliest years. Telepathy [is] a primitive means for the infant to communicate basic survival needs, since the infant has not yet developed the ability to use language."[4]

If mother and child telepathy is real, I thought, then what I was finding—that a mother's awareness can trigger a child's memory—is possible as well. Two more cases finally convinced me that this is a real phenomenon.

Elona, Anna, and Seth

At a Fourth of July party at my sister Barbara's house in upstate New York, I met her friend Elona, who has three kids. She and I were finishing our barbecue and discussing the logistics for taking all of the children to see the fireworks that evening. Naturally the conversation turned to another Fourth of July and the story of my children's past life memories. Elona was spellbound. She confessed that she had always believed that she had been a child who died in the Holocaust. But she had no idea how this could be possible because reincarnation wasn't something she thought about, and it had never been a part of her religious upbringing. Yet her feelings about her Holocaust life were so strong, they began to come up again as we sat and finished our watermelon. "I'm not ready for this," she said as she brushed back the tears.

A week later she and her five-year-old son Sagiv were riding in the car together when he had a spontaneous past life memory. She was sure of it. (Her full story is in the next chapter.) She was just as certain that our conversation on the Fourth of July had changed her own awareness of past lives, which had then triggered her son's memory. Another case of mother and child telepathy, I thought.

But there's more. Sometime later, in September, I mailed Elona the draft of her case that I had written for this book. She was just sitting down to review the write-up when her friend Anna stopped by for a visit.

"What's this?" Anna asked.

Elona showed her the draft. After reading it through, Anna's only comment was "This stuff couldn't be true. You must have dreamed this."

Elona explained how she was convinced that Sagiv had had a past life memory. She told the story of Chase and how his fear of loud noises had disappeared. But there was no convincing Anna. As a last shot Elona offered, "Well, your own son Seth is terrified of any kind of face painting. On Halloween he's a basket case. How do you explain that?"

"He probably gets it from me," she said, completely dismissing Elona's suggestion.

Two days later Anna called Elona, scared and distraught. Over the phone she spilled out what had happened with five-year-old Seth.

"My husband, Ben, and I were riding in the car with Seth. Seth, out of the blue, asked his father, 'Did your mother die?'

"Ben said, 'Of course not. You know Grandma is still alive.'

"Seth continued in a sad voice, 'My mother died.'

"Ben went nuts and blasted, 'Don't be silly! What are you saying! Your mother's right here.'

"Despite his father's anger, Seth couldn't hold back. 'My mother was very sick, and then she died.'

"I asked Seth what their names were, and he gave what sounded like Native American names. Then he added, 'She was very old, and I'm old too. She asked me before she died to find this person, and I can't find him.' Seth began to sob like a grown man, with tears rolling down his cheeks. He said he was sad that his mother had died, and he was deeply upset that he had broken the vow he had made to her to find that person."

When Anna was finished, Elona asked, "Now, do you see the connection with the painted faces?"

Anna's only reply was, "I'm scared. I look at Seth differently now, and I don't know what to do."

A few days later Elona called me and said, "When I talked with Anna, she was confused and upset because she saw the same signs in Seth that I had begun to describe to her. She saw the definite, grounded, 'this is it and I'm not kidding' look in her five-year-old's face as he spoke of this Native American life. I know she saw it because she described it: the adult integrity that comes over a child's face when they talk of these things, a look you can't convey to someone else—until you witness it in your own child. Anna saw it, and it scared her because it shattered her belief that we only live once. She refuses to discuss the memory any further with Seth, hoping that it will just go away."

Elona and I agreed that Seth was probably afraid of face paints because they triggered memories of his Native American lifetime and the deep sadness of his broken vow. It seemed to fit.

We spoke again a couple of weeks after Halloween. She reported: "I saw Seth on Halloween night, and he wasn't afraid of the costumes or face paints at all. He thought it was all great fun. And I know he had this problem in September, before he had the memory. It went away after he remembered that past life."

This was fascinating. Here, *despite* Anna's disbelief and resistance, Seth's memory emerged two days after Anna had been exposed to the idea of past lives. And simply by verbalizing the memory, Seth seemed to have benefited from it because his fear of painted faces vanished.

Elona was amazed by this chain of events. My telling the story of Chase's memory triggered her own memory. Then her awareness psychically triggered her son, Sagiv. Anna's awareness of the *possibility* of past lives, despite her doubts, triggered her son's past life memory, which cured his phobia.

"It's a web of triggers, all linked together," Elona suggested with wonder in her voice. "It's a chain reaction of awareness." Then she added, "Wow, what's going to happen when your book comes out?"

"I don't know," I answered her. "But I can imagine!"

CHAPTER 12

What a Parent Can Do

If, one day, your child suddenly experiences a past life memory, what do you do?

First, take comfort in the fact that other parents have been through this. With no guidance whatsoever, many have helped their children negotiate profound, life-changing experiences. Their only tools were love, intuition, and a desire to hear what their child had to say. The cases in this book show how they muddled through.

If they can do it, you can too. Actually, most of you will have it easier because you have the benefit of this overview of how past life memories work, and you have dozens of cases to refer to as models of how particular children's past life memories have unfolded.

Many of the pioneering parents who worked through the experience by themselves started out bewildered and confused because no one had told them that past life memories were even possible. They had to grapple with the fear that their children might be suffering strange fantasies or delusions. But from the scientific studies of Dr. Helen Wambach, you know that past life memories held up to statistical analysis in a sample of more than a thousand adults. Dr. Ian Stevenson's research and scientific documentation of more than 2,500 cases shows that *spontaneous* past life memories are a natural phenomenon in children. So if your child remembers a past life—and the four signs will help you decide if he does—you can proceed with the confidence that your child is normal and in good company.

You can proceed with the confidence that past life memories bring benefits. You know, from the work of past life therapists, that these memories are an opportunity to heal unfinished business that otherwise might cause problems as your child grows into an adult. You know, too, that past life memories bring blessings. They can be a source of spiritual insight and direction that inspires confident strides in this life.

Back to the original question: in that moment when your child begins speaking of a past life memory, what do you actually *do*?

How you respond is the heart of the matter. This is where you apply your understanding, and where reincarnation changes from a philosophical abstraction to a practical skill. To guide you, here are five steps that summarize what I have discovered about responding appropriately to a child's spontaneous past life memory. This is what you do in the moment when your child suddenly says, "When I was big, I had a different mommy":

1. Stay calm:

Breathe. Clear your mind so you can devote your full attention to your child.

2. Acknowledge:

With assuring words and a loving tone of voice, acknowledge your child and the truth of the memory. This keeps the memory flowing and ensures a positive outcome.

3. *Discern:*

Listen closely to discern the facts and emotions of the emerging story. Also, look for the underlying themes of the memory, and how they relate to your child's present life.

4. *Allow emotions:*

Always allow your child to follow the memory wherever it leads, and to express all emotions, no matter how disturbing or intense.

5. *Clarify past and present:*

With loving assurance, clarify for your child the difference between images from past lives and present reality.

Although I've organized my advice into steps, don't worry about following them in order. Every case is different. Sometimes the memories rush out all at once in a single session. If this happens with your child, you may find yourself doing all five steps simultaneously, responding intuitively with no time to think. In other cases the memories trickle out over several weeks and months, giving you plenty of time to ponder their meaning and plan your response. Whatever your case is, remember: you don't follow steps—you follow your child and the energy of the moment.

Don't worry, either, about committing this advice to memory. Responding to a past life memory is not a technical process; it's communication with your own child, and you already know how to do that. Trust that you will absorb everything you are now reading, and if your child has a past life memory anytime in the future, you will know what to do.

Above all, *always respond positively.* Respond by affirming, allowing, encouraging, acknowledging, explaining, clarifying, assuring—and always with love. I have never seen an instance where a negative response was appropriate. When responding to a past life memory, *never* correct or scold or argue with your child. Period.

Stay Calm

Imagine you are riding in your car, chatting with your three-year-old daughter. Suddenly her voice gets serious, she becomes unusually still, and says:

"When I was with my *other* mommy, I was a boy."

In that moment, thoughts and impressions swirl in your mind. You hear the matter-of-fact tone, you glance over at your darling three-year-old and notice that her face is calm, serious, *glowing*. And immediately *you* feel the energy. All of your senses come to attention. In a flash you know she is speaking about a past life memory.

What do you do first?

First, don't crash the car! This is not a joke. These memories pop up so often while riding in a car, the chances are good that this is where it will happen to you. If you feel unnerved, shaken, or in any way disturbed, pull over to the side of the road. Then direct your attention to your child. No matter where you are when the memory first comes up—at home, putting your little girl to bed, giving her a bath, or working in the kitchen—stop what you're doing. Focus on your child.

Almost all parents feel a bit frightened, excited, and off-balance when they sense this change in their child. Try to stay calm and collect yourself so you can be totally present. One way of doing this is to take full, deep breaths. Deep breathing assuages the shock and calms you down. It helps you find your center. If your mind is racing with wild thoughts or rebel doubts, breathing will quiet your mind so that you can give full attention to what your child is trying to tell you. Try to keep breathing deeply through the whole process.

Breathing consciously and staying calm and centered will enhance your receptivity. It will help you become more fully engaged and at one with your child. The emergence of a past life memory is an extraordinary, even mystical moment that breaks through the illusion of time. When you are fully present, you and your child enter a bubble of timeless space together. Your spirits touch. Centering and breathing opens your heart and intensifies this special connection.

During these moments, when it feels as if you and your child are enveloped in a bubble of energy, you are temporarily shut off from the commotion of the outside world and nothing else matters. Protect this feeling. Don't do anything abrupt that might pop the bubble. Don't run to bring in another member of the family, don't rush out to find a tape recorder, don't look for paper and pencil and try to write it down. If you leave the room or yell to summon another person, you may startle your child back to a normal state of consciousness. Don't worry that you won't remember every word your child says. You will remember what you need to and will be able to write it down later. Actually you'll probably discover in the following days that every word has been indelibly burned into your memory.

Acknowledge

If you do nothing else, remember to acknowledge the truth of your child's memories. Let her know you believe her and that what she is saying is important to you. This is crucial. With your questions and comments and your loving tone of voice, you communicate that you are truly interested in anything she has to say. By acknowledging your child, you are assuring her that it is safe to express whatever comes up, that she won't be ridiculed, and that she isn't somehow being a bad girl or doing something silly.

Ask questions to keep her talking about her memory. In the first few moments of the experience, your goal is simply to keep her talking so she will give you enough information to discern what the memory is about. The easiest questions to ask are what counselors and therapists call *restatements*. Simply repeat her words back to her with a questioning tone of voice. If she says, "When I had another mommy," you say, "You had another mommy?" If she says, "The bad guys shot me and I died underwater," you respond, "You died underwater?" or, "The bad guys shot you?" Restatements acknowledge the memory because they communicate that you're tracking with her and want to hear more. This is a powerful technique for keeping the flow of memory open.

It's okay to probe, to ask questions to test if this is really a past life memory. You can ask if she saw a story like this on TV, or heard it in preschool or from a brother or sister. But as you probe, don't criticize or express doubt in any way. Take care to ask in a loving "tell me about it" tone of voice, and *not* with an accusing "where did you hear such nonsense" attitude. Don't in any way hint that you think she is wrong, or crazy, or lying.

While asking questions, suspend judgment as to whether this is a true past life memory. It may not be. Allow, for now, that it *is* genuine, so you won't be distracted by a debate in your head. While the moment lasts, it doesn't matter where she got these ideas and images. Later, after things have returned to normal, you can decide what it was. But not now. While it's happening, open yourself fully to the reality of your child's experience. Defer judgment. Stay with the memory. If your faith doesn't allow for reincarnation, or if you fear that no one will believe what you are hearing, don't think about it now. You will have time later, after the moment has passed, to deliberate belief.

Acknowledging the truth of your child's words will have a profoundly good long-term effect on your relationship with your child. For when children communicate a past life memory, they are exposing an innermost part of their nature, something delicate and true. By acknowledging their memories, we are accepting *them* deeply. Your acknowledgment will keep these deep channels of communication open between you and your child for future days. It is through these channels that understanding and healing naturally occur. *Not* acknowledging, or denying your child's memory, could have an equally profound but *damaging* effect. If we deny our children's memories, or ridicule them for their remarks, we confuse them. It's like giving them a slap in the face for telling the truth. They may quickly get the message to doubt what they are experiencing, and they may seal off that deep part of themselves so they will never be judged or laughed at again. From this experience children may learn to doubt all inner or spiritual experiences. It may take them many years to rediscover and trust the truth that was so clear in their innocent hearts. We lose too. In closing that part of themselves off to us, we are deprived of a meaningful soul connection with our children—a priceless gift.

No matter what else you do, continue to acknowledge her, and her memories, throughout the experience.

Discern

Beginning with her first remark, your goal is to understand what your child is trying to express. You actually have two objectives: to discern the facts and feelings of the past life story, and to discern the themes implied by those facts. When you have a picture of what the past life memory is about and what emotion or unfinished business is pushing through, then you will be prepared to respond appropriately—to answer her needs with your understanding.

Listen closely and with an open mind to what your child is telling you. Use questions to keep her talking about the experience. Observe her facial expressions, body language, and gestures. Use your intuition too: pay attention to the way her statements make you feel, and to realizations that spring into your mind while you listen and watch.

More important than any technique, allow your child to lead the way. I can't emphasize this enough. You want to know what her experience is from *her* extraordinary perspective. Don't put ideas into her head, or assume you know where she is going with the memory. Let her do the talking. If she's talking freely, don't interrupt her with too many questions. Get in step with the rhythm of her conversation.

If the story tumbles out all at once, all you need to do is be attentive and listen. Simple phrases that acknowledge and encourage her—like "Oh, I see," or "That's interesting," or an occasional restatement—are all you need to say to keep her talking. Sustained eye contact, a nod of the head, or an occasional "uh-huh" will also do the trick. However, if your child hesitates, or has difficulty clarifying the memory, be patient. Wait. Breathe deeply. Then ask her an open-ended question, like "Then what happened?" "Now what do you see?" "Tell me more about it." Open-ended questions are those that *cannot* be answered with "yes" or "no" or a short reply. They are valuable for keeping the information flowing, without suggesting ideas or outcomes. Open questions allow your child to go where she needs to in the story.

Closed questions—those that *can* be answered yes or no or with a short reply—are useful for eliciting specific details. Questions like "Did you have brothers or sisters?" or "How old were you when you died?" or "Are you wearing a bathing suit?" will help you complete the picture of what happened. If she hesitates or seems to get stuck without moving along, asking the right closed question may strengthen and sharpen her mental image by focusing her attention on a specific detail.

Generally, open questions are best to draw out the most information. For example, instead of asking "Are you sad?" (closed), ask "How do you feel?" (open). You may be surprised to hear that, instead of being sad or not sad, she is angry, afraid, envious, or proud. The question may trigger a long and detailed description of her feelings and branch to new parts of the story. To a very small child with a limited vocabulary, you may want to offer a menu of choices: "Did you stay sick, or did you get better, or did you die?"

Avoid asking "Why?" questions. "Why's?" force your child to grope for an explanation or interpretation. They may interrupt the flow of memory by calling on rational thinking and bring the dialogue to an abrupt end.

Remember, your paramount goal is to keep her involved in the memory, to keep her talking. Stay with the rhythm and the pace she sets, and use questions to keep it flowing. As the story unfolds, you will find yourself asking open questions to expand the picture, followed by closed questions to focus and to clarify.

Match your tone of voice to hers. If she is enthusiastically describing her other life or even her death, match her enthusiasm. If she is sad, then respond with a serious, concerned voice, just as you would if she had come to tell you her pet hamster just died. Your genuine interest in what she is saying will encourage her to go deeper into her memory, to see more clearly, and to stay with the story.

These techniques are guidelines and suggestions only. Don't worry about making a mistake. When engrossed in a past life memory, children will hold tenaciously to the truth of their vision and are not easily swayed. Recall that in many of the cases in this book, the parents were so taken aback by their children's remarks that they fumbled for words and asked silly questions. Still, the children were tolerant of their parents' ineptness and patiently corrected them. In other cases, when a parent assumed too much and said, "You saw this on TV, right?" the child adamantly denied it. So don't fret or hesitate for fear of asking the wrong questions. It is far more important to be lovingly present for your child in these moments. Your unconditional acceptance of what she is experiencing is the key; your skill in questioning is only a useful tool.

Henry Bolduc, speaking from more than thirty years of experience as a past life regressionist, agrees that a relaxed pace is the best technique:

When children come up with these memories, I think it's important to acknowledge them without making a big deal about it. I ask as few specific questions as possible, and instead say, "Tell me more about it." It should never turn into an interrogation or a grilling or anything like that.

It's important to let them go at their own pace. That way you'll encourage the natural flow of information. Wait for them. Sometimes when I'm working with an adult client, I want to jump in and say something or ask a question. But I've found that it's better to silently count to ten—and wait. The process of memory is like the opening of a flower—you don't want to rush it.

Discern Facts and Feelings

The first objective of discerning is to discover the particulars of the story. Was she an adult or child in the past life? What sex? Did she have a family? What life-changing traumas did she go through? How did she die? You want to glean as much of the story as you can while this moment of lucidity lasts.

Be aware of your child's feelings as she talks about her memory. Is she sad, happy, scared, or excited? Is she distraught, bitter, guilty, remorseful? Tears usually indicate sadness, but not necessarily. They can be an indication of any deep emotion welling to the surface—even long-forgotten happiness. The strength of the emotional charge is the best indicator of the strength of the memory and its hold on her present life. Strong emotions point to the reason the memory is alive in your child, and to how you might respond. If she tells the story in a blasé, detached tone, then the emotional charge may be slight. On the other hand, if she appears to be deeply disturbed, or is crying or distraught, it could be a sign that the memory still has a strong grip on her, clouding and distorting her present reality.

Listen carefully to the verb tense of the story. It can be another clue to how your child is experiencing the memory. Is she speaking of something that she knows happened in the past? For example: "My other mommy used to put her hair up like that when she wanted to look pretty." Or does she speak as if the events are happening in the present? "My real mommy lives in Biloxi." Sometimes, as the story unfolds, a *change* in verb tense will reflect where the child is in the process of remembering and reveal how much she has let go of the past.

If she mentions dying, concentrate on the circumstances surrounding the moment of death. Ask questions like "How did you die?" "Who was with you when you died?" "What happened just before you died?" Use open questions, too, like "What happened next?" "How did you feel?" "What were you thinking?" Get as much information as you can, so you can discern what unfinished business might remain from the moment of death. Proceed gently, in an unexcited, matter-of-fact tone of voice. If she resists this line of questioning, don't push.

After she's told you as much as she can about the moment of death, ask her, "Right *after* you died, then what happened?" You may be rewarded with a full description of her journey through the after-life bardos and heaven. Or your child may simply say, "And then I came to you!" By tracing this transition from past life death to rebirth, she may come to understand for the first time that the past life is over, that she is now in a new lifetime. This could be just the understanding she needs to help her let go of the past and ground herself in present reality. This realization alone may neutralize the effects of an incomplete death.

Remember, it is not necessary to know names and dates in order to discern the meaning of the memory. Names and dates are irrelevant to the personal meaning of a past life, and proof is not the point. Don't probe or push too much for names and dates, because if she doesn't remember, she might begin to think that there is something wrong and freeze up, blocking the flow of memory. The same is true for apparent inconsistencies in detail and historical inaccuracies. Don't correct her if she says something that seems incongruous or inaccurate. Let it go without interrupting. By poking at an inconsistency, you may break a hole in this delicate web of memory as it is being spun. Concentrate instead on discerning the overall pattern of the story and the emotions behind it.

One more thing to watch for. Be alert for the instant the remembering is over. You'll know it by the look on her face as she snaps back to her playful, little-girl self, or when you feel a shift in the energy between you. Once the trance is over, there's nothing you can do to prolong it, so don't try. If more needs to be told, be assured that the memory will surface again.

Sagiv (Part 1)

This case is a good example of how one mother used questions to establish the facts of her son's past life story.

My first encounter with Elona at my sister's Fourth of July picnic is described in the previous chapter. A week later, when her son Sagiv began speaking of his past life, all she knew about past life memories was what she had learned from my brief account of Chase's story. But by using her instincts and common sense, and by employing a balance of open and closed questions, she was able, first, to determine that Sagiv was talking about a real past life memory, and then to follow the story where it naturally led. She was able to keep Sagiv talking, to keep the memory flowing. Keeping him engaged in the memory quickly led to a life-changing catharsis.

One night, four-and-a-half-year-old Sagiv and I were driving in the car to pick up some pizzas for dinner. We seldom drive alone together, since Sagiv is one of three children. He was sitting in the front seat with me and said, "When I was three years old, my mommy used to put me to sleep at night in the car." This statement threw me for a loop, because I had never done that, so I asked him, "Was it the same car?"

"Yes, it was blue like this one, but the top"——he pointed to the ceiling——"was different. It had no windows or ceiling." I guessed that he was talking about a convertible.

Then he said, sort of boasting, "My daddy has a speeding car."

This remark was really odd, since he never calls his father Daddy. My husband is Israeli, and the kids have always called him Abba, which is Hebrew for father. I was so surprised that I blurted out, "Your *daddy*?"

He said, "Yeah," but he seemed almost as confused about it as I was.

I said, "You mean Abba?"

"No," he insisted, "my *daddy*."

Okay, I thought, where is this going? He was really focusing, and I could tell by the seriousness on his face that he was not making this up. Kids are transparent. With a fantasy story I can see the eyes conjuring it up, and I can tell by the singsong quality of his voice: "And then the frog . . . uh . . ." But now he was looking down with his brow wrinkled in deep concentration, really trying to remember. Each time he came up with a piece of this, he would look up, almost surprised, as if he were saying "Yeah, that's it." He was really happy that he could remember and express it. Interestingly, Sagiv has always had a language retrieval problem, and he forgets words and gets frustrated when he can't express himself. But with this, he was concentrating, and the words were coming to him.

To keep the conversation going, I asked him, "Do you have any brothers or sisters?"

"No."

"How old were you when this happened?"

"Three."

I could feel a special connection between us, and I didn't want to taint it by asking questions that might spoil it. I just wanted information from him at this point. I just wanted to ask questions that would tell me where he was coming from, where *he* was trying to get to, and how I should deal with him appropriately as a parent—even whether I should be taking all of this seriously or not. But from the beginning I sensed that this was something very real. And while I'm driving! I'm trying to drive normally and ask him these questions at the same time.

I asked him where he lived, and he said that he didn't know. So I asked him, "Was it in the country, or like where we live now in the suburbs, or in the city?"

"It was in the city, like where Uncle Stacey lives. In an apartment."

"Did you grow up, or did you stay three years old?"

He said quietly and seriously, "No, I was shot."

"You were killed?" I asked, a little shocked.

"Yes. I was shot and killed."

I was very concerned at this point and asked him, "How?"

"Burglars. They didn't mean to. I wasn't doing anything. He just shot me for no reason. I was at the top of the stairs. First they shot my mother, and she was on the floor. And then they shot me."

Sagiv's story took a sharp turn at this point and is continued later in this chapter.

Discerning Themes and Needs

The second objective of discerning is to discover the meaning behind the past life story, beyond what your child is perceiving and describing. Then from this you decide what kind of help your child might need from you.

When young children talk about a past life memory, they tell their story by describing what they see in their mind's eye, what they feel, and by answering questions. But they have neither the maturity nor the objectivity to articulate how the experience relates to their present life. They are too young to analyze the story or to identify what issues from the past are still affecting them. This is where they need your help. As an adult, you know how to recognize underlying themes in a literal story—to read between the lines. Applying your analytical skills and your general understanding of how these memories work, you can discern how your child is being affected by the past life. You might also discover *why* the memory is pushing through by identifying the unfinished business behind it.

Recall that when Chase first spoke of his Civil War memory, he didn't explicitly talk about his guilt at being a soldier. He was too young to articulate the concept of guilt, but he told us that he "didn't want to be there and shoot other people." Norman Inge inferred through Chase's statements and body language that he was feeling guilty about being a soldier and killing others in battle. By properly identifying this theme and then addressing these unpleasant feelings in a way that a five-year-old could understand, Norman was able to help Chase release his guilt and its accompanying fear.

This level of discernment may require thought and reflection; you may have to ruminate for hours or days before you understand the issues from the past and how they connect to the present. Or you might see it in a flash. Each case is different.

How do you discern past life themes? First, put yourself in your child's shoes, and imagine what you would see, think, and feel if you were at the center of her past life scenario. For example, if she told you about dying alone on a battlefield, imagine yourself on that battlefield. How would *you* feel: Still angry at the enemy? Or angry at the stupidity of your own leaders? Disgusted with yourself for making a mistake that resulted in your being killed? Scared out of your mind by the confusion and gore around you? You might feel guilty about killing others who are similarly pawns in the game. Or grieving for the family and fiancée you left behind. Try to imagine how any one of these emotions could tint your view of reality in this life. Then think of everything you know about your child. Does she have any unexplained behavior, traits, physical symptoms, or emotional problems? Phobias, especially, are the first place to look. If she does have an unexplained behavior or trait, think how it might correspond with the facts and emotions of the past life story. This correspondence is the key—it's what you are looking for.

To see the variety of possibilities, think back to the correspondences between past life trauma and present life problems that Dr. Woolger discovered. Some of these correlations are simple and easy to identify. For example, if your child tells you a story of being mauled and killed by wild dogs in a past life, and now has a phobia of large animals, the connection is obvious. In other cases there may be no obvious connection. The link may be complex, involving layered themes and a tangle of unfinished business that make the correlation more difficult to see.

Use your intuition as well as your intellect to discern this correspondence. This is not a scientific process; there are no formulas to determine precisely how a past life experience will affect your child, or the definitive meaning of a memory. Open yourself to whatever inspiration comes to you. Knowing your child as intimately as you do, you may get a flash of insight about how this memory fits into your child's present life, or understanding may come to you in a dream. If so, give it credence, just as you would a direct statement from your child. Follow your hunches and see where they lead.

And remember, themes from past lives don't have to be negative or cause problems. Positive past life memories convey positive themes. A child may remember a beloved grandmother from a past life and be left with indelible feelings of love and belonging, causing this child to be secure and affectionate. Bountiful, uplifting memories are just as significant as troublesome ones. By understanding these positive themes, we can gain insight into our children's temperament, personality, and behavior. With such children there isn't necessarily anything else we, as parents, have to do.

Unblame Parents

The case of Donald Foster is one in which a mother discerned the correspondence between a past life theme and a present life problem. In a phone call from her home in Tennessee, Becky Foster told me what happened.

> When Donald was three, we were driving alone in the car, looking at the scenery, when he started talking about his *other* parents. As soon as he said that, it really hit something in me. He was in a serious mood, very genuine. I could tell that this wasn't a made-up story, he wasn't joking. I asked him what had happened to his other parents. He told me that he was very young when they died.
>
> "Where were you when they died?" I asked.
>
> "I was hiding in the bushes," he said.
>
> He didn't know how his parents had died, but I could tell by his voice that he was terrified. He went on to tell me more about that life, and it seemed to make him feel better to talk about it. Then his face lit up and he said, "And now I'm here with you and you're my mother, right?"
>
> I said, "That's right. And you're my son and I'm your mother. Poppa's your father, and Cassidy, Kelly, and Elizabeth are your sisters."
>
> He added, "And we're one big happy family!" By saying this, he knew that his experience was in the past and gone. He could be at ease with it.

When I asked Becky if Donald had any unusual behavior relating to this memory, she responded:

> Now that you mention it, for a long time Donald had terrible separation anxiety. He was the only one of my four

children to have it. He was fine if he could still see me when I walked out of a room. But if I walked out of the room and he couldn't see me, it didn't matter who was around, he would start screaming. To keep him from screaming, I had to pick him up and carry him around everywhere I went. It was really bad!

None of my other children had this problem at all. So I assumed it was all because of me, it was my fault. I blamed Donald's separation anxiety on my emotional state during pregnancy.

I had never put these two things together before, but now I see it. Donald probably was afraid I was going to abandon him because that is what happened to him after his past life parents were killed in front of him and he was left alone. Now it makes so much sense! And I don't have to feel guilty anymore.

Becky's story brings up a very important idea, a significant benefit for *parents* that derives from understanding how past life memories affect children. This benefit is to remove guilt—to *unblame* parents.

Because we generally don't accept reincarnation in our culture, conscientious parents often blame themselves and their parenting mistakes for any and all mental or behavioral problems their young children may have. Recent research has shown that babies in utero register impressions from the mother that affect the forming personality,[1] so now some mothers feel guilty even for incorrect thoughts and feelings during pregnancy, as Becky Foster did. This self-blame stems from our Western belief in the *tabula rasa* theory—the idea from the old paradigm that children come in as blank slates to be written on first by parents.

But now that we know how past lives influence a child's behavior and personality, parents don't have to be so hard on themselves. I'm not saying that all problems are the result of past lives—nothing's that simple. But parents shouldn't feel guilty for *everything* in their children's makeup. They should know, from the research presented in this book, that children *do* bring their own baggage with them from the past, and that not all of their feelings and behavior are a reflection of our parenting abilities.

Allow Emotions

No matter how sad, excited, happy, upset, or disturbed your child may be, allow her to express the emotions of the memory fully. If the memory is coming up because traumatic issues need to be resolved, she may arrive at a full resolution just by talking about it. The resolution may involve crying, even a full catharsis. Or there may be no emotion at all; she may be totally detached from the memory. Whatever happens, your response is the same: allow her to stay involved with the experience until the memory runs its course, as long as the energy lasts.

This is important because an emerging past life memory is a natural process guided by the unconscious. Exactly how the unconscious works is beyond our ability to comprehend, but you can trust its gentle wisdom. Past life therapists do. Every day, in case after case, they watch the unconscious mastermind impressive healings; the implicit wisdom of the unconscious is a given in their profession. You can trust your child's unconscious to know how much to reveal, how much she can take at any one time, and when to stop. It knows what is necessary for a complete healing. When you allow expression, you are getting out of the way so the unconscious can do its work. You are allowing the miracle of spontaneous past life healing to happen.

With some children, like Courtney, no heavy emotional issues seem to be involved—the memories are just there. They need only to tell their stories. These children are the ones most likely to interject snippets of their past life into a conversation anytime something triggers their memory. Even in cases where the death was sudden or traumatic, like Liia's drowning, the child may not be troubled. Allowing, in these benign cases, means resisting the temptation to exaggerate the issue. There may be no mystery to solve, no issues to understand or respond to. Just allow your child to talk about her past life as she will. You can relax and enjoy the wonder of it.

You may discern strong positive emotions when your child recalls her past life. She may tell you stories of love, fulfillment, and devotion. She may be excited, happy, or peaceful. She may weep tears of joy. Join in her happiness, exult together in the love, and explore the reasons for fulfillment. Delight in the gifts or talents she may have brought with her from the past. The memory of that life is good.

If your child shows negative emotions, if she is sad or scared or cries as she speaks of a tragic life, let her know that you understand how she feels. If she is speaking of a loss, even her own death, and tears are running down her cheeks, acknowledge her sadness: "You're really sad about this, aren't you?" Let her know that you are with her. Your understanding will make her feel safe and encourage her to express herself fully. When she is finished, the sad or scary memories will have lost their emotional charge and will soon be forgotten.

If very strong emotions are still tangled in the memory, you will likely hear about a traumatic death. Be prepared for these memories of death, for they are the most common. What you hear may not be pretty; it may be disturbing to you. But how *you* feel isn't the issue. Don't try to minimize these memories or divert her from talking about them. Instead, encourage her to stay with the images and feelings. Don't be afraid that these visions of death are a morbid fixation or in any way dangerous. They are not. They are valuable opportunities to let go of the troubling past, and a natural part of the healing process. As past life therapists have found, going back through the moment of a traumatic death releases and resolves its negative effects.

For most children talking through the past life trauma will be sufficient to clear strong negative emotions. Other children, though, may need a full catharsis. Catharsis is when pent-up emotions and thoughts come to a head and are released all at once. Your child may get angry and upset, cry, flail, and thrash about—she may even get hysterical. This is good. This is the memory coming out and letting go. Allow it to happen.

Of course, use your good sense in these situations. If your

daughter becomes hysterical and begins to thrash about, protect her from hitting the furniture or falling down. Hold her, if you sense she needs it. But *never* try to talk her out of her feelings. I know it's difficult to sit by and watch your child wrestle with such strong emotions. But this is the climax of the healing process, the crucial moment when your forbearing is the most loving thing you can do. Don't suddenly change the subject and say, "Well, let's go have some lunch" to make her feel better or to ease your own fear that she will get stuck in these bad feelings. She won't get stuck, and the catharsis will not last more than a few minutes. On the other hand, if you interrupt at this moment, you will yank your child out of the process prematurely and rob her of an opportunity for a complete release of the troubling emotions.

When she is finished, she'll snap out of it suddenly. If she has a complete release, you'll know it. She'll look like the sun shining through after a storm. You'll see radiance on her face and feel freshness in the air around her, as the clouds of emotion lift.

Sagiv (Part 2)

Elona's acceptance of what Sagiv was saying allowed him to proceed to a catharsis with life-changing results. Let's back up slightly to the point in Sagiv's story where he remembers being shot:

"Yes, I was shot and killed."

I was very concerned at this point and asked him, "How?"

"Burglars. They didn't mean to. I wasn't doing anything. He just shot me for no reason. I was at the top of the stairs. First they shot my mother, and she was on the floor. And then they shot me."

Then he looked at me, and in a loud and angry voice, he blasted, *"You didn't save me!"* He was really angry at me and started getting excited. Again he shouted, *"You didn't save me!"*

This floored me. I assured him, in a calm and authoritative voice, *"It wasn't me. It wasn't me. It was a different time. It was a different mother, someone I don't even know."*

He seemed to accept this immediately, then proceeded to tell me what happened next. He said, "Well, then I died. I was dead, but I grew up—you know what I mean. I stayed there until I came back to be a baby again." And then his eyebrows went up, his face lit up, and he said, "And then I chose you and Abba!" He said this like suddenly it all made perfect sense to him.

Believe me, our family doesn't normally discuss things like this. We live in a traditional Jewish household. We light candles every Friday night, but we don't discuss religious philosophy at all. I don't even know if he knew who God was at that point. So when he said this, it really blew me away. To me, it was just so real and beyond anything he could know. And the funny thing was, he was so happy about choosing us as his parents.

After all this, after talking so casually about his death and how he chose his parents, in the next breath he asked brightly:

"Are we at the pizza place yet?"

"Yeah," I told him, "we're almost there."

Elona's genuine concern for what Sagiv had to say about his death allowed him to move quickly to a catharsis, which came when he screamed at her, "You didn't save me! You didn't save me!"

A week later Elona brought up the memory again. This time, though, when Sagiv told his story, he was not emotional about it—his catharsis was complete, his anger was spent. And Elona began to notice a major change in his personality:

A week or so later I asked him about this again, right before he went to sleep. He repeated the story in exactly the same way, but he told me more details about his death. He said that his mother was standing at the top of the stairs, and he was in front of her. First they shot her, and then they shot him. He said that when he was shot, his mother was already dead on the floor at the bottom of the stairs. Again he repeated that his mother couldn't save him. *This time, though, he was not emotional about it.* Again I assured him that I was not that mother and that I would never let that happen to him. He was relieved.

It was after this that I noticed a huge change in Sagiv, especially in the way he related to me. He had never been a warm child. Since he was born, something was missing. He was never a cuddly baby. He was always tense and pushed me away. He didn't enjoy being cuddled by *anyone,* for that matter. This really hurt me, because his older sister had been such an affectionate baby. Sagiv was different, and I couldn't understand why. Was it something I had done?

But immediately after he told me the story, he changed. I remember this clearly, because it hit me like a bomb! Sagiv moved himself onto my lap, put his arms around me, and said, "I love you, Mommy." He became very cuddly and started hugging me. It was amazing. He now massages my neck if I'm tense and is very affectionate. Before this, he wouldn't even sit on my lap—ever! My mother even noticed this change and commented on how he had warmed up so much.

Looking back, I could see that he held *me* responsible for whatever had happened to him before in that other life. He had been angry at me for not saving him or protecting him from what happened. And, he had carried these feelings since birth. After he remembered this, he finally let go of his anger. Since then he hugs me all the time. It's amazing.

Clarify Past and Present

Some children, like Sagiv, need our help in clarifying the difference between what happened in the past and what is true now in the present. Even after talking about their memories and expressing their emotions, they may continue to wrestle with uncomfortable feelings from the past. They may need more than just our forbearance: they may need us to intervene and assure them that the images in their minds will no longer hurt them, that the past life is gone, and that they are now safe and secure in this new life with a family that will protect them.

Though it is hard for us to imagine, some children cannot distinguish between past and present. These children don't know that they have died, moved on to another lifetime, and are now in another body. Both past and present lifetimes merge in their awareness, and scenes and feelings from the past overlay their present reality.

This is dramatically clear in two cases from Ian Stevenson. In the first case, from Turkey, one of baby Celal Kapan's first full sentences was, "What am I doing here? I was at the port." As his language improved, he explained that he had been a dock worker who fell asleep in the hold of a ship that was being loaded. He was killed instantly when an oil drum was dropped on top of him. From Celal's point of view, when he awoke from his nap in the hold of the ship he was surprised to find himself in the body of a small child. He didn't know that he had died.[2] Parmod Sharma from India was similarly bewildered by his sudden transition to a new life. He remembered dozens of verified details of the life of a man who had died right after taking a curative bath. Some of Parmod's first words were: "I was sitting in a bath tub and my feet have become small."[3]

Some children still have one foot in the past and jump back and forth between lifetimes; they are blatantly confused about which life they are in. This is more likely to be true for very young children because they are closer on the continuum of memory to their past life. Their consciousness has not yet been fixed within the boundaries of a single lifetime. Their perceptions of time are blurred; past and present exist simultaneously. One reason this occurs, I believe, is that the shock of a sudden death freezes a part of their consciousness in their former experience: a part of them is truly held back in the past, and the transition is not complete.

We can help children complete the transition by telling them, "You are now safe in a new body. You are now in a different life," as Colleen did with Blake. The words act like a rescue rope to pull these children out of the past and anchor them completely in the present. Sometimes this understanding is all that is necessary for them to let go of the past, and the past life feelings and thoughts that had been troubling them vanish in an instant.

Along with this general clarification, you may need to give your daughter assurances that speak to *specific* troubling issues. Assure her that each unpleasant event she experienced is over and won't happen again. Use positive affirmations to reinforce the lessons learned from the memory. Repeat these assurances, if necessary, in the days, weeks, and months that follow, especially when she encounters situations that may remind her of the troubling past life experience.

For example, an appropriate affirmation in Billy's case, since he was troubled by his memories of poverty and starvation, would be: "You now have all the food you need." An affirmation that would be appropriate in almost all cases is: "You are part of our family now, and we all love you."

Natalie

Phyllis Elkins tracked me down shortly after I appeared on *Oprah*. She called me a couple of days after her two-year-old daughter, Natalie, gave what sounded like a premonition of her own imminent death. Notice in this case how Phyllis used questions to discern facts, how baby Natalie progressed over a few weeks to an eventual catharsis, and how her verb tenses flip back and forth, revealing that she is confused about time and reality.

The other morning Natalie and I came downstairs and were getting ready to have some cereal. She was just lying around on the floor and talking, when all of a sudden she looked up at me and said, in an unusually clear and articulate manner, "You will never see me again."

I said, "What do you mean?"

She said, "Bob and Randy put me in the water, and they killed me, and I went up to the blue," and she pointed up to the sky. Of course, I began to shake in my boots and asked her, "When did this happen?" She thought for a minute and looked over and said, "Tuesday." This was on a Monday.

As we were sitting at the table eating breakfast, she was staring at me, her eyes slightly glazed over and looking into my eyes the whole time. I could see in her eyes that there were moments when she was present and moments when she was in a trance. Her words were deliberate and crystal clear. Her behavior was suddenly different—she was calm and controlled and seemed more mature. Her words, tone, and behavior left me feeling completely unnerved.

I told my husband about this when he came home that evening. He was as distressed as I was. He tried to talk to her about it, but she just changed the subject and acted like a baby.

The next morning my instinct told me that the window was open when she would talk about it again. My husband had gone upstairs. I said to her, "Do you remember yesterday, when you talked about Bob and Randy?"

She said, "Yes, something about a swimming pool." She was very serious in the face, very articulate.

I said to her, "Tell me about the swimming pool."

She answered, very calmly, unafraid, "It has toys and fishies."

I continued, "Tell me about Bob and Randy. Are they kids?"

"They're boys," she immediately replied.

"Is this a dream?" I asked.

"No, no," she said without hesitating.

"Did you see this on TV?"

"No, it wasn't TV."

"Did this already happen?"

She said, "I've got to go soon, I've got to go up to the blue."

"Are you afraid of water?"

"No. I've got to go away soon, up to the blue."

And that was all I could get out of her. When she talked about this, she was especially articulate, almost older or more mature, serious, and unbelievably matter-of-fact.

My husband and I didn't know what to think or feel. We were both emotionally drained. That night I slept with

Natalie, because I was scared and wanted to be close to her. The next morning I again asked her about the pool. Immediately she said, "I floated up to the blue." [Note the past tense.]

"Were Bob and Randy there?"

"They were my friends, but they didn't want to play with me."

"Are you wearing a bathing suit?" I asked.

She looked down at herself and said, "Yes."

"Was Mom there?"

"No."

"Were you a little girl or a big girl?"

"Little girl."

"What is your name?"

"Natalie." [Notice that Phyllis used the present tense, *is*, and that Natalie gave her present life name.]

"What was the pool like?"

"Toys, a little pool with fishies. I was swimming around."

"What was it like to float up?"

"Nice."

I know this wasn't fantasy. She was a two-year-old, and the story was solid. It didn't change from day to day. When she tells a fantasy story, she will add pieces from other stories, from her imagination, and from fairy tales, mixing it all together with the story she's making up. I can identify these easily: she alters them and the stories always change. But in this past life story, there was no fantasy about it. She was very matter-of-fact and very clear about the details.

Natalie brought up her story again and again, always in the morning. These things would come to her when she first woke up and was very fresh. She would just come out with it. It was always consistent. I began using open-ended questions, like "Then what happened?" and I followed her lead. Then she would come up with what was in her head, not what I brought to the party.

And, when she was finished, she was finished. There was nothing I could say that would prolong it. I tried to talk to her before she went to bed, but it wouldn't work. And it's funny—Natalie is such a "Daddy's girl," but she wouldn't talk about it with him. She didn't achieve the memory with him.

Phyllis and I discussed the possibilities: was Natalie speaking of a past life memory, or was she foreseeing her own death? We were both leaning toward a past life memory. Although Natalie wasn't afraid of water, the other signs were there: the matter-of-fact tone, the consistency of her story, and her knowledge that drowning can kill you—something Phyllis assured me that her two-year-old couldn't possibly know.

She told me that they didn't know any boys by the names of Bob and Randy, but that she wasn't going to let Natalie anywhere near a swimming pool until this was resolved. In fact, she was even reluctant to bathe her!

I encouraged Phyllis to continue to talk to Natalie about it, to use open-ended questions, and to assure her that this was something that had happened before, when she was in a different body, and that Bob and Randy were no longer around and couldn't hurt her. I also warned Phyllis that a catharsis might be imminent. Natalie might reexperience the terror of that moment of drowning and cry and thrash around, but it would be okay. I told her that if this should happen, she should be present for her, let her go through it, and then give her love and reassurance that she is now safe and that the experience is over.

A few weeks later things began to shift. On Mother's Day Phyllis again asked Natalie about her experience.

"Did the baby hurt herself while playing in the swimming pool?"

"Yes," said Natalie. "The baby fell and hit herself on the head. Her cheek was red. She's not Natalie, she's Zack."

Surprised by this change, Phyllis asked, "Then what happened?"

"I went up to the sky."

"How old is Zack?"

"Two," she replied.

"Do you want to talk about it?"

"No," she answered, "I'm scared."

Phyllis assured her, "This will not happen again. It's okay to talk about it." But Natalie's trance was broken. She had nothing more to say.

At this point Natalie's feelings were becoming conscious enough that she could articulate them. She could finally say, "I'm scared."

Later that day the family was driving to Grandma's house. Phyllis recalls:

Natalie was in her car seat, very sleepy. My husband turned around and looked at her. She looked like something was wrong. She had a very contorted, grim face and was staring at the floor.

I said, "Do you want to talk about it?"

She kept saying, "I'm scared, I'm scared." As she said that, she was thrashing around in her car seat. She went through this little fit. Then suddenly her eyes got bright, and she was calm. By the time we got to Grandma's, it was gone, she had changed. I could see it in her face. She was real bright.

A few weeks later she surprised me when we were visiting my friend, and Natalie asked her, "Did you hear about Zack?" Then, in a very matter-of-fact way, Natalie told my friend that Zack was swimming and he breathed up too much water and fell, hit his head, and went down there with the fishies. She must have gone through some resolution of this on Mother's Day, because that was the end of it.

Natalie was able to move through her fear, I believe, because she knew that her mother fully supported her. She had the catharsis by herself, in her car seat. Then she was free of it. A few weeks later, confirmation that this episode was over came when Natalie told the family friend about her memory and referred to it in the *past tense* and in the *third person*. She was no longer emotional about it, she was no longer troubled. She told it as a story that had happened to somebody else. And Natalie never spoke of "going up to the blue" again.

Unfolding over Time

Resolving a memory may not happen all at once. In most cases the process of remembering and venting emotions unfolds gradually. The memories may come up repeatedly over a period of days, weeks, months, or even years. Your child may talk of her past life once, then again a year later, and never again after that. Or you may have one of those loquacious children who frequently drop casual references to their past life into their chatter seemingly at random, tickling you with surprise each time.

Because you never know whether your child is finished with the memory, you need to be careful not to say or do anything that might discourage her from bringing it up again. If you have the urge to share her amazing story with relatives and friends, *be discreet*. Don't make a big fuss about it, *especially in front of your child*—it could embarrass her. Some parents have told me that in their enthusiasm for telling others, the children became embarrassed by the attention and then denied they had ever remembered a past life. Protect her from direct criticism too. Don't mention it to friends or family members who you know will not believe it—especially within earshot of your child. It only takes a few discouraging words or a mocking joke for a youngster to get the message that past lives is something that adults ridicule.

A woman from South Carolina wrote to me about an unforgettable past life experience she had more than *sixty years ago,* when she was five years old. But her mother laughed at her. The stinging embarrassment of that incident remained with her for the rest of her life:

> I remember it as if it happened yesterday. Mother just hugged me and laughed. I was humiliated. I regretted that I had shared my vision with her, only to be laughed at. Later I heard Mother tell Father what I had said, and she laughed

again. When I heard that, I decided that I would *never again say anything serious that would make them laugh at me.*

Some parents have asked me if it's okay to try to bring up the memory again, rather than waiting for it to come up spontaneously. The answer is yes, if you summon it gently and don't pressure the child to remember. If the first spontaneous memory was brief, as it often is, you may not have had enough time to give your child clarification or assurances; or after reflecting on what she said, you may realize that she didn't get closure on an important issue. These are good reasons to bring up the memory again, and there's no harm in trying.

Use your instincts to determine the best time to ask. Wait until you are calm and your child is relaxed and you are both free from distractions. Colleen and Elona both brought up their children's memories at bedtime, when their kids were most receptive to their suggestions. Phyllis Elkins discovered that her daughter's time for remembering was first thing in the morning, during breakfast. Another parent told me that it *always* happens in the kitchen.

Then, when you feel the energy is right, casually remind her about what she said before. For example, ask: "Remember when you told me about your other mommy?" Let her know you are interested in what she said and would like to hear more of the story. If she still remembers and is able to talk about it, this might be all the prompting she needs. She might pick up where she left off in the memory, without missing a beat. Or she might not want to talk about it, or can't remember. If, after you have tendered your gentle offer, she acts as if she doesn't know what you're talking about, or says it was "just a dream," or changes the subject, let it go without making a big deal about it. If the door won't budge, there's nothing you can do to force it open.

If you can't get your child to talk about it further, you might try encouraging her to express her memory artistically. For some children, expressing a memory in a right-brain medium is easier than putting it into words. Suggest that she draw it, paint it, or reenact it with toys. Even if she ignores your suggestions, watch her casual drawings and play activity. If you see that she is drawing or reenacting scenes from her memory, show an interest in what she is doing and ask her to tell you about it. This may open the flow of memory again.

Postscript: Write It Down

Keep a record of your child's past life memory. Write it down immediately after it happens, while it's still fresh in your mind. Record everything you remember: the words she spoke, the look on her face, body language, signs of emotion, what you said and the questions you asked, and how you felt and what you thought as you listened. Also record what you and your child were doing at the time that might have triggered the memory.

If she talks about the memory more than once, your written record will make it easier for you to compare each instance for consistency and to notice added details. Also, some past life memories come in fragments that don't seem to have much significance at the time and are difficult to remember later. But if you keep a record of everything she said, you may see that these little bits, when strung together in your journal, form a pattern that does make sense.

Writing is an excellent way to sort out your own thoughts and open yourself to new insights about your child's experience. You may discover a correspondence between what your child said and her present personality. You may suddenly see a connection to an earlier remark or incident—like a nightmare or an unusual fear—that foreshadowed the memory. And writing about the experience may work as a meditation on the spiritual meaning of your child's memory for your child—and for you.

Writing it down will help other parents too. The study of children's past life memories is a new field, and much more research has to be done before we can understand the full importance of this phenomenon. Independent researchers like me must rely on parents like you for the cases. A written account of your story, if you choose to share it later, will be a valuable contribution to this research. Then other parents will be able to learn from your experience.

Be sure to archive your writings with your most valuable keepsakes, where it will be safe for the next twenty or thirty years. When your child is grown and has totally forgotten her past life memory, your journal of her actual words will show her what awareness she had when she was little. From the perspective of an adult, her past life memory may take on a deeper meaning. You both will marvel when you realize that her adult behavior, skills, interests, or career were presaged by her innocent remarks as a two-year-old.

John Van Dyk

John Van Dyk is now a grown man in his twenties—the same John Van Dyk who remembered being a young Indian forced into battle. When he was three he had another past life experience at the holy site of Saint Francis in Assisi, Italy. His mother, Alison, kept a journal and a scrapbook. As he grew older, this record of his memory proved to be a source of inspiration and guidance for him. It reminded him that he had received the first clues of his life purpose when he was a little boy.

John was three years old when we visited Assisi. Prior to this visit, his favorite book was *Saint Francis and the Wolf*, a little book for children that told about the life of this remarkable saint. He loved the story more than any other and asked me to read it over and over.

On our first day there, we visited the main church and then walked over to the little chapel where Saint Francis had his famous vision of Christ, who commanded him, "Francis, build my Church."

Like most energetic three-year-olds, John was always on the run and at least a half a block ahead of us. By the time my husband and I turned the corner on the path that opened onto the little chapel, to our astonishment, John was holding the hand of a Franciscan monk and patiently waiting for us. The monk introduced himself and then said that

John had asked him for a tour. The monk seemed taken aback but obviously intrigued by the openness of this American three-year-old.

As we followed behind the two new friends, we were amazed at the conversation that followed. John began the tour by asking to see certain areas of the chapel that I had never heard of and could not possibly have told him about. He was speaking like one who had been there before. The monk caught on to this time warp and continually modified his responses: "Well, *today* the monks eat there; well, *now* we sleep in that area, because there are more of us."

When we arrived at the chapel proper where Francis had his vision, John stood silently for a long time staring at the image of Christ—a highly unusual action for such an active three-year-old. By the time John had said good-bye to his new friend, we were convinced that he had a past life at Assisi.

John and I made a book of postcards and photographs of this trip. Even today it is one of his most prized possessions. I have only to say, "Remember when you were in Assisi?" and the memories come flooding back to us from those well-worn pages.

In his early twenties John joined a Christian student group in Colorado, where he attended college. On two occasions he traveled to Mexico to do missionary work with the Tarahumara Indians, and on another to Alaska to work with Eskimo villagers. He has decided to dedicate his life to working with the poor in the Third World. John's career choice, I believe, was in many ways determined by his past life experiences and memories.

As a parent and child psychotherapist, I believe that children between the ages of two and seven are particularly open to spontaneous past life memories. Our job as adults is to honor these experiences and perhaps, as I have done for my child, record these memories so that the wisdom is not lost.

CHAPTER 13

Dreaming Up
the Past

Past Life Memories Emerge in Dreams

"It never would have happened without the dream," begins Jenny Cockell's story of her childhood dreams and past life memories. As a young child in England in the 1950s, Jenny was plagued by the most vivid recurring dream. She saw herself as a grown woman, named Mary, lying in bed in a large white room and dying from a fever. Jenny would awaken from the dream sobbing with grief and tormented by guilt for the eight young children she was leaving behind. As she grew older, the recurring dream persisted, the guilt would not go away, and she couldn't shake the belief that her dream was of a real person in the past. From the time she was old enough to hold a pencil, she drew maps and pictures of the village she saw in her dream: detailed depictions of her home, the roads, the shops, the church, even gates and lanes. She "knew" that the village was in Ireland, and that someday she would find it.

By the time she was an adult, Jenny had enough information from her dream and from her waking visions to trace her former identity to Mary Sutton, a woman who had lived in a small town north of Dublin, and who had died of fever, leaving behind eight small children. Jenny's long quest to discover her past life identity culminated in an emotional reunion with Mary Sutton's grown children in Ireland. Almost every detail that Jenny remembered was confirmed, including some things Jenny knew about Mary that no one outside the family could have known. Most importantly, after this contact with her children from a former life, Jenny was healed of the guilt and sadness that had tormented her since she was a small child—since the dreams began.

Jenny Cockell's amazing story, which is fully documented in her book, *Across Time and Death,*[1] is a dramatic case of past life memory—a "solved" case in which the previous personality was identified and the memories verified. Her experience is strong evidence that past life memories can sometimes emerge in dreams. I have also seen past life dreams in cases I have collected, and in several of Dr. Stevenson's verified cases, where the content of the past life dream was confirmed to match the real life of the deceased.[2] Past life dreams are part of the phenomenon of children's past life memories; dreams can precede or accompany waking past life memories from the same lifetime. They are an additional place we can look for the memories to emerge.

It makes sense that past lives should show up in dreams. Past life memories reside in the unconscious, and dreams are an expression of the unconscious. While we sleep, when the conscious filters of rationality are down and the demands of practical awareness shut out, all sorts of unconscious material—images du jour, fantastic visions, symbolic expression of fear and desire—reel through our dreaming minds. But sometimes past life memories push aside the ordinary dream stuff and steal the show. Since young children's past life memories are so fresh and close to the surface, I suspect it is more common than we realize for those memories to leak into their dreams.

How early in childhood do past life dreams begin? Some children begin describing dreams and nightmares as soon as they can talk. And some of these same children have had a history, since infancy, of inexplicable screaming during the night, which suggests that past life dreams may begin at birth. Could past life dreams begin even earlier on the continuum of memory—in the womb? Recent scientific studies have shown that babies in utero, beginning at twenty-six to thirty weeks, exhibit the brain patterns of REM sleep, which scientists know indicate dreaming.[3] What could these unborn babies be dreaming about, since their only experiences have been in the confines of the womb? Past lives is the logical answer.

Curiously, an eleventh-century Tibetan medical text pinpoints the time when past life memories begin in utero, and agrees exactly with present-day scientific findings about the onset of REM sleep and dreaming. This text says: "In the 26th week in the womb, the child's awareness becomes very clear and it can see its former lives. It can see if it was a pure being or if it was an ordinary being, and what type of life it had before it took this birth."[4]

Dream Signs

The dynamics of a past life dream are mostly the same as those of a spontaneous past life memory. Most of what I said in Chapter 10 about identifying these memories using the four signs applies to dreams too. But there are three additional signs that help to distinguish a past life dream from an ordinary dream.

1. Vivid and Coherent

Vivid is the word most often heard from people who have had past life dreams. The quality of the dream is strikingly real and sharp. It is so vivid, it stamps a strong impression on the memory that remains for days, weeks, even years.

Unlike ordinary dreams, past life dreams do not veer into

a disjointed muddle of story fragments, fluid images, fantastical morphing, or flying people. The story itself is always a coherent and realistic scenario, with fully plausible details and action that describe a believable plot. Even if the dream scenes offer only fragmentary images, they imply a coherent story.

2. Recurring

Many past life dreams repeat. They usually start and stop in the same place in the story, like a video cued up to play the same segment over and over. Some are single, unmoving images that the dreamer sees in exactly the same way each time. Others progress, then stop unresolved just at the point of crisis. The crisis could be an imminent death, or the dream could end just before an important fact is revealed. Sometimes the story progresses slightly with each recurrence; in other cases, after making no progress in all previous dreams, the story jumps ahead suddenly to the point of crisis.

For example, in the recurring dream of my Holocaust life, each time I saw the same vivid, colorful images of the woman wearing a hat and maroon coat, carrying a shoulder bag, and walking down the boulevard with a stone wall behind her. This dream began as early as I can remember, and I always saw the same scene. It wasn't until I was an adult that the dream progressed beyond the previous stopping point—when I walked up to the government building to confront the German officers.

Sometimes these dreams become less frequent as a child grows older and eventually cease. But not always. Recurring dreams can begin in childhood and persist *long into adulthood*, without losing their vividness or emotional power. You will see in the following cases how a recurring past life nightmare can haunt a person to distraction and cause severe insomnia.

Of course, not all vivid, recurring dreams are past life dreams. A fear from present-day life can hound us in our sleep too—how common is it to have nightmares about being unprepared for a big exam in school? And not all past life dreams are recurring. I've heard reports of people having a dream that haunted them for years—a single dream so vivid and moving that they never forgot it.

3. Different Personae

Because past life dreams tap a real memory from another life, the dreamer may experience himself as another person in another time and place. If that person is of a different sex or a greatly different age, the dreamer, upon awakening, knows that this dream was "not like any other dream I've ever had."

In my recurring dream I saw myself as a grown woman in an unfamiliar city wearing clothes that were old-fashioned compared with the adults around me. Although I saw the woman as "someone else," I *knew* that she was really me in some form, just as Jenny Cockell knew, without a doubt, that she had been Mary Sutton. In a long case in Rabbi Gershom's *Beyond the Ashes,* a young boy had frequent nightmares in which he was a grown woman.[5] When this sign is present, it is a strong indication of a past life dream.

"J'ai Peur! Où Est Ma Mère?"

Some of the most graphic evidence that past life memories emerge in dreams is nighttime xenoglossy—speaking an unlearned language during sleep. This case is from the book *Lifetimes* by Dr. Frederick Lenz.

My husband and I were awakened one night by the sound of a strange voice coming from our six-year-old daughter's room. We got out of bed and went into her room but found her sleeping quietly. We were puzzled and were about to return to our own room when she began to talk in her sleep.

She spoke rapidly in French in an unfamiliar voice. My daughter is six and has never been outside this country and has never been exposed to anyone who speaks French.

She spoke in French for several nights in a row. Neither I nor my husband has ever had more than an elementary course in French in college, so we had trouble following what she was saying. My husband borrowed a portable tape recorder from his office, and we made a recording of one of her conversations. We brought the recording to the French teacher at our local high school. She listened to it and told us that the little girl (our daughter) on the tape was looking for her mother, who she had been separated from when her village was attacked by the Germans. She said the little girl seemed to be lost and, judging from her tone of voice, was very distressed.

It is my feeling that our daughter lived before in a village in France and probably died in one of the world wars.

This case is fascinating not only for the tape-recorded and verified xenoglossy but because it has all the hallmarks of a past life memory. The little girl's words described a typical past life story, reminiscent of so many other past life tragedies from recent wars.

The story sounds to me like unfinished business begging for attention. I suspect that in this child's former life, she died shortly after her traumatic separation from the mother, leaving her in a state of incompleteness at death and causing her to come into this life with residual feelings of abandonment and fear. I wondered if the girl suffered in this life from separation anxiety or phobias that would be explained by the past life trauma. But the published account said nothing more about how the memory might have affected the child.

Healing Nightmares

The past life dreams that we are most likely to hear about are nightmares. Children do have vivid dreams of pleasant and uneventful past lives, but they are not as likely to tell us about them. A dream of a traumatic past life death or trauma, however, alarms you into noticing it. It causes your child to wake up screaming, run into your room, and jump into your bed, whimpering for protection. For children with recurring nightmares, this scene repeats night after night, devastating the midnight peace of the whole family.

Some nightmares are past life memories screaming to be healed. As with waking past life memories, the past life dreams that we hear about are usually a manifestation of unfinished business from the past: a trauma or violent death that is begging to be brought to light and resolved. What a difference it makes in our response if we look at nightmares as *opportunities to heal* past life traumas still gripping the child.

This is an important difference. If past life nightmares are not recognized and resolved, they can cause fears, insomnia, low self-esteem, and other problems into adulthood. This is why parents must stop responding to nightmares the old-fashioned way—by brushing them off with "You'll be okay," by dismissing them as "just a dream" (implying that the dreaming reality has no meaning), or by trying to prove in a patronizing way that no monsters are in the closet or boogeymen under the bed. Never make light of your child's nightmares! Instead, approach every nightmare as a possible past life dream and an opportunity for healing. See the terror not as the problem but as a symptom of a troubling past life that needs to be understood and resolved.

How *should* you respond? The general principles of working with past life dreams are the same as those for past life memories. Once a memory is brought to consciousness and acknowledged, it fades and ceases to interfere with waking reality *or* sleeping dreams. There is an important difference, though: merely dreaming about a traumatic past life does not necessarily clear it. Unlike waking past life memories—which are already conscious—past life nightmares remain unconscious until your child *talks about them while awake.* Then, once the dream is made conscious, it acts very much like any spontaneous waking memory, and you can follow the gist of the advice in Chapter 12. Encourage your child to talk about the dream. Discern the facts and emotions of the story. Acknowledge the truth of his experience, and allow him to express his emotions fully. Then clarify past and present, assure him that he is now safe and loved, and address specific themes with specific clarifications.

Mary and the Bombs

The case of Mary, from Rabbi Gershom, is an example of how a traumatic past life memory can emerge first in dreams, then continue to disturb the child during waking hours. It's easy to see what Mary's parents *could* have done in this case if they had known what to look for.

> Mary was born in the Midwest. During the day she was a normal, happy baby, but at night she screamed in terror. As soon as she could talk she described vivid nightmares of being bombed, and she was absolutely terrified of sirens. Once while Mary was walking home from school, a siren went off. She started screaming and ran into the street, stopped a passing car and shouted, "We're going to be bombed! We're going to be bombed!"
>
> While still a little girl, she had visions of herself as a young woman, very gaunt, wide-eyed and frightened, asking, "Why, why, how can this be?" Mary, now an adult in her middle age, has never known hunger in this life, yet she has a deep fear of starving to death.
>
> Her parents always brushed off her weird behavior as "something she heard on the radio," but Mary always knew it was something more. She puzzled all her life about what was "wrong" with her, until years later, while traveling by train through Germany, she had a flashback. She finally saw that she had died in the Holocaust, and her nightmares and weird behavior suddenly made perfect sense.[6]

Mary's parents might have cured her fears when she was still a little girl by simply accepting her story as a literal past life memory and offering her comfort. They might have healed her by saying, "Yes, you were bombed in your other life. I understand that you are afraid of being bombed again, but the war is over. You are now safe with us, and we have plenty of food." They could also have asked her for more of her story: how she died, how old she was, who was with her, where her family was. Bringing the memory out into the open with a few simple words and questions might have spared Mary many years of confusion and anxiety.

Some children have what sleep specialists call *night terrors,* a serious sleep disturbance that is not in the same category as regular nightmares. In a typical night terror episode, the child screams, thrashes about, and may even walk or run around and get violent, all while appearing to be awake. But afterward, un- like a nightmare, the child has absolutely *no memory of the incident* and no dream story that might explain the bizarre behavior. This alone makes night terrors extremely difficult to treat. Scientists have no satisfactory explanation for what causes night terrors, and no reliable remedy. But they do know that they occur during the deepest sleep cycle, and that they commonly begin between the ages of three and four, and fade by the ages of five or six.[7]

Since we now know that some nightmares have a past life cause, it makes sense that some night terrors would too. Perhaps, during deepest sleep, a state furthest from waking consciousness, these children are being terrorized by vivid memories of a past life trauma. I think it's significant that night terrors occur at the same ages when children are most likely to have spontaneous past life memories.

As some of the cases later in this chapter show, when night- mares are treated as a form of past life memory, they can be healed. Perhaps some of the same techniques used for past life nightmares could help cure night terrors. If parents and scientists who are trying to understand night terrors would open their minds to the possibility of a past life cause, it might lead to genuine solutions for this baffling and terrifying sleep disorder.

Look to the Literal

Because most parents don't know that past lives are even possible, they unwittingly compound their children's despair and confusion by trying to explain away a past life dream. Typically they dismiss it as a replay of something seen on TV or in a scary picture book. Or, influenced by what they've read of Freudian psychology, they explain it as the symbolic representation of a repressed urge or fear. But they wouldn't have to resort to metaphorical thinking if they realized that, in truth, some dreams and nightmares are *literal* memories of real experiences from the past.

Dana Grabiner

Dana, who lives in Maryland, saw one of my published articles and wrote to tell me about a recurring childhood nightmare that had haunted her for years, causing severe insomnia. She was debilitated by this condition until a past life regression revealed the source of the nightmare. She believes that if her nightmare had been treated as a past life memory when she was a child, it would not have plagued her all those years and into adulthood.

"Tell parents in your book," she pleaded, "that these nightmares *don't* always go away when a child grows up, unless they are recognized as past life memories." I promised her I would share her story.

My worst childhood nightmares were underwater terrors. From the age of four or five, as I dozed in bed, I first would hear a faint buzzing, then swirling water would engulf me. Somehow I was paralyzed and couldn't cry out for my parents. But when I woke up from these dreams, I would scream for my parents and run into their room to tell them about my nightmare. My father would come into my room and check behind the bed, in the closet, and under the bureau, to show me there were no monsters there.

I had other recurring dreams in childhood, but these water nightmares were different. They were always more vivid: I was actually drowning in the dream; I could feel the water in my throat and nose. And these nightmares always left me absolutely terrified.

The nightmares continued through my childhood and teenage years. Finally, in late 1982, at age twenty-four, exhausted by intermittent insomnia, a friend suggested I try a past life regression to find the root of the dream. I agreed.

"Who are you?" the hypnotist asked during the regression. I identified myself as a young girl named Athene, a Greek house servant. Somehow I knew that I was this young girl. I was experiencing her thoughts and feelings. Resentful and defiant, one day I threw down my kitchen utensils and ran out of the house down some outdoor stairs toward a lagoon. I shed my clothes, leaving them on the ground, and jumped into the water. The water felt so good. Moments later a man appeared on the banks and ordered me out of the lagoon. He refused to toss my clothes to me, so I remained in the water. Then a storm hit suddenly, and I drowned.

Soon after this short regression, my insomnia went away. I have never been troubled by the underwater dream again.

Dana didn't say if she had ever consulted a therapist for her insomnia. But if she had, any traditional psychotherapist likely would have interpreted the water in her dream symbolically as a metaphor for a hidden cause from her childhood. Depending upon the therapist's training and orientation, he or she might have interpreted her drowning as a metaphor for engulfment by her mother, as a symptom of some other suffocating situation, as a reliving of a difficult birth experience, or as the effect of a toxic pregnancy. These interpretations might be correct for other people with different circumstances, but not for Dana.

The immediate and total cure of Dana's lifelong affliction with just one past life regression proves that her water nightmares were not metaphors, not unconscious symbols representing some complex syndrome. They were in fact *literal* images from a past life drowning. We will do our children a service if, in addition to speculating about symbolic meaning, we look to the literal story for a possible past life cause.

More Nightmares from the Old Paradigm of Psychology

Joan, like Dana, had been plagued by recurring nightmares since early childhood. Her parents sought professional help for her. But the well-meaning professionals had not been trained to look for past life memories, so none of their advice or prescriptions could cure her of her terrifying dream. Her terror continued for more than thirty years until, finally, she chanced on a therapist, Dr. Thelma Freedman, in upstate New York, who recognized a past life memory when she saw one. Dr. Freedman published her account of Joan's case in the *Journal of Regression Therapy*.[8]

> My client, Joan, was in her mid-thirties, married and with three children. She had a recurring nightmare all her life. To be accurate, it was actually a combination nightmare-apparition.
>
> It was, according to her, always the same: she would become cold and terrified in her sleep and would wake to find her room filled with an eerie silvery-blue light. Standing on the other side of the room watching her was an old man dressed in old-fashioned rumpled clothes. This figure never moved, but seemed to peer at her from beneath the brim of his battered hat, pulled down low over his forehead. Upon seeing him, Joan always screamed, and this broke the spell. The old man faded away and the silvery-blue light went with him.
>
> When Joan was three or four, her concerned parents consulted the family pediatrician about her nightmares. He assured them not to worry; it would go away in a few years.
>
> But, when Joan was eight, it had not gone away and they consulted a child psychiatrist. She visited him every week

for a year, but the nightmare continued as before. The psychiatrist finally told Joan's parents that she was a healthy, bright, normal, yet overly imaginative little girl. He assured them not to worry; it would go away in a few years.

By the time Joan was in her middle teens, the nightmare was occurring every two weeks or so. She and her family had learned to live with it. But, each time she had the nightmare, the dream figure moved a little closer to her bed. This was so terrifying that the family sought help from another psychologist. He administered "a lot of tests" over the first few sessions, and then began a six-month course of therapy in which they talked about Joan's childhood. The psychologist finally concluded that Joan was fine and healthy. He assured them not to worry; it would go away in a few years.

In college, when she was 20, Joan's roommate, alarmed by the terrifying nightmares, urged her to go to the counseling center for help. After a few sessions, Joan was told that she had deep-seated hostilities towards her parents and that the nightmares would go away in a few years as soon as she graduated from college and was truly independent from her parents. They advised Joan to begin an active sexual life at the college to relieve her tensions.

Her final therapy experience before she became my client came soon after she married, at age 26. Her new husband, alarmed by the terrifying nightmares, took her to a psychiatrist, who admitted her into a local mental health center for evaluation and observation. She stayed there three weeks and was released with a diagnosis of generalized anxiety and a prescription for a tranquilizer. She and her husband were told not to worry; the nightmares would go away in a few years.

Joan came to see me at the urging of her sister, who was alarmed because, even though Joan was now into her middle age, the terrifying nightmares had persisted. Her sister thought she should try hypnosis because none of the psychiatrists in Joan's long history had ever tried hypnosis with her before. Joan was desperate and willing to try anything, even though by this time she had no faith in therapy of any kind, and she didn't hesitate to say so. She never imagined her nightmare would lead to a past life.

Joan trembled with fear as she told her story of a lifetime of terror. And the dream was getting worse: in her childhood, the "old man" had stood across the room; over the years he had been getting closer until, by the time she came to me, he was standing very near her bed. Joan had learned to live with her nightmare, but now, in her thirties, she was terrified again because she was afraid of what would happen if the man got close enough to *touch* her, which she was sure would happen soon.

I was frank with Joan and told her it was possible that she had been sexually abused as a child, and that this "old man" was really a repressed memory. When I mentioned this, she laughed at me. Her last three therapists had told her they believed sexual abuse was the cause, and they did what they could to get her to remember it. The psychiatrist in her childhood, she thought, had probably believed it too, since Joan remembered a lot of playing with dolls with male and female body parts. But none of these therapists had been able to prove their theory, and the nightmare persisted. She was willing to see if hypnosis could reveal the truth, no matter what might turn up. She was ready.

I must admit that I, like those other therapists, assumed that Joan had probably been sexually abused in some way by the "old man." It did not occur to me that a past life might be involved. Joan went into hypnosis easily and I used guided imagery to lead her into a beautiful clearing in the woods. In the clearing, I brought down a white light which surrounded her with calm and safety. Then I asked her to bring the "old man" into the clearing, at the side opposite from her.

She had no trouble doing this. He stood just as he did in her nightmare, in his old-fashioned rumpled clothes, watching her from under his hat brim, although she could not actually see his eyes. At my instruction, she asked him to look directly at her, but after a moment she reported he would not do so.

However, she said that she now felt he wanted something from her. Naturally, I instructed her to ask him what it was, but again, after a few moments, she said that he would not reply. In short, he would neither talk to her nor look directly at her. He simply stood there.

At this point I asked her if she still wanted to explore any childhood experience she might have had with this man. She said she did. I then instructed her to calmly go back in time to a point five minutes before she had last seen him. I was still not considering the possibility of a past life, and expected a memory from her childhood to surface.

She found herself as an adult woman on a stony hillside, watching her little daughter gather wildflowers. The man was nowhere to be seen. However, as she described the scene, she became confused, because she wore a long old-fashioned skirt, and her daughter was not her present daughter. I realized now that she might have slipped into a past life and I asked her where she was. She said, "I think I'm in Spain."

I instructed her to go back to the time when she was a child in that lifetime. I reasoned that we might as well take the past life report chronologically. The "old man" would appear sooner or later. This suggestion took us to England.

Joan reported a life in the early 1800's. She was raised in an English seacoast town and when she was fifteen her widowed and impoverished mother arranged a marriage for her to a prosperous local shopkeeper. Her new husband was in his forties, a dour and upright citizen. He was the man of Joan's nightmare, her apparition. The young girl was at first entranced by her charming new home, her pretty new clothes, her status as the wife of a prosperous man. But he was too old and too settled in his ways for her. He had married her, he finally admitted, because he wanted a housekeeper and a hostess, and because he hoped for a son to inherit his business.

As time passed and she failed to become pregnant, he grew more and more distant toward her. She was soon lonely and bored, and the inevitable happened. Fishing ships put in to the town to sell their catches, and she fell in love with a young fisherman from one of these ships. She ran away with him to his village in Spain, where he introduced her as his wife. She settled into her new life as a village fisherman's wife, and soon had a baby daughter.

Her life in Spain was not altogether happy. Her "husband," like the other men of the village, was away for weeks at a time, and the village women never quite accepted her, the "foreign woman." Nevertheless, she was fairly content, raising her child and participating in the life of the village as much as she was allowed.

One day, when her "husband" was away on his ship, she and her daughter were gathering wildflowers on a hillside overlooking the sea. This was the initial scene she had experienced when we began the session. The child was a little distance away, picking flowers. When Joan looked up she saw her true English husband striding up the hillside toward her, his clothes travel-stained and rumpled. He had tracked her down. He was followed by the women of the village.

He came to her where she sat on the ground, wildflowers in her lap. He said nothing, but stood staring down at her, a look of scorn and hatred on his face. After a moment he gave her a savage kick. As if on cue, the village woman nearest to her scooped up a stone and threw it. Then the other women joined in, howling epithets at her and pelting her with stones. She died, stoned to death by the "virtuous" village women who were outraged by her English husband's indictment. The last thing she saw before she died was her husband, standing passively by, watching her writhing body from underneath his lowered hat brim. She could not see his eyes. The scene was diffused with the silvery-blue light of the sun reflecting off the sea.

After we finished exploring this past life I knew that these two people had unfinished business. They must forgive each other. Accordingly, I instructed Joan to place herself once more in the clearing in the woods that started the session. This time I gave her no white light and instructed her to confront her husband, ask him first what he wanted from her, and then ask his forgiveness for having run away from him. She must also forgive him for having acquiesced in her brutal death. He had been a cold and unforgiving man, and she, a romantic, dreaming girl. They had married for their own self-centered reasons, and the tragedy which followed was predictable.

Joan now realized this, and in the clearing she again asked the "old man" to come forward, calling him by his name, William. She was crying as she asked him what he wanted from her. This time she got an answer. He said he wanted her back as his wife.

At my direction, she explained to him that their time was long past, that she had moved into another life and that they must forgive each other so that he could do the same. He seemed to understand, looked at her, took her hands, and spoke to her, agreeing. Then he smiled and faded away. Still crying, Joan called "good-bye" to him as he went.

Before returning to alertness, Joan said she felt lighter and freer than she ever had before. She "knew" her English husband would not trouble her any longer. I was not too sure, but she was right. I talked with her recently, now more than nine years later, and she reports, gratefully, that she never had that nightmare again. But, she says, she sometimes wonders where her "husband" is now.

Dr. Freedman comments: "Had it been possible for Joan to be treated with past life therapy in her childhood, it is likely that she would have been freed from her nightmare. This would have saved her the time, expense, and embarrassment of years of inappropriate therapy.

"It is appalling to realize that large numbers of children suffer from recurring nightmares, as Joan did. Given the highly hypnotizable nature of most children over five years old, therapy for children's nightmares should require only one or two short sessions to free the child from whatever unfinished business the past life nightmare represents. With this approach the prognosis is excellent for the elimination of the nightmares, while at the same time, the child's personality and unique talents would not be threatened. If we approach it correctly, it should also be an enjoyable experience for the child."

Bruxism: A Success Story

I suspect there are thousands of children who suffer from past life nightmares and need help. Their perplexed parents may pay for psychological help, as Joan's did, and still the child gets no relief. This case from Florida is an exception. Keith's past life nightmares were recognized soon after they began and were immediately eradicated. His story inspires hope for other children with nightmares.

Eight-year-old Keith came to Dr. Ron De Vasto in search of a cure for his bruxism—the compulsive grinding of teeth. Keith's father had taken him to several dentists, but none of them could find any connection between the bruxism and the physiology of his teeth or jaw. Finally the last dentist who saw Keith suggested hypnosis and referred him to Dr. De Vasto. Dr. De Vasto tells what happened in his session with Keith:

> The father told me that Keith's problem started very suddenly one night six months earlier and seemed to get progressively worse. During the course of the initial interview, he mentioned, almost in passing, that Keith was having nightmares, which had started at about the same time as his grinding of teeth. In Keith's nightmares he was being suffocated. He didn't know what was suffocating him, but he had the feeling that he was being crushed. After each of these nightmares, Keith always woke up feeling very tense and filled with deep fear.
>
> Keith seemed to be a very pleasant, bright, and quiet sort of boy. We established a rapport right away. I knew from experience that he would be easy to work with. I used age regression to take him back to the time of his first nightmare. He easily regressed but seemed to resist my attempts

to get him to look at the situation. Gentle persistence paid off, though, and the story that unfolded had me on the edge of my seat with excitement—and his father on the edge of his seat, totally baffled!

Keith related the story of a fifteen-year-old boy in France during the time of the Nazi occupation. He began speaking from the perspective of this French boy, René. As Keith sat there with his eyes closed, he began to tremble and seemed to be experiencing a great deal of fear as he described what he saw. A long line of people from his village were being forced by German soldiers to march down the road in front of his family's farm. The soldiers came into the yard and grabbed René and his family and pushed them into the line with the others. Keith, still in trance with his eyes closed, started to scream and beg, "Please tell them I'm not a Jew! Please tell them I'm not a Jew!"

But his cries were not acknowledged. After many long and exhausting days of marching and riding on trains, René found himself being herded through an elaborate structure of barbed wire and fencing. He started to retch from the smell of death all around him. Then, along with many others, he was lined up in front of a ditch. Men in uniform with machine guns began firing. A bullet grazed the side of his head, and he fell into the ditch. He felt the suffocating weight and pressure of bodies as they fell on top of him. He gasped for air and tried to scream, but he couldn't open his jaw because of the mass of bodies on his head. So his screams remained silent and internalized. Filled with fear and anger, he finally died a slow and excruciating death.

The entire session with Keith lasted about three hours. When it was over, Keith breathed a wonderful sigh of release. His father could only say, "I can't believe it." After discussing and processing what had happened in the session, Keith and his father went home. That was the last of Keith's nightmares and grinding of teeth.

When the unexpressed terror of Keith's past life death began to seep into his dreams, it manifested at the same time in his jaw as bruxism. The simultaneity of the dream and the physical symptom was the clue that Dr. De Vasto used to trace the cause of the bruxism to a past life source.

Mother and Child Telepathy in Dreams

As other chapters have already shown, telepathic communication between mother and child can trigger past life memories. The following two cases show that telepathy connects mother and child through past life dreams as well. In each case the mother helped her child heal a troubling past life memory through this dream connection. These cases hint at how much more there is for us to learn about children's past life memories.

Through the medium of dreams, the inner lives of children and parents intersect. Dream telepathy adds a new dimension to the phenomenon of children's past life memories, raising to a higher power the number of ways that parents might help their children understand and process them.

Sharon and Joey

Sharon Benedetto's recurring dreams from her childhood led her to try a past life regression. That regression triggered nightmares in her son, Joey, of a past life they shared together. Then through their telepathic connection, Sharon healed Joey of his traumatic past life dream.

Sharon, who lives in Delaware, sent her story to me in a letter.

When I was in my late thirties, my therapist suggested I try a past life regression to understand why I continued to dream so often about a man I had known since I was a child. I had been dreaming about this man for thirty years.

With only the slightest hypnotic suggestion, I instantly saw myself walking barefoot down a dusty country road in what seemed to be rural Russia. I was a peasant, very happily married to the man I'd been dreaming about for so long. We had many children, including my present son, Joey. The feeling of calm and happiness began to dissolve, though, when the sky turned black with storm clouds. Even as I recall this now, it sends shivers down my spine. A devastating storm, like a tornado, took us by surprise and destroyed our house. We lost much, including a baby. Joey survived the storm.

Soon after this regression Joey, who is now five, had a nightmare. It was his first ever. I heard his crying and ran upstairs to him. I knew immediately, because he was crying and calling for the baby, that he was in the storm I had seen in my regression. I was amazed that he had tapped into this lifetime. I was equally amazed that I knew exactly what was happening to him, beyond any doubt. I comforted him back to sleep. The next night his nightmare happened again, and I took it a step further. I whispered in his ear as he slept and tossed and cried. I told him that the storm had happened a long time ago and that we're safe now. I told him in a totally calm and soothing voice, and he settled down.

But he was not finished. He had a third nightmare. This made me realize I had missed something, that he needed closure on the baby—he had been crying out for the baby in all three nightmares. This time when I whispered in his ear, I assured him that the baby was safe now and in a different place and body. I told him that this happened a long time ago and we were all okay now, and safe. He immediately settled down and slept peacefully. He was five then and hasn't had the nightmare again for the past seven years. It's gone.

I feel that this is a wonderful example of how my son and I healed our tragic past life through our dream connection. Trusting my intuition in the mother-son relationship was crucial. I knew instinctively what was happening with my son and what to do. The key was in actually following through and acting on what my intuition was telling me.

Sharon's experience shows that this unconscious dream connection is real, and it works. It suggests another way parents can respond to a child's past life nightmare—by talking him through it while he is still sleeping.

Gladys McGarey, M.D.

The following extraordinary case comes from Dr. Gladys McGarey, an obstetrician with a practice in Scottsdale, Arizona, and a longtime pioneer in holistic medicine. Her story adds a new twist to mother and child telepathy in dreams. It also is an example of past life memories affecting behavior in utero.

Dr. McGarey first published this case in her book *Born to Live:*

This case involving one of my obstetric patients really had an impact on me. During the last six weeks of her pregnancy, this new mother's baby was in a breech position (feet first) every time she came into my office. Each time, I would rotate the baby to a vertex (head first) presentation, and send the mother out, a normal pregnancy waiting to be delivered. But the next time she came back, the baby would be in breech position again. Finally, I taught her to rotate the baby herself, since it was the easiest rotation I had ever done.

This continued until she went into labor. When I arrived at the hospital, sure enough, the baby was in breech. But there was no problem in rotating him once more. He delivered in a vertex position and everything was fine. I didn't think anything more about it afterwards, but instead, tucked the incident away in my mind as an interesting medical phenomenon.

When the mother brought the baby in for his one-month check-up, she said, "I don't know why, but this baby is the most frightened child I've ever seen. He just screams. Every so often he just looks terrified and starts to scream. I haven't been able to do anything to get him to quiet down."

A week later, she came to see me again. This time she told me that she had gotten so frustrated with the screaming, she finally put the baby down on the bed in utter desperation and said to him, "Look—I don't know what to do with you. I've tried everything I know, and it hasn't worked. You obviously are frightened and there's something wrong with you. What is it? How can I help?"

No words came from the infant and I am sure she didn't expect any.

But that night she had a dream. In the dream, she was watching a battle between a large group of white men on horseback and a small band of Indians. The scene was a mountain near Phoenix, and the fight was going on perilously close to the edge of a tall cliff. One of the Indians near the edge suddenly lost his balance and fell precipitously, end over end, down hundreds of feet to his death on the rocks in the canyon below. The mother's dream perspective changed and she was standing in the dream near where the Indian's body had landed. She walked over to where the man had died. As she approached him, he got up, grew smaller and smaller, and she recognized him as her newborn child.

Then, as she awakened and the meaning of the dream sunk in, it all began to make sense. If her son in his last lifetime was the Indian who fell down a precipice to his death, then his turning in the womb from vertex to breech, over and over again, was a repetition of his falling off that cliff, head over heels.

After she had the dream, the baby was still terrified and screaming. But now the mother understood what had happened. She talked to him as he was falling asleep: "If that is what happened, then it happened. It's done, it's over with, and you don't need to go through that experience again. You've been born into a new life, and you don't have to be full of fear and terror any more. We love you and we will help you get rid of your fear."

After she talked to him like that, he never had the screaming fits again. He was no longer frightened. From then on he was a happy and peaceful baby.

Dr. McGarey adds this historical note:

Arizona history tells that soldiers from a Company "B" of the Arizona Volunteers climbed up a secret path to the top of Big Picacho Mountain near Phoenix and cornered seventy-five Apaches on Big Picacho cliff. Shots were fired, there were war whoops, and Indians jumped off the cliff and fell to the rocks below. Legend has it that fifty Indians were killed in the first volley and that twenty-five more jumped off the cliff rather than be taken prisoner.[9]

This story is extraordinary in three ways.

First, while still in the womb, the baby was reenacting his head-over-heels fall to death. This seems to demonstrate that some past life *behavior* begins *before* birth. Past life therapists are familiar with this phenomenon and often see examples of it in their work. They find that a wide range of prenatal and birth experiences appear to be a replay of past life deaths. Roger Woolger writes: "Whenever there is a severe trauma in the struggle to be born, the form of the trauma commonly proves to be an exact and faithful symbolic mirror of accumulated past life death experiences."[10] For example, a child born with the umbilical cord wrapped around his neck may have died before by hanging.

Second, when the exasperated mother in this story asked her infant son, "How can I help?" she was answered in a past life dream. The dream explained her son's behavior in the womb and his present terror and anguish.

Finally, using the information from the dream, this mother was able to help her baby by talking to him—acknowledging his past life experience and assuring him that he was now safe—the same techniques mothers use with older children to clear past life memories. Of course, the baby couldn't understand his mother's language in the normal sense, but somehow the mother's intentions came through.

This mother shows us, as Sharon did, that dreams can be a real means of communication between mother and child. And she shows us that past life memories can be understood and cleared through the telepathic dream connection.

PART THREE

Listen to
the Children

CHAPTER 14

Adults and Their Religions

Grown men may learn from very little children for the hearts of little children are pure, and, therefore, the Great Spirit may show to them many things which older people miss.

—BLACK ELK OF THE OGLALA SIOUX[1]

Face to Face with Reincarnation

Parents who witness their own children speak of past lives inevitably must come to terms with the idea of reincarnation.

For some, the encounter causes distress because reincarnation conflicts with their religious beliefs; others welcome it as a confirmation of what they had suspected to be true. For all of the parents I spoke to, the power of their children's memories was stronger than any religious doctrine they had been taught. Their sudden awareness of reincarnation as a practical reality expanded their former concept of what is possible in the universe and in their own lives. They all admitted that their beliefs had been profoundly changed when their young children innocently spoke of having lived before.

Lisa credits her daughter Courtney with jolting her out of her spiritual complacency and forcing her to reconsider her beliefs.

I was not a believer in reincarnation before Courtney started telling me these things. I was brought up a Missouri-style Lutheran—all hellfire and brimstone, and every word of the Bible was exact. I was brought up in a very structured religion.

But Courtney has caused a revolution in our entire family. There's something very real here, although I haven't worked it out yet. I intended to contemplate these things while sitting back in my rocking chair when I was in my sixties. I wasn't expecting this kind of thinking to be prompted by a two-year-old.

Sometimes I feel like I'm out on a limb, and I don't want to get so far out that I can't get back. And Courtney is dragging me all the way. It's funny, though—I have enjoyed it. I just didn't expect it. I thought that it would be at a later time . . . she has made it a little more necessary now.

Mary Fleming, the mother of the artist twins, tells how her children's remarks have expanded her thinking:

There's something quite unsettling when your own children begin talking so frankly about God, death, reincarnation, and heaven. But because it was coming from my own children, I couldn't push it aside. I had to reevaluate all my beliefs and ideas about life and why we are here on earth.

Our family is quite active in the local Roman Catholic parish, and I'm not quite sure what the Church would think of all this. But I have to believe my own children when they talk of these things.

The truth of a child's memories initiates a chain reaction of new understanding, not only about life and death but about the unseen spiritual world that moves through and around us. When children speak so innocently of death and rebirth—mysteries that we presume are outside their ken—we know what they say is true because it pulsates through our bodies. This witness to the truth coming through our own children stirs something within us. We awaken to another reality. We begin to notice things that we hadn't before.

It's like stumbling upon a dewy spider's web, with the sun glistening on it at just the right angle. We suddenly see the intricate strands that connect us to all people and events in our lives. We realize that nothing happens by chance; coincidences suddenly have meaning. We get a glimpse of the gossamer patterns that connect all things between the inner and outer worlds. But we might have missed it if our small child hadn't pulled us by the hand and pointed it out to us.

Pat Carroll, Billy's mother, describes this shift in perception:

> The experience with Billy opened my mind significantly. I see everything so differently now. I was just so superficial before. Billy's memory made me think more. I feel like I'm stretching out—no idea is impossible now. I was so closed before to the possibilities of life.
>
> I *feel* things now. I am much more intuitively alert and aware; I can feel whether there is something with me that is good or wrong. I don't have to be hit over the head now to pick up the subtle messages. Now that I've opened up, I see miracles everywhere! This never would have happened before Billy's experience.

If we believe what our children are saying, we open ourselves to the possibility that we too have lived before and will live again. We feel greatly expanded and alive from this realization, knowing that the deepest part of us will always exist. We feel connected to a greater power, the source of all energy and life. Our minds and hearts expand with new vibrancy.

For Phyllis Elkins, her experiences with Natalie gave her a different view of the world, full of hope and meaning.

> I was raised Catholic. But at this point I am not a church-going person. I believe in God on my own terms. We have

never really talked about religion with Natalie, except that we believe in God. My husband is a very open-minded person too. But the first time we went through this, it was like we were slammed against a wall. It's like when you give birth—you instantly have a different view of the big picture of life. You have a different view of what's important.

I used to think that it would be comforting to know that when we die, we have a chance to come back and work things out and maybe even be with our family again. Because of Natalie, now I really believe we do.

The lives and perceptions of these parents changed because they believed their children. They didn't let their formal religion get in the way. Either they changed their minds about the religious doctrine they had been taught, or they found a way to stretch their religious beliefs to make room for reincarnation.

But for others it's not that easy. When I talked to some parents, they were nervous, unsure of what they should think or believe about what their child had said. They would say to me in a hushed voice, "This may sound weird, but . . ." or, "Please don't think I'm crazy, but . . ." I assured them they were in good company, that they weren't the only ones seeing and hearing these things in their own children. They were relieved to hear this and to finally find someone who understood. They were grateful for the opportunity to discuss their experiences without feeling embarrassed, guilty, crazy, or afraid for believing their child. They confessed that they couldn't talk about these experiences with their family or friends—or heaven forbid, with their priests, rabbis, or ministers—because they were afraid. They knew that these experiences didn't conform to their religious doctrine and that they might be laughed at or ostracized for believing "nonsense" that contradicted their faith.

I thought about this. If these parents who had enough confidence to seek me out were still this nervous, how many other parents keep their children's memories a secret altogether? Or worse, how many silence their own children and deny what they see with their own eyes and feel in their hearts because they are afraid of being criticized by their neighbors or their church?

This fear, as I see it, is the biggest obstacle to a widespread acceptance of children's past life memories. I decided to do some research to understand it better. I wanted to see if I could discover why reincarnation has such a bad public image in Western culture. In jokes on TV and in cartoons, reincarnation always gets a laugh when lampooned as superstitious nonsense. For many people the very word conjures up images of cow worship or the notion that if you do something bad, you will come back as a slug. Sometimes when I talk to people about my work, they begin singing the "do do do do" of the *Twilight Zone* theme, a polite way of labeling these ideas as weird and out of bounds. Since Shirley MacLaine so courageously published her personal experiences with reincarnation, her name has become synonymous with reincarnation jokes.

But there's something interesting going on here, because reincarnation's public image does not jibe with what people believe in private. According to a recent Gallup poll, 27 percent of adult Americans admit anonymously that they believe in reincarnation. And though people joke about Shirley MacLaine, millions have bought and read her books on reincarnation. Why this strange double standard? Where does this fear and denial come from?

A Generic Spiritual Idea

Part of the problem is simple ignorance of the facts. Because reincarnation is rarely discussed as a serious spiritual idea in mainstream media or in schools and certainly not in most churches, most Westerners know only what they absorb about reincarnation from the jokes and cartoons.

Reincarnation is *not*, as many people in our culture think, a belief tied to India or to any particular religion or culture. It has been an enduring spiritual belief for billions of people for thousands of years all over the world, a global idea that sprang up independently among peoples on every continent, from the Celts and Teutons of northern Europe, to the indigenous peoples of Africa, Australia, and the Americas. Hundreds of millions of

Hindus and Buddhists in the world today believe in reincarnation. It is tolerated by Islam—the Islamic mystical sect, the Sufis, make it the cornerstone of their faith. From the point of view of most of the rest of the world, our Judeo-Christian culture, with its denial of reincarnation, is in the minority.

In truth, there is no such thing as a single, fixed doctrine of reincarnation. It is impossible to say that reincarnation is this and not that. It is a generic spiritual idea, like a belief in deities, that in interpretation and practice is as diverse as the peoples of the world. Some notions of how reincarnation works *are* superstitious nonsense—notions that clearly are an embarrassment to our modern minds. But in other places reincarnation has developed into a philosophy of natural laws and spiritual insight that could make a valuable contribution to Western thinking.

On any single question of the mechanics of reincarnation, there are a confusing range of beliefs from around the world. For example, on the question of how long a soul waits to be reborn, some believe that the interval is hundreds of years, while others believe it is fixed at seven or twenty years. The Druses of Lebanon hold the extreme belief that rebirth happens immediately after death, with no interval whatsoever—they say that the last dying breath is followed, without pause, by the first breath of the reincarnated newborn.[2]

As some cultures, religions, and sects interpret it, reincarnation is a dogmatic and punitive idea, institutionalized into rules and rituals; the fear of an unfortunate rebirth is wielded as a tool to intimidate and control the masses. The caste system of India, for example, is structured on the idea that souls reincarnate up the caste ladder a few steps at a time and only after performing excessive rituals.[3] In another example, some local Buddhist sects believe that even accidentally denying a holy statue in the family chapel its daily water offering will be punished by poverty in the next life.[4]

In other cultures, reincarnation is a profoundly liberating and life-affirming concept. Anthropologist Margaret Mead found that both the Balinese and Eskimos honor the cycle of rebirth in their attitude toward learning. They believe that their children have prophetic gifts, and "early on, they teach their children to do complicated things and trust that they can perform them, because, in truth, they are adults. Even old people continue to learn, because they trust their efforts will not be wasted."[5]

The versions of reincarnation taught by the esoteric traditions of the Hindus and the Tibetan Buddhists are most uplifting and most compatible with the Western mind. But even Buddhists and Hindus disagree on exactly what is transmitted from lifetime to lifetime. Hindus believe it is a traveling soul identity; Buddhists say it is continuous stream of consciousness, a cause-and-effect relationship, but without a traveling soul identity. They do both agree, however, that a natural law, called karma, governs the particulars of rebirth.

Karma is another idea, closely related to reincarnation, that is wide open to interpretation and is often misunderstood by Westerners. On the simplest level karma is the same as the physical laws of cause and effect, action and reaction. Christians know it as the teaching "You reap what you sow." But karma operates across many lifetimes. By this principle, everything we do, good or bad, has an effect on ourselves and others; and the consequences of each action eventually come around to us again, if not in this lifetime then in another.

As the Buddhists teach it, karma is *not* a law of predestination, as some Westerners fear. Rather, it allows for free will. The law of karma does not dictate how we act. It is an impartial law, asking only that we learn from our mistakes. When we create "bad" karma by acting selfishly, hurting others or ourselves, disrupting the harmony of the Universe (acts that some call "sin"), the Universe doesn't judge us. It simply loops the disharmony back at us, offering us another opportunity to respond correctly. We create good karma when we act with awareness and in harmony with the connectedness of all things—in other words, with love and compassion. The compelling message of karma is that we are responsible for our actions.

Reincarnation and the law of karma explain the paradox we ponder in the West: why do horrible things happen to good people, while scoundrels seem to run free and easy? Without seeing the cumulative aspect of karma, life seems random and unfair—a cosmic roll of the dice. Indeed, it is often impossible to see any moral justice or meaning within the confines of a single life when, for example, an innocent child dies, or is born blind or homeless. But if we look at each lifetime as only one frame of a movie composed of many frames, our perspective changes. We understand that the movie seen as a whole makes sense and tells a story of balance, justice, and order.

So if reincarnation is a generic spiritual idea, not tied to any one religion or culture, why is it resisted in the West? Why is the Judeo-Christian culture different from most of the rest of the world? I turned to sources on Jewish and Christian history for answers. Now, I'm not the kind of person who usually enjoys digging into ancient history—especially religious history—but what I found was so fascinating and revealing, it was worth the effort.

I looked first at Christianity and discovered that nowhere in the Bible is reincarnation addressed, let alone banned. There is no scripture that repudiates reincarnation. In fact, many biblical scholars and devout Christians believe that Jesus tacitly endorsed the idea.[6] Historians know that reincarnation was a widely held belief in the Middle East at the time, and Jesus seems to assume it as an accepted idea of the day, not worthy of explicit comment one way or the other.

Two incidents from Jesus' teachings that demonstrate this are cited most often. In Matthew 17:10–13 Jesus is talking with his disciples about the well-known Old Testament prophecy that the return of the prophet Elias would precede the coming of the Messiah:

> The disciples asked him, "Why then do the teachers of the law say that Elias must come first?"
>
> Jesus replied, "To be sure, Elias comes and will restore all things. But I tell you, Elias has already come, and they did not recognize him, but have done to him everything they wished. In the same way the Son of Man is going to suffer at their hands." Then the disciples understood that he was talking to them about John the Baptist.[7]

How can these direct statements, this direct acknowledgment by Jesus that Elias has returned as John the Baptist, be interpreted as anything but reincarnation?

Another incident often cited is from John 9:2. The disciples pointed to a man who had been *born* blind and asked,

> Who did sin, this man or his parents, that he was born blind?

Jesus used the question to make a point about sin, but it is significant that he did not repudiate the obvious assumption behind the statement. How else could the man have sinned *before* he was born unless he had lived a past life? If Jesus had wanted to mark reincarnation as a false doctrine, this was his opportunity to criticize or condemn it, but he didn't.[8]

So where do Christians get the notion that reincarnation is a sin, as I've heard some people claim? The answer lies not in the words of Jesus but in the origins of the Roman Church. Most interesting is the story of what happened in the three hundred years between the time of Jesus' humble ministry in the desert, and the fixing of the doctrine and creed that Christians take for granted today.

Dogma Bites Man

The awesome charisma of Jesus Christ and his good-news ministry profoundly changed the lives of those who knew him and who followed soon after.[9] The enthusiasm and spirit of the first Christians spread through the Middle East until what had begun as an inspired cult of Jews in dusty Judea grew to be a revolutionary religious movement pervading the whole Roman Empire.

As the ideas spread, they percolated through the practices and theologies of existing religions and took on forms that Jesus would not have recognized—especially the institution of a formal priesthood to mediate between man and God. Throughout the first three centuries of the Christian era, there was no single Christian doctrine. Christian theology and doctrine—interpretations of Christ's teachings blended with ideas from other philosophies and religions—were hotly debated for at least three hundred years.[10] Many of the tenets of the faith that Christians take for granted today were, during this long period of flux, simply a few ideas among many.

It is a fact that some Christian sects and writers accepted reincarnation as an enhancement to the teachings of Christ. Origen, one of the heralded Fathers of the Church and described by Saint Gregory as "the Prince of Christian learning in the third century," wrote: "Every soul comes into this world strengthened by the victories and weakened by the defeats of its previous life."[11]

So if reincarnation was an idea in currency with early Christians, why have all traces of it disappeared from the Christian religion we know today?

By the early fourth century, strong Christian factions were vying with each other for influence and power, while at the same time the Roman Empire was beginning to fall apart. In A.D. 325, in a move to renew the unity of the empire, the absolute dictator Emperor Constantine convened the leaders of the feuding Christian factions at the Council of Nicaea. He offered to throw his imperial power behind the Christians if they would settle their differences and agree on a single creed. Decisions made at this first council set the foundation for the Roman Catholic Church. (Soon after, the books of the Bible were fixed too.) For the sake of unity, all beliefs that conflicted with the new creed were banished, and in the process the factions and writings that supported reincarnation were thrown out.

Then, with the applause and support of the Christian leaders, Constantine moved to eliminate competing religions and make his personal grip on the empire even more absolute.[12] The result of the marriage between church and imperial state was a new Church made in the image of the autocratic Roman Empire. This is why, according to some historians, the Church exalts unquestioned central authority, imposes a singular dogmatic creed on its followers, and works so hard to stamp out divergent ideas.[13] This is important, because reincarnation fell outside the official creed.

Apparently some Christians continued to believe in reincarnation even after the Council of Nicaea, because in A.D. 553 the Church found the need to single out reincarnation and condemn it explicitly. At the Second Council of Constantinople the concept of reincarnation, bundled together with other ideas under the term "pre-existence of the soul," was decreed to be a crime worthy of excommunication and damnation ("anathema"):

If anyone assert the fabulous pre-existence of souls, and shall assert the monstrous restoration which follows from it: let him be anathema.[14]

Why would the Church go to such lengths to discredit reincarnation? The implicit psychology of reincarnation may be the best explanation. A person who believes in reincarnation assumes responsibility for his own spiritual evolution through rebirth. He does not need priests, confessionals, and rituals to ward off damnation (all ideas, incidentally, that were not part of Jesus' teachings). He needs only to heed his own acts to himself and others. A belief in reincarnation eliminates the fear of eternal hell that the Church uses to discipline the flock. In other words, reincarnation directly undermines the authority and power of the dogmatic Church. No wonder reincarnation made the Defenders of the Faith so nervous.[15]

Despite the decree of 553, belief in reincarnation persisted among the rank and file. It took another thousand years and much bloodshed to completely stamp out the idea. In the early thirteenth century, the Cathars, a devout and enlightened sect of Christians who believed in reincarnation, flourished in Italy and southern France.[16] The pope launched a crusade to stop the heresy, a half million people were massacred—whole villages at a time—and the Cathars were totally wiped out.[17] This purging set the tone for the brutal Inquisition that began soon after. Not only was a belief in reincarnation cause for persecution, but so was belief in *any* metaphysical idea that fell outside the bounds of Church dogma.

The murderous efficiency of the Inquisition proved effective. The persecution by the institutional Church has scarred our col-

lective psyche, and it has surrounded us with an invisible fence
dividing what is safe from what is dangerous to believe. Since
then, people who harbor forbidden ideas have learned to keep
their thoughts to themselves. Our cultural memory still carries
the fear of reprisal for publicly associating with any occult practices, the use of psychic powers, or a belief in reincarnation.

Here it is, the source of the double standard. No wonder so
many people today believe in reincarnation privately but are
afraid that if they come out publicly, they will be attacked for
being weird—the modern word for heresy. Maybe by understanding where this fear comes from, we can negate its hold on us
and turn off the invisible fence. So when our children speak of
past lives, we can follow our hearts and not our fears—and believe them.

Victoria Bragg and the New Testament

Victoria Bragg, a devout Christian, discovered that reincarnation
was the missing piece she needed to solidify her faith.

> I had two years of Bible College in which nothing clicked. I
> was constantly asking questions, I was constantly the
> rebel—the troublemaker who didn't believe in form, be-
> cause I always felt that there was something else they
> weren't telling us. I was constantly asking them questions
> that no one could answer.
>
> After doing the regression and experiencing all of this
> with four-year-old Mark, I finally felt that I was moving in
> the right direction. This made everything click. It means so
> much more to me because I wasn't *forced* to believe in this
> way, it's not what they wanted me to believe. I believe this
> way because I really believe it. I worked it out for myself.
>
> It helped my New Testament faith because reincarnation
> doesn't take away anything the Bible teaches—it only en-
> hances my beliefs and what the Scripture says. It brought it
> all back to a perfect little bundle, whereas before, I couldn't
> understand many things. Like in Matthew 17:10–13, in
> which Jesus is speaking of Elias coming back as John the

Baptist. Now I know what this means—John the Baptist was Elias reincarnated.

I think that Jesus Christ was saying to us that it is okay to come back again and learn. I do believe in the karmic laws as well. As the Bible says, you reap what you sow. I really believe we create our own destinies on Earth and create our own heavens and hells.

The Book of Splendor

Is it possible for observant Jews to believe in reincarnation—to believe their own children's past life memories—without contradicting their faith? Most Jews will be as surprised as I was to learn that reincarnation is at the heart of esoteric Judaism, called the Kabbalah. Until I started doing this research, I had always thought that Judaism ignored reincarnation. It had never been mentioned in any of my religious training or by anyone in my family. Yet it's there. Jewish scholar Simcha Paull Raphael emphatically proclaims: "Yes, kabbalists do believe in reincarnation! Reincarnation is as kosher to Judaism as Mogen David wine."[18]

The Jewish religion has no single doctrine or dogma, no one book that defines its faith, as the Bible does for Christianity. Instead, Jews draw their inspiration and spiritual guidance from a number of sacred texts. One of them is a book of mystical teachings, the principal text of the Kabbalah, called the *Zohar*, or *The Book of Splendor*. This book has guided Jewish mystics since at least the thirteenth century when it first appeared in Spain, though some scholars believe it records secret teachings that were handed down since before the time of Christ.

The Book of Splendor traces the cycle of death and rebirth, called *gilgul*, which means both "wheel" and "transformations." It teaches that each incarnation is a unique mission comprising lessons to be learned, commandments to be fulfilled, and deeds to be performed to balance wrongs committed in former lifetimes—in other words, to take care of unfinished business. The

ultimate purpose of *gilgul* is the purification of the soul and a
release from the cycle of earthly lives.

The more I learned, the more I was amazed to discover how
closely *The Book of Splendor* parallels the mystical beliefs of the
Hindus and Buddhists, especially of *The Tibetan Book of the Dead*.
Both books were written to guide the soul on its journey through
the after-death states and on to rebirth. *The Book of Splendor* describes cycles of evolutionary development where death is merely
one stage in the journey of the soul, a door to other realms of
consciousness on its way back to another earthly existence. It
agrees with the Buddhists that the most important point on the
cycle of consciousness is the moment of death, and that the
thoughts held in the mind at that moment most strongly influence the character of the next life.[19]

What a surprise to find this treasure of wisdom buried in my
own spiritual back yard, the same jewels of insight that had
attracted me to the esoteric writings of the Buddhists and
Hindus. I wondered how my quest would have been different if I
had learned about the Kabbalah when I was younger. If I had
been familiar with these teachings when my memories of the
Holocaust were breaking forth, I might not have gone through so
much confusion and uncertainty about what was happening to
me.

Why don't more Jews today know about these beautiful insights into death, the afterlife, and rebirth? From what I could
tell, they had been a vital element of Jewish teachings in the
Middle Ages but somehow got buried and obscured from the
mainstream of Jewish thought. I found that the answer has a lot
to do with the treatment, since the Middle Ages, of the Jews by
the Roman Catholic Church. When the Church dominated all of
the institutions of Europe, it pressured the Jews to abandon their
religion and accept the Christian theology. The Church insisted
that it controlled the *only* door to the afterlife. An official Church
decree from the Council of Florence in 1442 leaves no doubt:

None of those outside the Catholic Church, not Jews, nor
heretics, nor schismatics, can participate in eternal life, but

will go into the eternal fire prepared for the devil and his angels.

Centuries of this kind of persecution took its toll on the modern Jewish psyche. Surrounded by Christian teachings of an afterlife that explicitly assigned them to hell, many Jews decided to opt out of the whole system, completely eliminating any idea of the afterlife from their beliefs—including their mystical tradition of *gilgul*.[20]

Today, however, we are seeing a flourishing of interest in all mystical traditions and a revival of the Kabbalah. *The Book of Splendor* is being resurrected with new translations and interpretations, reaching a wider audience than ever before. From what I've learned, I feel confident in telling any Jew that accepting a child's past life memory is in complete harmony with Jewish tradition. If anything, belief in reincarnation taps into the deep and ancient heart of Jewish mysticism.

"Yes, There Is a God!"

When a child speaks of a past life memory, the effects ripple far. At the center is the child, who is directly healed and changed. The parents standing close by are rocked by the truth of the experience—a truth powerful enough to dislodge deeply entrenched beliefs. For observers removed from the actual event—even those just reading about it—reports of a child's past life memory can jostle the soul toward new understanding. Children's past life memories have the power to change lives.

Colleen Hocken describes how her life was changed:

> I think that Blake's experience was something that I needed to start me on my own spiritual journey. Before it happened, I really was an atheist. I thought that God didn't exist. Before, there were things I just couldn't understand, like why three-month-old babies had to die. I couldn't understand how God could be so cruel.

Since Blake's experience I did research and read about reincarnation and began to understand how this all works—that we have many lives and we learn things in different lives. We also choose the body we're in, like a handicapped body or that of a retarded person, for the purpose of learning. Before this I thought that God was so cruel to do this to one person, while another person was given a wonderful life.

Then, knowing that past lives are possible, everything seemed to fit together and I realized, yes, there is a God!

CHAPTER 15

Death Is a Revolving Door

Forget not that I shall come back to you. . . . A little while,
a moment of rest upon the wind,
and another woman shall bear me.

—KAHLIL GIBRAN[1]

Losing a Child

There is no greater tragedy than the death of a child, no greater agony, no grief that tears more viciously at the soul and rips at the heart.

When a child dies, parents search desperately for meaning in the torment. They cry in anguish, "How could God be so cruel as to take my child?" They grope in vain for reasons: "What did my baby do to deserve this?" Inevitably they blame themselves, crushing their spirits with incredible guilt: "What did *I* do to deserve this?" If we believe that we have only one life to live, the death of a child seems a senseless, unfathomable waste.

Nothing can erase the sorrow and pain of such a terrible loss. But if we believe that death is not the end, that we live more than once, and that souls—especially those of children—are reborn quickly, we may take solace in the thought that the child will soon be back on Earth to start over again.

Parents do not have to lose faith in the order and justice of the universe if they believe that their child's death has a purpose, however harsh the grief is at the time. Every death is a supreme karmic event for the soul who passes on, as well as for those left behind to suffer the loss. We can trust the logic of the cosmic pattern that the death has meaning, even if that meaning is hidden from us. This eases the despair a little and, as time passes, can lead us to see much deeper meaning in our own lives than we ever saw before.

Reincarnation offers plausible hope for a real, honest-to-goodness miracle. It is entirely possible that a child lost to death may turn around and be reborn into the same family—a cosmic turnabout. As these next two cases show, fervent prayer and stubborn faith also play their healing part.

The Power of Prayer

This case is well documented and well known in England. Some of the account came from the London-based magazine *Reincarnation International*. Dr. Stevenson followed up with his own verification and published it in *Children Who Remember Previous Lives*.[2]

Jennifer and Gillian Pollack

On May 5, 1957, the Pollack family in England suffered an unthinkable tragedy when their two daughters, eleven-year-old Joanna and six-year-old Jacqueline, both died in the same accident. The girls were walking to Sunday mass when a crazed driver careened onto the sidewalk and hit the children, throwing them into the air and killing them instantly.

For years before the accident, their father John Pollack, a devout Roman Catholic who also believed firmly in reincarnation, had prayed to God asking for proof of reincarnation.

Now he prayed that God would send his daughters back to him.

Within a year his wife, Florence, became pregnant. John assured her that their two daughters were returning to their family as twins. John persisted in this belief, contradicting their gynecologist who maintained that only one baby was growing in Florence's womb. Each man kept stubbornly to his opinion right up to the time of delivery. On October 4, 1958, Florence gave birth to identical twin girls; they named the twins Jennifer and Gillian.

Immediately they noticed that Jennifer, *but not Gillian*, had two birthmarks—a white line on her forehead and a brown birthmark on her waist—that matched the size, shape, and location of a scar and a congenital birthmark that had been on Jacqueline's forehead and waist. This is remarkable because identical twins, if they share identical genetic material (Stevenson had tests done to prove this was the case) will have identical birthmarks too. Therefore, these marks were caused by something other than heredity.

When the girls were old enough to talk, they remembered details of their deceased sisters that they had no normal way of knowing. In a test, they correctly identified toys that had belonged to Joanna and Jacqueline. When visiting for the first time the town where Joanna and Jacqueline had lived (the Pollacks had moved away when the twins were infants), they correctly picked out the former Pollack house, led the way unassisted to the park and the playground, and spontaneously described a school and swings before these came into view. Once, when the little girls were playing, Florence overheard them re-enacting the accident: "Gillian was holding Jennifer's head and saying that blood was coming from her eyes because that's where the car hit her."[3]

This case has all the signs of a classic past life memory—especially the birthmarks. John Pollack was certain that God had answered his prayers, and that both of the daughters he had lost in the terrible accident had come back to him.

Family Return

The Pollacks' story of twin deaths and twin rebirths is very dramatic. But it is neither unique nor just wishful thinking. The phenomenon of *family return*—reincarnating back into the same family—is surprisingly common. Ian Stevenson documented many cases all over the world of children who reincarnated back into the same families; the Harrisons found this phenomenon too. Statistics compiled from the cases of Stevenson and other researchers show that as many as 10 percent of the children they investigated had returned to the family of the previous personality.[4]

In some cultures, such as those in West Africa, Bali, and Burma, as well as among Native Americans and Eskimos, it is *expected* that a person who dies, whether young or old, will reincarnate into at least the same tribe or community, if not into the same family. When a child is born, they look for signs—birthmarks, especially—to learn which of their recently deceased tribesmen has returned. Later, to prove this identity, they test the young child's ability to recognize personal objects of the deceased. Among the Yorubas of West Africa, it is customary to greet a newborn with the salutation: "Thou art come!" They name boys Babatunde, which means "Father has returned," and they name girls Yetunde, which means "Mother has returned."

This next case came to me through my network of friends. It is told by Hilda Swiger, a grandmother from Florida, who had strong faith that her prayers would bring back her dead son.

Randy Swiger

I was born into a strict religious family. My father was a minister in the Church of God in Indiana. He thought that reincarnation was of the Devil. Some people are like that.

But me, I always believed in reincarnation. You see, there are references to reincarnation in the Bible, like in Matthew

17:10–13, when Jesus told his disciples that John the Baptist was Elias reborn. People just overlook these things, but they're there. People miss so much when they aren't willing to look.

My son Richard was killed in a car accident in 1977. He was twenty-eight.

I prayed and prayed that he would come back. And I dreamed of him all the time. The last dream I had of Richard was when my other son's wife was pregnant. In this dream I begged him to come back to Earth again. He said, "No, I've been here on the other side a long time, and I don't want to come back." I was crying, and I pleaded with him, saying, "I'll be so good to you." That was the last dream I had of Richard.

Shortly after that dream, my grandson Randy was born. The first time I saw him, when he was two weeks old, he put his hands up to my face and looked me in the eye, and I said, "Uh-oh, I know who this baby is." I could see his soul in his eyes. I immediately felt a strong connection with this baby. I knew he was Richard reborn.

When Randy was two and a half, he said something for the first time that made us really believe that he was Richard reborn and that it was not just wishful thinking on our part. I had just moved, and we were unpacking from the move. I found a canvas of an angel that Richard had painted. When Randy saw the painting, he immediately grabbed it and ran to his father, all excited, and said, "Lookie, Daddy, lookie. Me painted this. Me painted this a long time ago."

Another time, when he was three and a half, he said to me, "I was in your belly before I went to my mommy. But then I died and went to heaven and I saw Grandpa John. But I knew you needed me, so I came down here in my mommy's belly so I could be with you." John was my father—*Richard's* grandpa, Randy's great-grandpa—but Randy called him *Grandpa* John.

A couple of years ago, when Randy was four, we all took him on his first trip to Epcot Center. We were headed into a restaurant, when suddenly Randy said to his daddy, "You're going the wrong way. You sit right there." Randy pointed to a particular table on the side. "That's where you sat before."

Suddenly my son realized that Randy was right. They sat at that very table on their last visit to Epcot Center, soon after Randy was conceived. My son asked Randy, surprised, "How did you know that?"

Randy's reply took us all aback. "Oh, I was following you and Mommy around that day when you came here before I was born."

The whole family is convinced that Randy is Richard reborn. After my son was killed, I really began to search for answers, because I was in so much pain. There's nothing in the world as bad as losing a child—nothing! That is the worst grief any person can have. Each year on the anniversary of Richard's death, I would sit on his grave and grieve. I would just sit there and cry for hours. Then Randy was born. He filled the hole where the grief was. I knew that he was my son come back to me. I didn't have to go to the cemetery anymore.

CHAPTER 16

See Children Differently

Our birth is but a sleep and a forgetting:
The soul that rises with us, our life's star,
Hath had elsewhere its setting.
And cometh from afar:
Not in entire forgetfulness,
And not in utter nakedness,
But trailing clouds of glory do we come
From God, who is our home:
Heaven lies about us in our infancy!

—WILLIAM WORDSWORTH[1]

Once we accept the fact that some children have lived before, we see all children differently. It changes our concept of what children are. We can no longer see them as inferior to us simply because they are little and can't reach the faucets or tie a shoe. For we know now that children are *more* than just biological beings shaped by heredity and environment. They are spiritual beings, too, who bring with them wisdom and experience gathered from other lives on Earth. If we accept this view—that children are experienced souls in little bodies—we realize that they have more available to them, and more to offer us, than we ever thought possible before.

At first this realization can be overwhelming, even upsetting, because it is so drastically different from what we were taught to believe about children. It's a big and sudden change, like being "slammed against a wall."

As Charlotte Swenson found out, it takes a while to get used to this new perception:

At first, when my kids started saying these things, it disturbed me. "I just don't want to hear it," I said. "Just let me be in ignorance." Because what they said forced me to think and not just float along. It made me feel uncomfortable, because the things they said were too shocking and surprising, things that shouldn't be coming out of the mouths of little kids. You think that when kids are born, they don't know much, and when they're four, they're four—not thirty or sixty.

Now I realize that children really are tuned in to the creative force. I want to keep those channels open, keep the flow going, for them *and* for me. And now I realize that my kids teach me more than I teach them. They show me there's more out there than meets the eye. Now, because of them, I believe in things that are outside the frame of a birth-to-death "normal" life.

When we accept the truth of past life memories, we begin to accept our children as souls who have lived before, will live again, and who are here with us for a purpose. The poet Kahlil Gibran said, "Children come through you, but not from you." In truth, they are God's creations, not ours. They are born to us according to a plan that is vaster than we can imagine.

This subtle shift in attitude, this new humility, changes our role as parents. We see that our children's development is not totally dependent on us. It is, at the core, an unfolding of the individual destiny and purpose they were born with. This is more valuable and real than any plan we might have for them.

Of course, it is still our duty to protect and nurture our young children, to guide them in the ways of the world, to prepare them to survive on their own. And it is our pleasure and privilege to share with them our own interests and dreams and the lessons we have learned along the way. But we have to rethink our roles as all-knowing parents and enter into a new relationship with our children, one of *mutual* respect and learning. There are times when we need to step back and allow them to share what they know with us. Then we can marvel at their originality and ask, "What can *you* teach me?" This is the recipe for a parent/child relationship rooted in the spiritual, making life much more interesting for us, and giving the unique individuality of the child the opportunity to flourish.

According to the principles of rebirth and karma, we come together in each life with people we have known before to continue our karmic lessons. Every person who is important to us now came into our lives for a reason. And we constantly switch roles. Your child in this life could have been your parent, wife, brother, teacher, persecutor, rival, or lover in the past. On the soul level you are both equal—the only difference is that this time around one of you arrived on Earth twenty or so years before the other.

This new perception increases the wonder and meaning of our relationships with our own children. Once we make the shift, to see children differently, we greet them as the souls they are and ask, "Who are you? Why did you come to me?" If we open ourselves to this spiritual level and listen to our children, while at the same time observing our own feelings, we will begin to understand our mutual destinies more completely.

Colleen Hocken knows that Blake came to her for a reason:

I recalled something my mother-in-law, who seems to have a sixth sense about things, said when Blake was born: "Look at his eyes. This is an old soul in a baby's body." I realize now that she said something very profound. She saw it. I now look at children differently too and say, "Who is that old soul in there?"

I really needed this experience with Blake because I was so lost before. Maybe my spiritual guides or angels knew that I needed something drastic to get me to open my eyes.

All children, not just your own, are spiritual beings. If they cross your path, it's for a reason. Even a brief encounter with a child, as Victoria Bragg learned, can change your life if you are open to it.

Meeting little Mark opened the door to help me understand everything happening in my life now. Before I met him, I was struggling spiritually and did not know it. He helped by showing me there's a bigger picture than just this one life. He's saying that it's okay to believe that we were together before, it's okay to be sad about it. And he's letting me know I don't have to worry about him anymore. He's saying, "Here I am, and I miss you because we were together before."

He helped me understand where I was going with my own spiritual growth, and he gave me the confidence to keep going. He made it all come together. I think that is why I met him. After all the spiritual teachers I've had, my best teacher came in the form of a four-year-old boy.

Beginner's Mind

When children speak directly from their hearts about heaven, death, and rebirth, they are commenting on the big questions of man's existence—the same questions that adults created philosophy, religion, and myths to answer. It is astounding, and a bit unnerving, when little children, whose biggest conquests so far are using the potty for the first time, or going to the back yard alone, blurt out confident insights into these greatest of mysteries. But it makes sense when we realize that they are speaking from direct experience. Their memories of the spiritual realms are still fresh. They still remember their most recent sojourn in the timeless, boundless space of God, Christ, Allah, Buddha-nature, Jehovah, the Great Spirit, or whatever name you want to give to the fountainhead of universal love and wisdom.

When children speak to us of these things, it is with a mind unprejudiced by adult limits or conceptual clichés—"beginner's mind," as Buddhists call it. Their understanding of spirit is still a direct, unadulterated experience. I wonder if this is what Jesus meant when he told us that we must be like children if we are to enter the Kingdom of God.

Yet because they speak with such disarming innocence, you must listen carefully to discern the spiritual nuggets from common fantasy babble. Listen for the sincerity in their voices. And be alert for telltale feelings of spiritual energy in your own body. This is how Mary Fleming knew that her children, sounding at first as though they were making up stories, were actually reporting what they remembered from before they were born:

> One night when Alan and Michael were six and their sister Colleen was about eight, we were all riding in the car and the discussion turned to a pet goldfish who had just died.
> Michael said, "Will our goldfish come back to life?"
> I said, "I'm not sure I know what you mean."
> "Will he come back to life as another fish?"
> "Do you mean like that saying, 'a cat has nine lives'?"
> Michael said in an exasperated voice, "Like people do. Will our fish come back and live another fish life like people come back to live another people life?"
> His tone of voice got to me. I looked at him and asked, "Who told you this, about coming back and living another life?"
> Michael said confidently, "Nobody had to tell us about it. We *just know it*." I saw nodding of heads all around as the other children agreed. I tried to avoid crashing the car!

Mary continued:

> The first talk I recall of the children discussing life before birth was when Colleen was five or six and the boys were three or four. It was before the baby was born. We were sitting at the kitchen table, and somehow the conversation turned to heaven and what it was like before they were born. They became very animated and were interrupting each other to talk.

Colleen said, "When I was in heaven waiting to be born, there were a lot of us there. Some of my friends were waiting too. There were two angels watching over us, and if anybody cried, the angel would come over and pick you up. There was a long line of us waiting to be born."

Michael interrupted, "God held me right before I came down to be born."

I said, "That's wonderful, Michael. Alan, did God hold you before you were born too?"

Michael gave me a withering look and said, "Mom, God held me and the Mother held Alan. Don't you remember?"

At that moment, I felt very strange, sort of chilled. I had assumed that it was make-believe up to that point, but something about the exasperated look he gave me and the matter-of-fact way they were describing things made me pay attention.

After a few years, the memories begin to fade. Even the children themselves realized this:

> Ever since Eileen, my fourth child, was born, the children have been saying that they can't wait until she can talk so she can tell them about heaven, *because they are starting to forget.*

"A Deep Integration of Beliefs"

Mary Fleming's children described their spiritual memories with childlike images of the places and events they remembered. Some children are born not only with these memories but also with a gift for comprehending and articulating sophisticated spiritual concepts. Lisa's daughter Courtney is one of these children:

> One day my son, Joey, was looking at a baby picture of his older sister Aubrey. He asked where he had been when the

picture had been taken. Aubrey replied, "You were in baby heaven waiting to be born, Joey."

Courtney got very indignant at this and said, "That's not how it works! That is just not how it works!"

She then clarified this by telling us: "You go to heaven, then you have a little time to rest, kind of like a vacation, but then you have to get to work. You have to start thinking about what you have to learn in your *next* life. You have to start picking out your next family, one that will help you learn whatever it is you need to learn next. Heaven isn't just a place you go to hang around forever. It's not just a place to relax and kick back. You have work to do there."

Courtney was very serious about this, very. She was four and a half at the time. This was not a childlike concept of heaven. This is a place where things must be accomplished.

I decided to confront her a little bit, so I said, "Courtney, if you have been in heaven, do you remember it?"

She said, "Yah."

"Well, then," I said, "you must have seen God."

She nodded and told me that she had. I thought to myself, I'm going to pin her down now. I said, "I really don't remember God. Could you please tell me what he looked like?"

Well, I was expecting the Hollywood version—a bright light or some warm feeling. She looked at me with eyes that went straight through me and said, "Don't you know, I only saw God with my soul."

I should have known I wasn't going to pin her into a corner.

Sometimes a child's understanding of the patterns of life can go beyond that of most adults, including their parents. When this happens, all we can do is open to the lessons and be grateful for the wisdom this child brings to us so freely. Lisa continues:

Courtney is now six. Most of her past life recollections have slowed down, but not completely.

She said something I found really interesting a few

months ago. We were in the kitchen, and she was breezing through in a sequined tutu. Courtney is a very dramatic, creative person, so she just came fluttering through the kitchen. The TV was on showing a news story of some kind. I wasn't paying attention, but Courtney asked me why that lady on TV was crying. Well, I tuned in mentally for the first time and realized they were talking about how this woman's son was going to be executed for a crime he had committed. I tried to explain this to Courtney in a nice way without going into detail about what *rape* means.

Courtney said, "Well, Mom, she just doesn't understand. That's why she's sad."

I said, "Courtney, what do you mean she doesn't understand?"

"Well," she replied, "she just doesn't understand that when someone has messed up their lives as badly as this man has, that it's really not a punishment to die. Because when he dies, he gets to start over again and be a baby in a new family without any bad things that he's done following him. And that's really a lot better for him because he won't waste his energy, and he'll be able to learn what he needs to learn a lot easier if he starts over. And she just doesn't understand this, Momma, because if she did, she wouldn't be sad." With that, Courtney flitted out of the room.

I get goose bumps when I talk about this. It took me about three hours to really contemplate what she had said. To me, that is a deep integration of her beliefs, especially for someone who is six years old. Believe me, it did not come from us. We attend a Presbyterian church and I consider us open-minded, but this does not come from religious dogma she has picked up. She never heard this kind of reasoning before. It was all her own.

I feel a great responsibility toward Courtney to nurture whatever this is in her. I feel that I have a child who is a more advanced soul than I am. At the moment I felt like I was the child and I had asked a childish question. Without being sassy or rude, she succinctly put me in my place.

Chase and Sarah

Some people ask me how my kids' past life experiences have affected them over the years. Certainly it hasn't harmed them, and I'm convinced it has helped them become strong individuals.

More than eight years have passed since Chase and Sarah first spoke of their past lives, and they are now both thriving teen-agers. Next year Sarah will be leaving for college, and Chase will be starting high school. Sarah is always on the go. She wins medals in sports, acts and sings, and does very well in school. She does *everything* with zest. She has a reputation for spontaneously breaking into a dance anytime, any place—in the halls in school, in the aisles of the supermarket, and especially in our kitchen. She makes us laugh.

Chase isn't a little kid anymore: he's six feet tall. He has his sights set on being a writer, and his passion for drumming has grown into a serious occupation. He plays in a rock and roll band whose business cards read, "Live music is great at parties." He still makes loud but syncopated booming sounds all the time. His intensity amazes us.

Both of my children are creative and full of curiosity, which I attribute, in part, to their experiences with past life memories. They know that Steve and I accept their nonordinary experiences, and I believe this has encouraged them to push the limits of what is possible or normal. Most importantly, they learned to trust their own intuition and inspiration, keeping their channels open to the source of creativity.

My work is as remote to them as most parents' jobs are to their own children. Rarely do they mention their past life experiences, and the images that were once so vivid to them have faded. Occasionally, though, they will ask questions that show me that their past life experiences have shaped their thinking and beliefs: "I wonder what my relationship was with my friend in a past life. We can almost read each other's minds." Or "How much of your karma do you take from lifetime to lifetime?" I usually respond by saying, "I'm not sure. What do you think?" Then I listen as they go deeply into themselves and draw out a far more interesting answer to their own question than I could have given them. I'm still learning from them.

Sometimes it hits me how much my life has changed since that day in my kitchen. This book, and my new career, all began that moment Norman Inge asked Chase to sit on my lap and close his eyes. I try to imagine how different my life would have been if I had *not* believed what Chase and Sarah said that day. Or if I had believed them but had kept it to myself and then stored their experiences away in a corner of the attic with the Barbie dolls and Lego sets. I would probably still be groping for something—a job, a hobby, an adventure—to give meaning to my life.

But ignoring the power of my children's memories was never an option. In retrospect I can see that what happened that day in my kitchen was part of a larger plan: the time, place, and conditions were perfect for me to appreciate the significance of the event, and to push ahead and learn all I could about children's past life memories to share with you. Now I see my story as more than just a personal tale, but as an example of what can happen when you open to these greater forces in general. And in particular, what can happen when you listen to your children—*really* listen with all your heart and all your soul.

Notes

Chapter 2: Prelude

1. T. S. Eliot, *Four Quartets* (New York: Harcourt, Brace and World, 1971), p. 16.
2. Ibid., p. 15.
3. W. Y. Evans-Wentz, trans., *The Tibetan Book of the Dead* (London: Oxford University Press, 1960), p. 96.
4. Swami Prabhavananda and Frederick Manchester, eds., *The Upanishads* (New York: New American Library, 1957).
5. William Blake, "A Memorable Fancy," in *English Romantic Poetry and Prose,* edited by Russell Noyes (London: Oxford University Press, 1956), p. 212.
6. T. S. Eliot, *Four Quartets.*

Chapter 4: The Moment of Death

1. Helen Wambach, *Reliving Past Lives: The Evidence Under Hypnosis* (New York: Bantam Books, 1979), p. 2.
2. Ibid., p. 62.
3. Ibid., p. 144.
4. Ibid., p. 146.
5. Edith Fiore, *You Have Been Here Before* (New York: Ballantine Books, 1978), p. 3.
6. Ibid., p. 216.
7. Ibid., pp. 148–59.
8. Roger Woolger, *Other Lives, Other Selves* (New York: Bantam Books, 1988), p. 84.
9. Ibid., pp. 144–47.
10. Ibid., pp. 220–24.
11. Ibid., p. 142.
12. Sogyal Rinpoche, *The Tibetan Book of Living and Dying* (New York: HarperCollins, 1994), p. 47.

13. Ibid., p. 224.

14. Dr. Winafred Blake Lucas, *Regression Therapy: A Handbook for Professionals,* vol. 2 (Crest Park, CA: Deep Forest Press, 1993), p. 431.

15. Woolger, *Other Lives,* pp. 174–76.

Chapter 6: Dr. Ian Stevenson

1. Ian Stevenson, *Twenty Cases Suggestive of Reincarnation* (Charlottesville: University Press of Virginia, 1974), pp. 109–27.

2. Ian Stevenson, *Children Who Remember Previous Lives* (Charlottesville: University Press of Virginia, 1987), pp. 84–88.

3. Stevenson, *Twenty Cases,* pp. 52–67.

4. Dr. Stevenson on psychoanalysis: "Psychoanalysis isn't really based on scientific inquiry. In fact, it's largely misguided in both doctrine and practice. I am sure that Freud will some day be considered a figure of fun." In the same vein, Dr. Stevenson rejects behaviorism because it "considers human personality as a mere machine responding to external stimuli." Quoted in Ken Adelman, "Everlasting Life?" *Washingtonian* (June 1995), p. 30.

5. For a thorough and objective overview of the entire field, including descriptions of researchers who have followed Dr. Stevenson's lead and a review of critics who challenge his evidence, see the article "Past Life Memory Case Studies" by James G. Matlock, in *Advances in Parapsychological Research,* vol. 6 (Jefferson, NC: McFarland and Co., 1990). The publisher's address is P.O. Box 611, Jefferson, NC 28640. The article includes an extensive bibliography that references all of the significant resources in the field.

6. Adelman, "Everlasting Life?" p. 30.

7. See bibliography in Matlock, "Past Life Memory Case Studies."

8. Matlock, "Past Life Memory Case Studies," p. 200.

9. Stevenson, *Twenty Cases,* pp. 67–91.

10. Stevenson, *Children Who Remember,* p. 116.

11. Ibid.

12. Ibid., p. 114.

13. Dr. Winafred Blake Lucas, *Regression Therapy: A Handbook for*

Professionals, vol. 2 (Crest Park, CA: Deep Forest Press, 1993), p. 431.

14. Stevenson, *Twenty Cases,* p. 117.

15. This case is summarized in Stevenson, *Children Who Remember,* pp. 62–64, with additional details from Adelman, "Everlasting Life?" p. 31.

16. Stevenson, *Twenty Cases,* pp. 91–108.

17. Ibid., p. 101.

18. Ian Stevenson, "Birthmarks and Birth Defects Corresponding to Wounds on Deceased Persons," *Journal of Scientific Exploration,* vol. 7, no. 4 (1993), p. 403. This article, which includes photographs, gives a preview of Dr. Stevenson's forthcoming volumes on birthmarks. This, and other articles by Stevenson, can be obtained by contacting: *Journal of Scientific Exploration,* P.O. Box 5848, Stanford, CA 94309-5848. Or on the internet: www.jse.com

19. Ibid., p. 411.

20. Ibid., p. 410.

21. Ibid., p. 413.

22. Ibid., p. 404.

23. Ibid., p. 410.

24. Stevenson, *Children Who Remember,* p. 158.

25. Stevenson, "Phobias in Children Who Claim to Remember Previous Lives," *Journal of Scientific Exploration,* vol. 4, no. 2 (1990), p. 246.

26. Stevenson, *Children Who Remember,* p. 163.

27. Stevenson, *Twenty Cases,* p. 329.

28. Dr. Winafred Blake Lucas, *Regression Therapy: A Handbook for Professionals,* vol. 2 (Crest Park, CA: Deep Forest Press, 1993), p. 431.

29. Stevenson, *Children Who Remember,* p. 212.

Chapter 7: Children's Past Life Memories

1. Peter and Mary Harrison, *The Children That Time Forgot* (New York: Berkley Publishing Group, 1991), p. 122.

2. Ibid., p. 133.

3. Ibid., p. 70.

4. Ibid., p. 75.
5. Ibid., p. 27.
6. Ibid., p. 121.
7. Ibid., p. 176.
8. Ibid.
9. Ibid., p. 11.
10. Ibid., p. 13.
11. Ibid.

Chapter 10: The Four Signs

1. Joseph Head and Sylvia Cranston, *Reincarnation: The Phoenix Fire Mystery* (Pasadena, CA: Theosophical University Press, 1994), pp. 401–2.
2. Peter and Mary Harrison, *The Children That Time Forgot* (New York: Berkley Publishing Group, 1991), p. 30.
3. Ibid., pp. 19–27.
4. Ibid., p. 46.
5. Ibid., pp. 41–46.

Chapter 11: Triggers

1. Yonassan Gershom, *Beyond the Ashes* (Virginia Beach: ARE Press, 1992), p. 135.
2. Peter and Mary Harrison, *The Children That Time Forgot* (New York: Berkley Publishing Group, 1991), pp. 58–62.
3. Ibid., p. 133.
4. Thomas Armstrong, *The Radiant Child* (Wheaton, IL: Theosophical Publishing House, 1985), p. 29.

Chapter 12: What a Parent Can Do

1. Thomas Verny and John Kelly, *The Secret Life of the Unborn Child* (New York: Dell Publishing, 1991). B. R. H. Van den Bergh, "The Influence of Maternal Emotions During Pregnancy on Fetal and Neonatal Behavior," *Pre- and Peri-Natal Psychology*, 5(2) (Winter 1990), pp. 119–29.

2. Ian Stevenson, *Children Who Remember Previous Lives* (Charlottesville: University Press of Virginia, 1987), p. 105.

3. Ibid., p. 109.

Chapter 13: Dreaming Up the Past

1. Jenny Cockell, *Across Time and Death* (New York: Simon & Schuster, 1993).

2. Ian Stevenson, *Children Who Remember Previous Lives* (Charlottesville: University Press of Virginia, 1987), p. 50.

3. Richard Ferber, *Solve Your Child's Sleep Problems* (New York: Simon & Schuster, 1985), p. 27.

4. Quoted in Dr. Winafred Blake Lucas, *Regression Therapy: A Handbook for Professionals*, vol. 2 (Crest Park, CA: Deep Forest Press, 1993), p. 270.

5. Yonassan Gershom, *Beyond the Ashes* (Virginia Beach: ARE Press, 1992), pp. 106–9.

6. Ibid., pp. 128–29.

7. Ferber, *Sleep Problems*, p. 147.

8. Thelma Freedman, "Treating Children's Nightmares with Past Life Report Therapy: A Case and a Discussion," *Journal of Regression Therapy*, vol. 5, no. 1 (December 1991), pp. 48–54.

9. Gladys McGarey, *Born to Live* (Phoenix, AZ: Gabriel Press, 1980), pp. 21–23. Available from author: 7350 E. Stetson Drive, Suite 208, Scottsdale, AZ 85251.

10. Dr. Winafred Blake Lucas, *Regression Therapy: A Handbook for Professionals*, vol. 2 (Crest Park, CA: Deep Forest Press, 1993), p. 33.

Chapter 14: Adults and Their Religions

1. Quoted in Thomas Armstrong, *The Radiant Child* (Wheaton, IL: Theosophical Publishing House, 1985), p. 82.

2. Ian Stevenson, *Cases of the Reincarnation Type*, vol. 2, *Lebanon and Turkey* (Charlottesville: University Press of Virginia, 1980), p. 3.

3. Hans Ten Dam, *Exploring Reincarnation* (London: Arkana, 1987), p. 37.

4. Ibid., p. 39.

5. Ibid., p. 31.

6. Leslie D. Weatherhead, *The Case for Reincarnation* (Surrey, England: M. C. Peto, 1966), pp. 3–5.

7. From the New International Version of the Bible.

8. Charles Hampton, *Reincarnation, A Christian Doctrine* (Los Angeles: St. Albans Press, 1925), p. 7.

9. H. G. Wells, *The Outline of History* (Garden City, NY: Garden City Books, 1961), pp. 429–30.

10. Ibid., pp. 433–34.

11. Sogyal Rinpoche, *The Tibetan Book of Living and Dying* (New York: HarperCollins, 1994), p. 82.

12. H. G. Wells, *The Outline of History*, pp. 429–30.

13. Ibid., p. 439.

14. Joseph Head and Sylvia Cranston, *Reincarnation: The Phoenix Fire Mystery* (Pasadena, CA: Theosophical University Press, 1994), p. 159.

15. Ibid., p. 164.

16. Hans Ten Dam, *Exploring Reincarnation*, p. 45.

17. Arthur Guirdham, *The Cathars and Reincarnation* (London: Spearman, 1970), p. 29.

18. Simcha Paull Raphael, *Jewish Views of the Afterlife* (Northvale, NJ: Jason Aronson, 1994), p. 314.

19. Edward Hoffman, *The Way of Splendor* (Northvale, NJ: Jason Aronson, 1981), p. 191.

20. Simcha Paull Raphael, *Jewish Views*, p. 28.

Chapter 15: Death Is a Revolving Door

1. Quoted in Joseph Head and Sylvia Cranston, *Reincarnation: The Phoenix Fire Mystery* (Pasadena, CA: Theosophical University Press, 1994), p. 380.

2. Ian Stevenson, *Children Who Remember Previous Lives* (Charlottesville: University Press of Virginia, 1987), pp. 71–73. "Sisters Return as Twins," *Reincarnation International*, no. 3 (July 1994), p. 26. Sybil Leek, *Reincarnation: The Second Chance* (New York: Bantam Books, 1974), pp. 23–24.

3. "Sisters Return as Twins," *Reincarnation International*, no. 3 (July 1994), p. 26.
4. Hans Ten Dam, *Exploring Reincarnation* (London: Arkana, 1987), pp. 120–21.

Chapter 16: See Children Differently

1. William Wordsworth, "Intimations of Immortality from Recollections of Early Childhood."

Bibliography

Adelman, Ken. "Everlasting Life?" *Washingtonian* (June 1995).

Armstrong, Thomas. *The Radiant Child.* Wheaton, IL: Theosophical Publishing House, 1985.

Bolduc, Henry Leo. *Life Patterns.* Independence, VA: Into Time Publishers, 1994.

Chamberlain, David B. "Babies Are Not What We Thought: Call for a New Paradigm." *International Journal of Prenatal and Perinatal Studies,* vol. 4, no. 3/4 (1992), pp. 1–17.

———. "The Expanding Boundaries of Memory." *Pre- and Perinatal Psychology,* vol. 4, no. 3 (Spring 1990), pp. 171–89.

———. *Babies Remember Birth.* New York: Ballantine Books, 1988.

Cockell, Jenny. *Across Time and Death.* New York: Simon & Schuster, 1993.

Eason, Cassandra. *The Psychic Power of Children.* London: Rider, 1990.

Eliot, T. S. *Four Quartets.* New York: Harcourt, Brace and World, 1971.

Evans-Wentz, W. Y., trans. *The Tibetan Book of the Dead.* London: Oxford University Press, 1960.

Ferber, Richard. *Solve Your Child's Sleep Problems.* New York: Simon & Schuster, 1985.

Fiore, Edith. *You Have Been Here Before.* New York: Ballantine Books, 1978.

Freedman, Thelma. "Treating Children's Nightmares with Past Life Report Therapy: A Case and a Discussion." *Journal of Regression Therapy,* vol. 5, no. 1 (1991), pp. 48–54.

Fremantle, Francesca, and Chögyam Trungpa, trans. *The Tibetan Book of the Dead.* Boston: Shambhala, 1987.

Gabriel, Michael. *Voices from the Womb.* Lower Lake, CA: Aslan Publishing, 1992.

Gershom, Yonassan. *Beyond the Ashes.* Virginia Beach, VA: ARE Press, 1992.

Grof, Stanislav. *Beyond the Brain.* Albany: State University of New York Press, 1985.

Hampton, Charles. *Reincarnation: A Christian Doctrine.* Los Angeles: St. Albans Press, 1925.

Harrison, Peter, and Mary Harrison. *The Children That Time Forgot.* New York: Berkley Publishing Group, 1991.

Head, Joseph, and Sylvia Cranston. *Reincarnation: The Phoenix Fire Mystery.* Pasadena, CA: Theosophical University Press, 1994.

Hoffman, Edward. *Visions of Innocence.* Boston: Shambhala, 1992.

———. *The Way of Splendor.* Northvale, NJ: Jason Aronson, 1981.

Kamenetz, Rodger. *The Jew in the Lotus.* New York: HarperCollins, 1994.

Kapleau, Philip. *The Wheel of Life and Death.* New York: Doubleday, 1989.

Lenz, Frederick. *Lifetimes.* New York: Ballantine Books, 1979.

Lucas, Winafred Blake. *Regression Therapy: A Handbook for Professionals,* vols. 1 and 2. Crest Park, CA: Deep Forest Press, 1993.

Matlock, James G. "Past Life Memory Case Studies." In Stanley Krippner and Mary Lou Carlson, eds., *Advances in Parapsychological Research.* Jefferson, NC: McFarland & Co., 1990.

McGarey, Gladys. *Born to Live.* Phoenix: Gabriel Press, 1980.

Moody, Raymond A., Jr. *Life After Life.* New York: Bantam Books, 1975.

———, and Paul Perry. *Coming Back: A Psychiatrist Explores Past-Life Journeys.* New York: Bantam Books, 1990.

Moore, Marcia. *Hypersentience.* New York: Crown Publishers, 1976.

Morse, Melvin, and Paul Perry. *Closer to the Light.* New York: Ivy Books, 1992.

Motoyama, Hiroshi. *Karma and Reincarnation.* New York: Avon Books, 1992.

Netherton, Morris, and Nancy Shiffren. *Past Lives Therapy.* New York: William Morrow & Co., 1978.

Pearce, Joseph Chilton. *Magical Child.* New York: Penguin Books, 1977.

Peterson, James. *The Secret Life of Kids.* Wheaton, IL: Theosophical Publishing House, 1987.

Piontelli, Alessandra. *From Fetus to Child.* New York: Tavistock/Routledge, 1992.

Prabhavananda, Swami, trans. *The Upanishads.* New York: New American Library, 1957.

Raphael, Simcha Paull. *Jewish Views of the Afterlife.* Northvale, NJ: Jason Aronson, 1994.

"Birthmarks and Birth Defects." *Reincarnation International*, no. 2 (April 1994), pp. 20–21.

"Sisters Return as Twins." *Reincarnation International*, no. 3 (July 1994), p. 26.

Rinpoche, Sogyal. *The Tibetan Book of Living and Dying*. New York: HarperCollins, 1994.

Schlotterbeck, Karl. *Living Your Past Lives: The Psychology of Past-Life Regression*. New York: Ballantine Books, 1987.

Stevenson, Ian. "Birthmarks and Birth Defects Corresponding to Wounds on Deceased Persons." *Journal of Scientific Exploration*, vol. 7, no. 4 (1993), pp. 403–10.

———. "Phobias in Children Who Claim to Remember Previous Lives." *Journal of Scientific Exploration*, vol. 4, no. 2 (1990), pp. 243–54.

———. *Children Who Remember Previous Lives*. Charlottesville: University Press of Virginia, 1987.

———. "American Children Who Claim to Remember Previous Lives." *Journal of Nervous and Mental Disease*, vol. 171, no. 12 (1983), pp. 742–48.

———. *Cases of the Reincarnation Type*, vol. 3, *Twelve Cases in Lebanon and Turkey*. Charlottesville: University Press of Virginia, 1980.

———. *Cases of the Reincarnation Type*, vol. 1, *Ten Cases in India*. Charlottesville: Univeristy Press of Virginia, 1975.

———. *Twenty Cases Suggestive of Reincarnation*. Charlottesville: University Press of Virginia, 1974.

Sutphen, Dick, and Lauren Leigh Taylor. *Past-Life Therapy in Action*. Malibu, CA: Valley of the Sun, 1987.

Ten Dam, Hans. *Exploring Reincarnation*. London: Arkana (The Penguin Group), 1987.

Thurman, Robert A. F., trans. *The Tibetan Book of the Dead*. New York: Bantam Books, 1994.

Van den Bergh, B. R. H. "The Influence of Maternal Emotions During Pregnancy on Fetal and Neonatal Behavior." *Pre- and Peri-Natal Psychology*, vol. 5, no. 2 (Winter 1990), pp. 119–29.

Verny, Thomas, and John Kelly. *The Secret Life of the Unborn Child*. New York: Dell Publishing, 1981.

Wambach, Helen. *Reliving Past Lives: The Evidence Under Hypnosis*. New York: Bantam Books, 1979.

Weatherhead, Leslie D. *The Case for Reincarnation.* London: M. C. Peto, 1966.

Weiss, Brian. *Through Time into Healing.* New York: Simon & Schuster, 1992.

——. *Many Lives, Many Masters.* New York: Simon & Schuster, 1988.

Wells, H. G. *The Outline of History,* vols. 1 and 2. Garden City, NY: Garden City Books, 1961.

Wester, William, II, and Donald O'Grady. *Clinical Hypnosis with Children.* New York: Bruner/Mazel, 1991.

Whitton, Joel, and Joe Fisher. *Life Between Life.* New York: Warner Books, 1986.

Wickes, Frances. *The Inner World of Childhood.* Boston: Sigo Press, 1927.

Woolger, Roger. *Other Lives, Other Selves.* New York: Doubleday, 1987.

For information on past-life regression therapy, contact:
The Association for Past-life Research and Therapies (APRT)
P.O. Box 20151
Riverside, CA 92516-0151
909-784-1570

About the Author

CAROL BOWMAN lives with her husband and two children near Philadelphia. Since beginning her research into children's past lives, she has become recognized as a pioneer and leading expert in this new field. She lectures and writes to share the news of children's past life memories with professional therapists as well as parents. Bowman continues to research the phenomenon of children's past life memories, and wants to hear from anyone who has a story to share. She can be reached by mail at Bantam Books, or by email at cbowman@childpastlives.org.

For more information and discussion on children's past lives, join Carol on the World Wide Web at www.childpastlives.org.